PRAISE FOR

Nature-Based Learning for Young Children: Anytime, Anywhere, on Any Budget

by Julie Powers and Sheila Williams Ridge

"*Nature-Based Learning for Young Children* re-energized my excitement about the power of nature to make learning at the early childhood level a deeply meaningful and joyful experience. The guidance offered here is practical, inspirational, and truly impressive."

—**Ruth Wilson, PhD,** research library curator, Children & Nature Network, author of *Nature and Young Children*

"Engaging and practical . . . this is a must-read for both the novice and the experienced early childhood educator. Weaving stories from the field; encouraging risk-taking; honoring inclusivity of all children, families, and communities, we are drawn into a myriad of lively nature-based learning opportunities that truly speak to the subtitle: *Anytime, Anywhere, on Any Budget.*"

—**Dilafruz Williams,** professor and coauthor of *Learning Gardens and Sustainability Education*

"There is increasing evidence that spending time in nature benefits children's learning and their emotional well-being. This much-needed book provides practical advice to teachers who want to promote nature learning for their children. Designed to address the needs of teachers who live in many different settings, some conducive to nature learning and some challenging, everyone should find help in these pages. This is a gem of a book!"

—**Megan Gunnar,** PhD, department chair, Institute of Child Development, University of Minnesota

"As a growing body of research and common sense tell us, spending time in natural environments supports the healthy development of children. *Nature-Based Learning for Young Children* is an important, easy to use, and practical resource for anyone looking to support children in reaching their full potential. This book doesn't take the reader back, but rather forward to nature!"

—**Sarah Milligan-Toffler,** executive director, Children & Nature Network

"Whatever your comfort level in bringing the natural world to your early childhood classroom, *Nature-Based Learning for Young Children* provides inspiration, enthusiasm, and practical instruction on how to get children connected to what's right outside our doors."

—**Megan Regnerus,** publications manager, Project WET Foundation (Water Education for Teachers)

"For those of us who have wondered on how to take the first steps in nature-based play, here is your guide! Rooted in the solid principles of connecting with the natural world, the authors provide practical and sensible strategies. This remarkable book makes a joyful case for connecting to the natural world once again."

—**Luis A. Hernandez,** early childhood education specialist

D1605340

Nature-Based Learning for Young Children

Other Redleaf Press Books by Julie Powers

Parent Engagement in Early Learning: Strategies for Working with Families

NATURE-BASED LEARNING FOR YOUNG CHILDREN

Anytime, Anywhere, on Any Budget

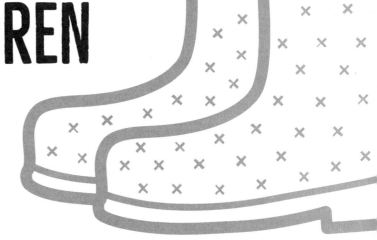

JULIE POWERS
SHEILA WILLIAMS RIDGE

 **Redleaf Press®**
www.redleafpress.org
800-423-8309

Published by Redleaf Press
10 Yorkton Court
St. Paul, MN 55117
www.redleafpress.org

First edition 2019
Cover design by Jim Handrigan
Cover photograph © iStock.com/debibishop
Interior design by Percolator
Typeset in Tiempos Text
Printed in the United States of America
25 24 23 22 21 20 19 18   1 2 3 4 5 6 7 8

Library of Congress Cataloging-in-Publication Data

Names: Powers, Julie, 1957- author. | Ridge, Sheila Williams, author.
Title: Nature-based learning for young children : anytime, anywhere, on any
    budget / Julie Powers, Sheila Williams Ridge.
Description: St. Paul, MN : Redleaf Press, [2018] | Includes bibliographical
    references.
Identifiers: LCCN 2018029071 (print) | LCCN 2018043132 (ebook) | ISBN
    9781605545974 (electronic) | ISBN 9781605545967 (pbk. : acid-free paper)
Subjects: LCSH: Science--Study and teaching (Early childhood)--Activity
    programs. | Nature study--Activity programs. | Environmental education. |
    Outdoor education.
Classification: LCC LB1139.5.S35 (ebook) | LCC LB1139.5.S35 P68 2018 (print)
    | DDC 372.35/044--dc23

Printed on acid-free paper

To our families

Julie's family—Margarita Kay, Marty Rosenthal, and Gabriel Powers

Sheila's family—Robert and Jeannette Williams, Faruk Williams, Kimson Ridge,
Faline Williams, Hailey Williams, Sierra Williams, and Olivia Williams Ridge

CONTENTS

ACKNOWLEDGMENTS

From Julie: Mama (Margarita Kay), thank you for letting me play outdoors unsupervised in the desert, on empty lots, and around the neighborhood when I was very young.

I have had many amazing mentors and colleagues who have inspired and encouraged me. Marcie Oltman has been the best mentor I could have had for my entrance into nature education, and Elaine Yamashita, the best colleague I could ask for in this time in my life. I would also like to thank my coauthor, Sheila Williams Ridge, for eighteen years of friendship, mentoring, humor, and acting as both my literal and metaphorical GPS!

From Sheila: Mom and Dad, thank you for your continuous support and encouragement, and for my dog Cinnamon, a wonderful friend to explore the desert with for many years. Kimson and our amazing daughters, Faline, Hailey, Sierra, and Olivia, thank you for taking time for hikes, canoeing, camping, snorkeling, biking, bonfires, and going on many other adventures. Our times spent exploring, especially those days in Yosemite and Hawaii, are some of the best moments of my life. Faruk, Aunt Sandra, Grandma Renate, Sameerah, Jody, and Uncle Larry, thank you all for your care and inspiration. Julie, you have been an amazing mentor and friend—thank you for believing in me and nurturing me and my family with your love and support.

We would both like to acknowledge Alyson Quinn, Amanda Janquart, Amy Vavricka, Ayuko Boomer, Cherie Lazaroff, Elizabeth Criswell, Jenny Hanlon, Kit Harrington, Marcie Oltman, Marie Lister, Natalie Gilmore, Patti Bailie, Rachel Larimore, Ruth Wilson, and Sarah Sivright for sharing their stories of experiences with young children in nature; Faline Williams, Sierra Williams, Hailey Williams, and Olivia Williams Ridge for research and editing support; Gabriel Powers for his encouragement; our editors, Kara Lomen and Stephanie Schempp, for their great support and leadership on this book; Marty Rosenthal, who tolerated us taking over the house when Sheila came to Telluride to work with Julie and for responding to Julie's calling out, "How do you spell . . . ?" (Oh, and also for his love and support.); and Carl Marcus for his patience taking our photo while fighting off mosquitoes.

We would like to thank the schools that were used in examples of best practice in early childhood nature education, including All Seasons Preschool, Dodge Nature Preschool, Minneapolis Nature Preschool, My Nature Preschool at Tamarack Nature Center, Nature Preschool at Chippewa Nature Center, Shirley G. Moore Laboratory School at the University of Minnesota, Tucson Community School, University of Hawai'i at Mānoa Children's Center, and Valley View Preschool.

INTRODUCTION

From Julie: For those of you readers who are new to nature education, welcome to our world! You will find the connections between early childhood education philosophies and nature a comfortable fit. Your experience may closely mirror my journey. After twenty-five years in the field as a teacher and/or director in early care settings including Head Start, parent-cooperative nursery schools, for profit and nonprofit child care centers, and an inclusion-based public preschool, I set off on a new adventure: starting a preschool at a nature center. I found many similarities between the people drawn to each field. Both chose their fields because of deep convictions, got lousy salaries, worked hard, and played hard. There were also differences. A good example was when a preschool educator came across a dead creature in the wild and her reaction was, "So sad." I heard the naturalists instead say, "Cool!" I began to appreciate learning experiences, even dead creatures, as I broadened my educational practices to include what I learned working with dedicated naturalists. In the years after my time working as a teacher, director, and later as a consultant for nature-focused organizations, I have brought my newfound understanding to other jobs, including my current position as associate professor of early childhood education at University of Hawai'i Maui College. I wish a book like this existed when I first went to work at Dodge Nature Center, or even before when I worked with young children and their families, and moved from Arizona to Minnesota to Colorado to Hawaii and could no longer use my own childhood experiences to guide me.

From Sheila: For those of you who are already comfortable with nature education and are looking for ways to take your explorations with young children deeper, we hope this book will offer inspiration and community that will allow you to reflect on your teaching practices and nurture the relationship between children and nature. I entered the field from the opposite direction of Julie. I was focused on business management, health and safety, and environmental conservation. My background in biology fostered my love of nature as well as my work with the Minnesota Public Interest Research Group (MPIRG) around air quality and the Endangered Species Act (ESA), and working with children in local Kids for Saving Earth groups gave me an opportunity to focus on environmental issues with elementary children and college students. When I began at Dodge Nature Center, the extent of my early childhood education experience came from my own children and from our Early Childhood Family Education (ECFE) groups.

We have designed this book to meet the needs of a variety of readers. You can read the book from cover to cover and realize how much nature education you already offer and discover ways to increase the focus. You can select chapters to read to gain specific information on a particular area of nature education. You will find chapters on setting up your indoor and outdoor environments, on specific topics such as mammals and plants, and on children with special needs and their families. We recommend that all readers begin with chapter 1 to provide a framework for what the rest of the book offers. We have also included resources for you to use: sample letters for families at the end of each chapter, sample lessons for each topic, suggested children's books, books and other resources for adult learning, and suggested materials, supplies, and equipment.

We do not view ourselves as experts on early childhood nature education, but rather as voices from the trenches. We have included short stories from a variety of experts working in our field that are meant to inspire you.

CHAPTER 1

NATURE EDUCATION

Building a Connection with the Natural World

Julie's group of three-year-old children were in the classroom. Outside a thunderstorm with pounding rain was underway. Tommy couldn't settle into an indoor activity. He approached the teacher and said in a pleading voice, "Mrs. Powers, can't we go outside to play?" Julie responded, "Let's go look out the window and see." She took his hand, and they went to the window. Tommy saw the pouring rain and flash of lightning, sighed, and said, "I guess not." Julie responded, "We can go outside when it stops and look for puddles. Would you like to read a book about rain?" Tommy agreed, and they walked to the book corner together. By the time the rain had stopped and the group could go outdoors, Tommy had a better understanding of rain. What does this story tell us?

- **Like most young children, Tommy loves to play outdoors.** Many children must be coerced to come indoors from the playground; these are often the same children who dislike sedentary activities. This is a good reason to integrate outdoor experiences into many areas of your curriculum.

- **Nature gives us the chance to support inquiry.** Julie could have just told Tommy they couldn't go out because it was raining. Instead, she gave him support for finding the answer to his own question, "Can't we go outside?" Inquiry is how children begin learning to use their senses to find answers to what they truly care about, rather than counting on adults for the answers. Nature provides many opportunities to develop inquiry skills.

- **Taking the time for impromptu nature education will help children develop self-regulation skills.** Because Tommy could see the limits for himself, he was less likely to have a meltdown. As Tommy was invited to see the connection between his desires (playing outdoors) and the natural limits (thunder, lightning, and pouring rain), he could understand that this wasn't an adult just saying no, and a power struggle was averted. The more children can gather their own data regarding limits, the greater sense of control they have. Tommy was ready to hear that the chance to play outdoors was in his future.

- **Nature education provides opportunities to stretch children's interests.** Tommy might not be a child who enjoys listening to books, but because he had an immediate need to understand thunderstorms, he was easily drawn into hearing a story.

THE VALUE OF NATURE EXPERIENCES

Is nature education the newest thing? Early childhood education (ECE) programs have focused on nature experiences for generations. The ECE field has recently refocused on nature experiences in response to research showing the importance of connection to nature and the loss of these experiences as programs have been pressured to meet external standards and prepare for kindergarten. The good news is you don't have to choose! As you will see in this book, you can meet standards, prepare children for future learning, and meet your curriculum goals through nature experiences. Your program is special and your place in your community and in the world is unique. Using place-based education principles can help you and your children connect with nature in your own backyard and beyond. David Sobel (2004, 7) explains, "Place-based education is the process of using the local community and environment as a starting point to teach concepts in language arts, mathematics, social studies, science, and other subjects across the curriculum." This starting point can lead to deeper understanding and inspire more questions about the natural world that help foster children's explorations.

A Lifelong Gift

In *Happiness and Education*, Nel Noddings (2003, 240) states, "Happiness is not best construed as a state earned or promised for future life. Happiness in the present is not incompatible with future happiness and it may even be instrumental for future happiness. Educators should therefore give attention to the quality of students' present experience." She lays a foundation for creating happiness in the classroom, and this can start with you. Providing opportunities for children to find joy and happiness in nature is a lifelong gift that we can give to every child everywhere. The sense of awe and wonder that children find when deeply exploring in nature is unparalleled, and that type of happiness is a feeling we all strive for throughout our lives. Let's give this to our children right now.

> *From Sheila:* My seventh-grade teacher, Mr. Jackson, took us into the desert for a "surviving in the wild" walk. He gave us, a group of semi-interested adolescents, time to explore on our own. He asked us to look for "signs of danger" and showed us examples of safe, wild edibles in the Las Vegas valley. In this single class, I learned many facts about my nearby wild space. This field trip wasn't the beginning of my love for the desert, but it piqued my interest and helped me build a deeper understanding of the land. My love for the desert came years earlier when my parents let me explore on my own with my dog. Those early experiences with small pieces of nature in our own backyards are the foundation for building deeper experiences with nature. If we can

continue to foster the wonder and build understanding and awareness for the importance of natural spaces, we will give a lifelong gift to our children, communities, and planet.

Spending time in nature, and even viewing nature from an indoor space, has been shown to improve the mental health, well-being, and behavior of children and adults (Bowler et al. 2010; Townsend and Weerasuriya 2010). Unstructured outdoor free play provides children with cognitive, social, and health benefits (Burdette and Whitaker 2005; Matsuoka 2008). Additionally, children with ADHD have demonstrated improved outcomes when spending time in nature (Faber Taylor and Kuo 2011).

As Richard Louv coined in 2005, "nature-deficit disorder" describes the conditions he noticed occurring in children and society from the loss of a relationship with nature. Louv (2005, 36) defines nature-deficit disorder as "the human costs of alienation from nature, among them: diminished use of the senses, attention difficulties, and higher rates of physical and emotional illnesses." The Children and Nature Network's online research library deeply examines the positive outcomes of interactions with nature for children and families, including physical and mental health benefits, academic and cognitive benefits, and effects on conservation values, knowledge, and behaviors.

Nature Activities Provide Development Opportunities

The National Association for the Education of Young Children (NAEYC) states, "The development of children's perceptual abilities may suffer when so much of their experience is through television, computers, books, worksheets, and media that require only two senses. The senses of smell, touch, and taste, and the sense of motion through space are powerful modes of learning" (1998).

Children today spend more time in front of televisions, computers, and other screens than outdoors (American Academy of Pediatrics 2013). According to the American Academy of Child and Adolescent Psychiatry, "Children and adolescents spend a significant amount of time watching screens each day—including televisions, gaming consoles, computers, tablet devices, and smartphones. Children in the United States ages 8–18 spend on average 7.5 hours a day with media and technology screens" (AACAP 2015). The National Recreation and Park Association adds, "Children today spend less time outdoors than any other generation, devoting only four to seven minutes to unstructured outdoor play per day, while spending an average of seven and a half hours in front of electronic media" (NRPA 2017).

Theorist John Dewey warned of human dependence on secondary experiences, especially in early childhood. He cautioned that those secondary experiences could depersonalize human life and lead to lack of connection with the world and others (Louv 2005). Secondary experiences like those through photos or the internet limit children's role to that of a consumer of information and not an integral part of the dialogue of nature. Photographs, videos, and interactive 3-D simulators can give children a glimpse of spaces they may never experience, but they are not a substitute nor are they equivalent to time spent picking flowers, following a fox's tracks through the woods, or planting a garden. Primary experiences in nature allow children to explore their part in the natural world, and that is how the relationship between children and nature grows and flourishes.

Many barriers, such as fear of violence, limited access, and busy schedules, can prevent children from spending much time outdoors. However, because researchers have discovered many benefits of outdoor nature play, a growing number of educators are recognizing the importance of experiences outdoors and are finding ways to include these experiences during the significant time periods that children spend at school. These outdoor experiences through educational settings may provide the ideal opportunity for experiential learning that fosters the development of cognitive, social, emotional, and physical skills. Outdoor experiences in school also help develop positive environmental attitudes that can help lead to sustainable behaviors, thus improving the health of the earth and the lives of people globally.

In 1965 Rachel Carson wrote, "If facts are the seeds that later produce knowledge and wisdom, then the emotions and the impressions of the senses are the fertile soil in which the seeds must grow. The years of early childhood are the time to prepare the soil" (56).

These early experiences in and with nature can help us prepare citizens of the Earth with the connection, interest, and ability to care that is needed to be stewards of our home. As stated in the Oceans Exhibit at the Smithsonian's Museum of Natural History, "Society has choices to make. Doing nothing is a choice."

Adding Nature Experiences Incrementally

Working on a new focus for your curriculum can feel overwhelming. Find your comfort zone for how much to include nature experiences. Once you experience success, you are likely to add more.

Try adding a nature activity on occasion. You might start by looking at how to add a nature experience into each new curriculum topic you offer. You will find examples of activities throughout this book. Once you are comfortable adding some nature experiences, you might be ready to offer curriculum studies that are centered on nature topics. Eventually you may have nature education as the foundation of your curriculum. In each chapter, you will find information on adding a little or a lot of nature experiences for each potential topic.

Challenges to Incorporating Nature Experiences

Every program has access to nature experiences if you know where to look. In this book, we offer ideas for a wide range of ecosystems and school environments. The following illustrates examples of challenges you may encounter in a variety of settings and ways to overcome those challenges.

Licensing limitations

Some programs are limited by regional licensing standards. For example, some creatures, such as reptiles, birds, or amphibians, are not allowed in some classrooms, food preparation may not be allowed, and limitations on field trips may affect nature opportunities. In this book, we include ideas so you can offer nature experiences without breaking rules.

Urban areas

Many children living in urban areas lack access to nature for a variety of reasons. Sometimes the neighborhoods are unsafe, either from crime or pollution, and others lack resources and places for children to play outdoors. However, there are many examples in cities like New York, Chicago, Baltimore, and Minneapolis where vacant lots and building rooftops have been turned into places of refuge and play. The adults in these areas prioritized natural spaces and have worked to make them safe and accessible for young children and families.

Natural phenomena and severe weather

Earthquakes, tsunamis, tornados, hurricanes, wildfires, and other disasters may affect programs. If we don't help children understand what each phenomenon is and how to be safe, they may fear nature. Schools should develop emergency action plans and practice drills to help children and adults prepare for emergencies. As climate change continues to reshape our environment, we have seen increases in severe weather across the country. During these times, finding developmentally appropriate curricular ideas to continue to build on experiences with nature is important. After a severe storm is also a wonderful time to engage children in working in and with their community to do cleanup, trail repair, and healing.

Desert environments

Seeing lesson plans for falling leaves can be frustrating if your environment does not include deciduous trees. The desert is alive with wonderful nature opportunities. In this book, you will find ideas involving weather changes, plants, animals, and minerals to make studying nature in desert environments exciting.

Coastal environments

Programs that are near the ocean have very different opportunities. We offer ideas for activities involving ocean safety, creatures of the ocean, plants, and minerals.

Benefits for Children with Behavioral Challenges

Nature experiences can support and inspire children who are experiencing behavior challenges. Children who are less interested in typical preschool skills-based activities, such as reading in a large group setting or doing fine-motor projects at a table, may find passion in nature experiences, especially outdoor activities. The story of Tommy at the beginning of this chapter provided an example. For many children, using nature experiences to hook their interest can help them develop confidence, enjoy school more, and learn necessary skills through activities that interest them. Throughout this book, we provide suggestions for using nature activities to support a wide variety of development.

Connecting Nature to Learning Standards

In early childhood programs, you may have state early learning standards to assess children's progress as well as NAEYC or local Quality Rating and Improvement System (QRIS) for classroom communities or program expectations. These standards help build high-quality programs and provide meaningful experiences for children, and incorporating authentic nature activities into the classroom and utilizing spaces outdoors can help you meet these standards. If your program is focused on kindergarten readiness, Next Generation Science Standards (NGSS), Head Start standards, or the federal Title 1 testing in reading and math, experiences with nature can build these skills and knowledge that help learning become concrete for young children. The benefits for children's emotional and cognitive development continue to be researched, such as a 2014 study in Massachusetts, which found that the green areas surrounding elementary schools led to academic benefits in both reading and math performance (Wu et al. 2014).

Meeting children's individual learning goals, building a sense of community, increasing executive function skills, and fostering an environmental ethic can be achieved through nature-based experiences. You will find examples of standards that help connect nature-based curriculum to learning goals in the sample lessons in appendix 1.

Opportunities for Risk-Taking

Risk-taking is important for growth. We learn that it is either safe to take a risk or it is not. School success depends on the willingness to risk the wrong answer, approach a potential friend, or work on a new physical ability. Nature activities provide real opportunities for children to take part in physical, social, and emotional risk assessment and challenge.

One example comes from our experience at Dodge Nature Preschool. The children found a rather steep hill on the grounds they named "challenge hill." Some children climbed it easily from the first day, scampering up like mountain goats. Other children were more cautious, either because they were less physically daring or because they lacked the gross-motor skills to climb the hill. The class returned to the hill often, and eventually all the children could climb it, to the cheers of their classmates. New challenges and risks came throughout the seasons as the hill became covered with snow, ice, or mud. Each child had to reevaluate the risk of climbing the hill and using new strategies to match the challenge.

Risk-taking and skills at analyzing risks are not just important for school success, they are important for life success. Research supports that adults are not very good at risk assessment.

From Julie: I am noticing a generation who has mostly experienced highly controlled contact with nature and are particularly bad at risk assessment. I call this the "theme park" expectation of nature. In Hawaii tourists are washed out to sea every year by rogue waves. Tourists visiting the lava fields on the island of Hawaii stand on hot coals until their tennis shoes melt. I am convinced that they believe, "If it is dangerous, they wouldn't let me do it," because we have so many simulated experiences, such as amusement park rides, that seem dangerous but are safe.

We act contrary to accurate data—that is, we are more frightened of terrorist attacks than pandemic diseases, of plane crashes than car crashes, of bee stings than mosquito bites. Such poor risk assessment can cause parents to make uninformed choices for their children, voters to make uninformed choices in politicians, and investors to make uninformed choices with their money. Childhood experiences assessing physical risks, learning to take care in risky situations, and developing the skills needed to successfully climb a tree, jump over a puddle without landing in mud, or avoid touching a sea urchin can transfer to risk-taking skills as adults. Several studies over the past twenty years have found that most playground injuries are scrapes, bruises, contusions, concussions, and fractures, which have resulted from falls from playground structures or collisions with swings or other equipment (Ball 2002; Bienefeld, Pickett, and Carr 1996; Mack, Hudson, and Thompson 1997; Phelan et al. 2001; Sawyers 1994; Swartz 1992). This demonstrates that natural playgrounds are a great option for your early childhood outdoor environment and can add an appropriate level of risk while balancing the safety of young children.

Family Engagement

Most of us want to find authentic ways to engage families in their children's learning. By focusing on nature experiences, we can involve family members who might be less interested in the typical "read to your child" experiences we encourage. Experiences in nature allow for community building activities like gardening, cleanup projects, and play. In this book, we will provide sample letters to parents for each chapter that you can use as you see fit to help engage your families in the learning and joy you are experiencing in nature.

From Sheila: Whether you remember long walks with your grandparents, helping around the yard with your parents, fishing with your uncle or aunt, picnics with your cousins, or playing in a vacant lot with friends, chances are that some of your best childhood memories occurred outside with a loved one. Those moments of peace, connection, and wonder are some of the best parts of childhood, and that connection is something all children should experience. Sometimes as adults we don't remember specific early moments, but we recognize those moments as foundational to our development. As an adult with my own children, I went back to visit my elementary school because one of my early teachers was going to retire soon. I entered a classroom full of aquariums and terrariums, photos of nature and bugs, and posters about the things we can do to protect the planet. It felt like home, and I realized more clearly that this teacher had an influence in my early development as a person, as a steward, and as a scientist of the world.

When choosing an elementary school for my oldest daughter, Faline, we easily decided on the environmental magnet school—it had all the natural elements, an environmental educator, and access to a wonderful creek outside. I really loved the school. Faline was happy although more interested in dance and music, which were offered occasionally but were not a priority at this school. After a couple of years of evening and weekend dance classes and music lessons, we found an art magnet where she could study the Russian language, violin, and many styles of dance during the day, and our evenings and weekends were now free for taking walks, exploring nature, and spending more quality time together as a family. Her art school also had a wonderful after-school nature program. This was the perfect balance, and now, with a bachelor's degree in environmental science, Faline is pursuing a law degree with a focus on environmental law.

Stories from the Field

I was doing an outreach program for a local high-rise apartment complex with a high Somali population in Minneapolis. I visited once a week to focus on nature education and experiences with children. My previous programs had been mildly successful, with the children's attitude fluctuating between interest and silliness. The last week I was there, our program was about worms, and it was really popular. We went into the alley to a small patch of grass by the back of the building—a space between the asphalt and a chain-link fence. I gave them all small bait coolers to use as mini worm bins. One little boy, Abdi, was hanging out along the edge and acting kind of interested at the beginning, but also making fun of our activity with some of the older kids. I think that was due to peer pressure. But there was something about the worms that drew him in, and he fell in love with investigating worms very quickly. Abdi was at my side the entire rest of the afternoon, asking all kinds of questions about the worms. We had a party at the end of the program, and the families all came. I read *Wonderful Worms* to the children and their parents, and we enjoyed snacks and drinks. Abdi contently sat against the wall with his worm farm in one hand and the book in the other. He wasn't the least bit interested in the party. He continued to ask me questions throughout the rest of the celebration about worms, like, "Do worms climb walls?" For Abdi the program initiated a transformation—a real connection with the natural world. —**Marcie Oltman, MA, MEd, director, Tamarack Nature Center, White Bear Lake, Minnesota**

• • •

I am continually amazed by children. They are aware of and knowledgable about the world if we only pay attention. I am particularly amazed at the role nature-based education plays in children's scientific knowledge. It seems so simple, but their insights can be quite profound.

A prime example of this was last fall when I was walking through a Michigan forest with a group of preschoolers. We were headed out to the woods to build forts. I was toward the back of the group with a handful of children clearly in no hurry and walking at their own thoughtful pace. The recently fallen leaves were swooshing and crunching under our feet. Suddenly one of the young boys stopped, looked up at a maple tree missing its leaves, and said, "That tree is dead." Not wanting to stifle the potential conversation, I said, "How do you know?"

As he thought about the answer to my question, we both looked up and noticed a white pine tree. Not being able to help myself, I pointed and added, "Is that tree dead too?" He suddenly responded, "No. It's different. It's like when . . ." He took a long pause and continued talking about the maple tree. "You know how sometimes flowers close up at night? And then the next day they open up?" I wasn't quite sure what he was thinking when he added, "Or like we go to sleep at night and then wake up in the morning. That tree is like that." Suddenly I realized what he was saying. He was describing dormancy but didn't have the vocabulary word. His reference to the closed flower and sleeping at night showed he didn't really mean dead, or gone forever, but rather a temporary stop in activity. That is the very definition of dormancy.

My realization of his understanding of the scientific concept of dormancy came about because of an open-ended question, time, patience, and application of my own knowledge of plants. Again, children have a great deal of knowledge and wisdom about the world if we pay attention. —**Rachel Larimore**, MA, Nature Preschool at Chippewa Nature Center, Midland, Michigan

ORGANIZATION OF THE BOOK

Readers will have different comfort levels with adding nature opportunities to their classrooms. Some of your comfort will depend on the flexibility of your curriculum, some on your knowledge about or enthusiasm for a specific area of nature studies. Even teachers who have always provided a nature focus may find that a new group of children or families offer challenges they haven't experienced before.

In each chapter, we will provide simple ways to offer nature experiences we refer to as "Dipping Your Toe In" (the water). Examples include spontaneous teachable moments to look for, simple materials and props to add to the classroom, and stories to read.

The next level is called "Wading In." This section offers ideas for adding more complexity in what you offer to teach children about a nature topic. Examples include activities, displays, visitors, and field trips.

The most complex level we call "Diving In." This section offers ideas for complex activities or topics of study surrounding an area of nature. Figure 1.1 is a topic web for a study of flowers as an example of how you can use your ideas to create in-depth curriculum.

ENVIRONMENTAL CHANGES TO INCREASE NATURE OPPORTUNITIES

Below are some general recommendations for changes you can make to your indoor or outdoor spaces. These adaptations to your environment will allow children to have hands-on opportunities with natural elements through play.

Figure 1.1 Flower Topic Web

SCIENCE
- Taking flowers apart and examining with a microscope
- Observing insects on flowers
- Germinating seeds from flowers
- Seed socks

LITERACY
- *Flower Garden*
- *Sunflower House*
- *Seed Song*
- *Tia Maria's Garden*
- *Incredible Plants*
- *Planting a Rainbow*
- *The Tiny Seed*
- *The Reason for a Flower*
- *The Dandelion Seed*

ART
- Flower petal collage
- Flower rubbings or pressings
- Painting with flowers as brushes
- Flowers as a centerpiece in painting area

BLOCKS & CONSTRUCTION
- Making flower boxes
- Adding artificial flowers to block area for use in construction

SOCIAL STUDIES
- Florist area or flower stand in dramatic play
- Visit to a garden center
- Visit from a lei maker or florist

MATHEMATICS
- Measuring height of flowers
- Comparing or counting sunflower seeds
- Making patterns with flower petals
- Matching flowers and seed packets

TECHNOLOGY
- Photographing flowers
- Watching video of seed germination and flower growth

Flowers

MUSIC & MOVEMENT
- "The Green Grass Grows All Around"
- "Sing a Song of Flowers"
- "I'm a Little Flower Pot"
- Moving like flowers in the wind to music

FINE MOTOR & SENSORY
- Potting soil and artificial flowers in sensory table
- Matching flowers to soaps with similar scents
- Matching leis

LARGE MOTOR
- Planting a flower garden
- Walking around the community looking for flowers
- Chasing dandelion seeds

COOKING & FOOD
- Sunflower butter on celery
- Sunflower seeds and cream cheese on crackers
- Edible flower salad

Access to Handling Natural Substances

As early childhood settings are becoming more focused on safe/commercial/tested/liability-proof materials and equipment, children often have less access to objects found in nature. Natural materials have their own nonuniform texture, smell, and look. They may not hold up as well as plastic, but the weathering of natural materials to the point of needing to be replaced is part of nature. Children who only touch objects made of plastic will not learn strategies for avoiding splinters, estimating how heavy an object is before lifting it, and truly understanding how nature interacts with itself. Look for ways to add natural elements to your outdoor play area. If you are saddled with a plastic "super" climbing structure, you can still add tree stumps for climbing on, stepping stones for jumping to, hollow wooden blocks for building with, and fencing made from sticks, straw, bamboo, stones, and bricks. If you have the space, planting trees for climbing and shade can be a great investment.

From Julie: At Tucson Community School, the climbing arrangement was a group of sturdy wooden boxes with pallet-like tops, giant wooden electrical spools, and sturdy boards with cleats on the edges to catch on the boxes and spools. Each day, a group of children was assigned to add the boards to the boxes and spools to create a new and interesting arrangement. Teachers always checked to ensure safety before children began to climb on the structures. This daily experience gave children opportunities for assessing risk, handling natural materials, solving problems, and working out mathematical puzzles. It also made children more likely to take part in gross-motor activities.

You can also collect natural objects for all parts of the classroom. Below are some examples of how to bring nature into the classroom:

- **You can increase the powers of imagination through adding natural objects like rocks, pine cones, leaves, or large seeds in the pretend play center in place of purchased replicas.** Wooden bowls and spoons are used to symbolize many things, and leaves can become pretend food.

- **Natural objects can be added to the block area to increase problem solving.** Sticks, boards, and branches of nonuniform size create different mathematical challenges from unit blocks.

- **The art center can be enlivened with nature.** Real clay has completely different properties than play dough. Natural objects can be used in collage. Damp sand or soil becomes highly textural fingerpaint.

- **The science center should have changing nature-based experiences to encourage inquiry.** You will find many ideas in this book for natural science experiences.

You can provide live, growing plants even if you have a tiny outdoor play area. Research supports the positive effects of access to live plants. *The International Journal for the Advancement of Counseling* shared a research article on the benefits of including more nature into counseling titled "Nature-Based Counseling: Integrating the Healing Benefits of Nature into Practice" (Greenleaf, Bryant, and Pollock 2014). This article highlighted the psychological benefits of utilizing nature as a treatment for emotional and behavioral challenges. Another study titled "Health Benefits of a View of Nature through the Window: a Quasi-experimental Study of Patients in a Residential Rehabilitation Center" found that "an unobstructed bedroom view to natural surroundings appears to have better supported improvement in self-reported physical and mental health during a residential rehabilitation program" (Raanaas, Patil, and Hartig 2011).

- **Find a space for plants outdoors.** Concentrate on native plants, which are most likely to handle weather well. Fight to keep trees that others might want to remove because they are "messy" or use water. Be sure to communicate your strategy with whoever takes care of your grounds. Too often we experience frustration when a new worker mows the prairie grasses or moves a few logs to mow, not knowing that our protected asparagus was just beginning to sprout.

- **Plant a garden.** You will find ideas for gardening in chapter 8.

- **Include plants indoors.** Real plants don't take up any more room than artificial plants, and they have more value from a curricular standpoint. Real plants change, need care, blossom, clean the air, and more.

Because more of us live in cities rather than on farms or in rural areas with access to wildlife, many children have fewer direct daily experiences with animals than past generations have enjoyed. Not only do animals bring joy to children's lives, but they provide experiences with the life cycle, providing care, and seeing how animals change and grow. Moreover, when the first death children face is that of a classroom pet, having the support of their family and classroom community in dealing with the loss is a valuable experience.

- **If possible, have a class pet.** You will find suggestions for a wide variety of pets throughout this book. Choosing the right pet for your classroom by considering safety, curricular needs, and resources is important. Make sure that the pet you select will have a positive experience in your setting, keeping in mind the attention this pet will need, facility accommodations when school isn't in session (will it get too hot or cold in the classroom), noise level tolerance of the pet, and preparation for the long or short life cycle of the animal.

- **Find community resources for observing and interacting with animals.** Zoos are not the only resource. Look for wild animal rehabilitation programs, aquariums, aviaries, farms, ranches, pet stores, groomers, and so on.

- **Invite families to bring their pets to school.** Bringing a pet to school can be a real treat for the child as well as for the other children in the class. Please be sure to check with other families ahead of time to incorporate any concerns about allergies, fears, or religious beliefs.

Weather can change quickly, and children benefit from observing different phases of weather. This is especially important for dealing with weather-related fears.

- **If possible, include architectural features that allow children to observe weather.** If windows are too high, create a platform for observation.

- **Give children access to screened porches.** Too often, screened or three-season porches are used for storage or cubbies, or have too much clutter for children to use them for observation.

- **Create wild animal observation stations near classroom windows.** Bird feeders, salt licks, and milkweed plants will all draw wildlife close enough to be observed.

RESOURCES

Author Favorites

- **Julie's favorite:** *Roxaboxen* by Alice McLerran. 1991. New York: HarperCollins. This book takes place in my native Arizona and tells the story of a group of children who create a world of their own in the desert. I love the absence of adults because it reminds me of my own childhood in the desert.

- **Sheila's favorite:** *Play with Me* by Marie Hall Ets. 1976. New York: Viking. This picture book explores the simple dream of having a relationship with animals. The main character first tries to play with different animals by approaching or chasing them but then learns that she must be patient and let them approach her and "play" in their own way.

Resource Books for Adults

- *Worms, Shadows, and Whirlpools* by Karen Worth and Sharon Grollman. 2003. Washington DC: NAEYC.

- *Natural Wonders: A Guide to Early Childhood for Environmental Educators.* 2002. Minnesota Early Childhood Environmental Education Consortium. This book is a free resource available online at www.seek.state.mn.us/sites/default/files /naturalwonders.pdf.

Sample Letter to Families

Each chapter will have a letter you can copy, personalize, and share with your families. This chapter provides a letter explaining to parents why we focus on nature.

NATURE PLAY

Dear Families,

The special memories and joys of childhood that have often been associated with the outdoors are different for this generation, and in many ways are more limited. The outdoors that many of us grew up experiencing is disappearing from the lives of our children. To fight this trend, we regularly implement practices at school that encourage a healthy relationship between children and nature.

Although real barriers exist that prevent many children from spending an optimal amount of time outdoors, researchers have discovered many benefits of outdoor nature play. A growing number of educators are recognizing the importance of experiences outdoors as well. These outdoor experiences may provide the ideal opportunities for experiential learning that fosters the development of cognitive, social, emotional, executive function, and physical skills. Outdoor experiences also aid in the development of positive environmental attitudes, leading to sustainable behaviors that will improve the health of the earth and the lives of people globally.

We know that while this play is engaging, it can also be messy, so we truly appreciate your washing extra laundry, packing extra clothing, and possibly even cleaning your car when your children so thoroughly explore their world. Thank you for all that you do in support of our nature engagement and exploration, and please let us know if there is anything we can do to support you.

CHAPTER 2

DOES IT WORK FOR MY KIDS?

Individual Needs in Your Setting

Children with varying capabilities benefit from experiences in nature. The children in our classrooms have many varying abilities, and knowing how to include everyone in nature experiences can seem difficult. If we plan ahead and consider each individual child, we can create an experience from which every child will benefit.

From Sheila: All children deserve access to and time in nature. Many nature-based programs have shared that their populations lack diversity in their children and families, and this can have far-reaching consequences for children and the environment. If only children with privilege can enjoy the many benefits of a relationship with the natural world—like lower stress levels and higher cognitive and social gains—we will further disadvantage many young children and their families. However, as nature-based programs continue to grow, I am certain they will reach more families and appeal to their needs of connecting with the natural world. As a person of color, I understand the deep love that many of us share for the natural world. I have been fortunate enough to grow up with two parents who loved camping, hiking, and exploring. I learned to swim at an early age, hiked, climbed, and played alone in the desert near our home. As an adult, I continue to nurture this passion and have joined several outdoor groups, including Outdoor Afro and the Sierra Club, that help keep my relationship with the natural world strong. Organizations like this can reconnect people of color to the outdoors. Whether the families in your program enjoy swimming at the beach, barbecues and parties in the park, or climbing around the rocky deserts, they all have a connection with the outdoors that can be supported and encouraged through our work with their children.

From Julie: Another population that can be left out of nature experiences is children who are dual-language learners. All cultures have a connection with nature, and all languages have vocabulary for nature. Take advantage of these teachable opportunities to encourage adults to learn the first language and culture of the children they work with, encourage children to learn English as well as their home language, and build a love of learning through meaningful experiences.

Stories from the Field

One of the most memorable moments I had while supervising a student teacher focused on a four-year-old girl with autism and her experience with a baby chick. I arrived at the school early while the children were entering the classroom. Jodi—the little girl with autism—entered the room with her mother. She didn't greet the teacher or the other children. In fact, she didn't even seem to notice them. Jodi walked directly to a table where an incubator with eggs was displayed. Jodi's mother was talking with the teacher when Jodi came running back to her. Jodi reached for her mother's hand, pointed toward the table, and said, "Look!" The response from both Jodi's mother and the teacher was of surprise—almost disbelief. This was early November. Jodi had been in this class since the beginning of September and had not uttered one word in the classroom until that morning, nor had she tried to communicate with the teacher. Now she was animated and wanted to share a message. Jodi pulled her mother over to the table and pointed to a baby chick struggling its way out of an egg. Again, Jodi said, "Look," while also reaching for her teacher's hand. Jodi was looking at her teacher and her mother. She was also looking at the other children who had gathered around the table. Jodi's mother couldn't hold back the tears as she first hugged Jodi and then the teacher. This was a significant breakthrough for Jodi. The teacher had tried in so many ways to get Jodi to interact with her and the other children. Nothing had worked. This morning it was more than a baby chick that broke through a shell. The excitement of watching it happen helped Jodi break through a shell of her own. —**Ruth A. Wilson**, PhD, author and educator, Albuquerque, New Mexico

• • •

I came from a farm-based nature preschool and my coteacher came from the zoo, so we both missed observing animal interactions with children. We were limited with what types of animals we could bring into our classroom, however, and we eventually settled on rats.

I had known Ryan from a previous program I had worked in. I knew he was shy and nervous around other children. Ryan was instantly drawn to our class pets. Each morning as he'd enter our classroom, he'd pop over to check on the rats and say hello to them before heading outdoors. The days that we played in our indoor classroom, Ryan initially spent much of his time interacting with the rats. This was a safe place for him. As he played with the rats, he'd stop and observe the play of his peers. Occasionally his classmates would come over to him to see what he was doing and also to check on the rats. Conversations about the rats would casually start, and Ryan would talk to his classmates. His social worries seemed to go away when the rats were involved.

Every day Ryan seemed to have a new idea as to what the rats might like. One day as some of his classmates were playing with the plastic wild animals with their block structures, Ryan picked up a toy bison and showed it to one of the rats. He was intrigued with the rat's response. Ryan created his own animal enrichment activities and quickly became an expert on the rats in our classroom. —**Jenny Hanlon**, MEd, preschool teacher, Tamarack Nature Center, White Bear Lake, Minnesota

DIPPING YOUR TOE IN

Plan your curriculum based on the interests and needs of your current group of children rather than simply thinking, "It's October, time for pumpkins."

Invite a naturalist or other expert in natural history. Many cities have nature centers or staff in their parks and recreation departments who know the community and can offer experiences for young children at your school or center. To make the biggest impact, these visits should occur as often as possible and ensure that the guest speakers always keep in mind the developmental stages of the children in your program. They generally have access to many natural items that can complement your curriculum.

Get outdoors every day. Aim to go outside every day, even if you have children who don't enjoy it or parents who don't value it, or if it means having to give up something else in your schedule. Offer a variety of outdoor activities so children and families who are not yet comfortable outdoors will find things that are familiar, engaging, or inspiring. The benefits of getting children outdoors every day, even if it is just for a few minutes, are worth it. You can find more information on the benefits of spending time outdoors in chapter 3.

WADING IN

Offer small-group investigations. Utilizing small groups can allow you to effectively meet the needs of your class or larger group of children. You can have several small groups concurrently explore similar or very different topics. Small groups can be assigned or selected by the children. When assigning small groups, you can consider age, temperament, and interest. For instance, if a classroom had many children interested in animals but different age groups or levels of understanding about animals, one group could focus on pets and caring for pets, while the other could look for tracks or finding signs of animals on a walk.

Make your curriculum as place-based and child-centered as possible. For example, if you live in an ecosystem where you can garden year-round, it is appropriate for gardening to be a part of your daily curriculum. However, in places where the growing season is only six months long, wait for natural cues to introduce gardening or harvest.

Explore your natural surroundings on a field trip. This can feel different from a field trip to the theater or museum because what happens will be driven by the state of the local environment. A recent storm could lead to a community service project. If it recently snowed, you could spend the time following animal tracks.

DIVING IN

Hiring specialized staff as additional resources can help the children, teacher, and classroom. Adding staff to your program who have worked with children with special needs, who are from your local community, and who are naturalists/environmental educators can accelerate the pace and improve the quality of implementing an individualized nature-based curriculum that meets the needs of your community. If you are not able to influence hiring, reach out to find volunteers in these areas.

Offering regular small-group experiences to your schedule can allow for more one-on-one contact with each child. If small group experiences become a regular part of your day, whether they are hiking/exploration groups or groups that meet around the school, you can continue to explore more deeply, work on projects with a focus, and help children more fully investigate their own questions.

INCLUSION OF ALL CHILDREN

Preschoolers are beginning to understand that people are individuals with different experiences, needs, and wants. This is prime time for learning about the perspective of others and makes exploration so much fun. When a child mentions something that is different at his home, it is an opportunity for developing understanding. Talking about differences with children and encouraging dialogue about what it looks like to meet each child's needs is important. For example, some children may need to have gum to focus or not put toys in their mouths, while some may need to sit on a special seat at group time. Acknowledging human differences also supports understanding of nature with all its differences, and nature in its turn helps children honor differences between people.

Below is a list of a few physical or cognitive conditions that may limit a person's movements, senses, or activities, and examples of how you can improvise to make it work in your setting.

Children with Behavioral Issues

- Be ready to run with the children yourself, and have other teachers available to support the other children.

- Wear a backpack so you can be mobile and yet have all the items you need for being outdoors with children.

- Have the best ratio your program can afford to allow teachers to work one-on-one with children whenever needed.

- Engage support staff and administrators to provide supervision at times when behavior issues most often occur. These tend to be transition times, whole group times, and times with lots of rules and expectations, but you will learn the patterns of children in your group.

- If a child is attempting to hurt other children, having an adult stay with that child at difficult times during the day is critical. Being proactive and preventing the behavior helps to keep the behavior pattern from becoming ingrained and protects relationships between children.

Children with Limited Mobility

- Before enrolling new children with mobility issues, tour the program, especially the outdoor spaces, with the family before they accept so that they fully understand what their child will experience.

- Have a plan for inclement weather transportation—sleds for the snow, wagons for small trails, umbrellas for rainy days.

- Ensure that your entire space meets Americans with Disabilities Act (ADA) regulations. This isn't important only for children with mobility issues, but also for staff and family members. Some regional licensing agencies have appropriately stringent regulations about meeting ADA regulations. Some areas grandfather in or exempt many programs. Don't depend only on licensing or funding agencies to set the bar for you. Continue to strive for the highest quality experiences for everyone in your program.

Children Who Are Deaf or Hearing Impaired

- Be sure to communicate with the other staff in your program about any hearing difficulties a child may experience—this is for safety as well as guidance concerns.

- If a child has a cochlear implant, be sure they are able to use the playground slide— sometimes the static can damage the processors.

- Share information about an implant with all children in the group in a matter-of-fact way. Curious peers have been known to grab or pull on implants.

Children Who Are Blind or Have Low Vision

- Before enrolling new children with vision issues, tour the program, especially the outdoor spaces, with the family before they accept so that they fully understand what their child will experience.

- Provide as many sensory experiences as possible throughout the classroom and outdoors.

- On your daily checks of the school, remember to look for new items, such as fallen logs or puddles, and walk children with low vision through these areas to acquaint them with the changes.

Children Who Are Nonverbal or Mute

- Offer experiences that do not rely on the child participating orally (writing is a form of verbalization according to reading specialists), such as writing in journals, story dictation, and acting, or listening and moving music experiences. This allows the child to continue to build community without verbal interactions.

- Teach the other children in the class ways they can communicate with the child, and help them understand that they can hear and understand them, but just isn't able to respond to them with words.

CULTURAL CONSIDERATIONS

Building trust with families is an essential part of any educational and child care setting. Hiring a diverse staff that understands child development and is willing to continue learning about the variety of children's needs is also important. Learning about their child's special needs can be difficult for families, and they must research, learn, and incorporate new routines into their daily lives. They often don't want teachers to take on that "burden," so you need to continue to assure them that working with a child with any need is not a burden but a joyous part of your work.

It also takes time for families to trust that we can care for their physically vulnerable children when outdoors, on trips, or in less controlled environments. Resist feeling defensive if parents with children who have special needs ask a lot of questions or even choose not to allow their child to take part in some activities. Inviting parents to join in, videotaping the experience, and listening to their suggestions for keeping their children safe all help build trust.

Collaborating with Parents

Including children with special needs can be anxiety provoking for many educators. The Individuals with Disabilities Education Act (IDEA) is often misunderstood. Some educators either find excuses for restricting enrollment or eliminate too many activities due to lack of understanding. One important aspect of the law to understand is that even private programs are required to include children with special needs with a few exceptions:

It would place an undue burden on the program.
The exception that is most abused is claiming that an accommodation places an undue burden on the program. A small program likely cannot afford a nurse. But even for children who are medically fragile, there are often ways to make nature programs work. The easiest challenges to solve are those of physical access. More challenging are those that relate to personnel. In one nature-based program, the staff and parents worked together to write a grant proposal to a philanthropic organization asking for funds for a special education assistant to help a child with autism take full advantage of the program. Challenge yourself to find creative solutions with parents.

It would change the nature of the program.

Solutions can often be found to the challenge that an accommodation would change the nature of the program. The need might be for a shorter day for a child who is medically fragile. We want all children to attend school as much as possible for inclusion in the community, but there may be days when a child's white blood cell count may be too low to make it safe for the child to be around certain animals. The families and staff should work together to find solutions for those times.

> *From Julie:* One time a parent with a severely medically and mentally challenged child contacted me about registering her child at our nature-based program. Rather than tell her the reasons it might not work, I invited her to come meet with me. We walked the grounds, and she saw the program in action and read the brochure that described the goals of our program. She concluded that her child would not thrive in this program but was highly appreciative of my openness to exploring the idea.

Children with Health Challenges

You will read many ideas in other chapters regarding how to include children with allergies or impulse control issues. The ADA statute Title III Section 301, Public Law 101–336 explains that programs must make adaptations to meet the needs of children in child care by removing physical barriers to access and safety as long as it is "easily accomplished and able to be carried out without much difficulty or expense." This law tends to be overinterpreted to keep children on the autism spectrum out of classrooms. The ADA also clearly prohibits the "imposition or application of eligibility criteria that screen out or tend to screen out an individual with a disability . . . from fully and equally enjoying goods, services, facilities, advances and accommodations" (Title III Section 302, PL 101–336 [2] [i]). However, it does acknowledge that programs do not have to do things that involve "significant difficulty or expense."

Rarely does including a child in a preschool classroom constitute a danger to others if adults are willing to examine their teaching practices. To borrow an idea from Harvard law professor and political activist Lani Guinier when she wrote about affirmative action, children with special needs can be the "canaries in the coal mine" of our preschools (Guinier and Torres 2002). If children with special needs are struggling, more typically developing children are likely also struggling. The difference is that typically developing children tend to be better at faking understanding than children who have special needs.

HEALTH, SAFETY, AND GUIDANCE ISSUES

Children who are impulsive can put themselves and others in danger when we take them outside of the boundaries of playgrounds and classrooms. Having general guidelines for the children so they know what the expectations are in the space is essential. Teacher preparation and support is critical to making this successful. Having proper ratios to support children, as well as appropriate training in child development and risk assessment will all help provide the best structure to support young children exploring.

For example, if you have trees on the playground, establish rules about climbing, such as how high children can climb and that a teacher must be present. Be sure you are in communication with your teaching team and set clear supervision roles for children who have impulse control issues or are continuously testing the boundaries of the guidelines or the space. For example, if you have a child who doesn't observe boundaries around water, be sure that any excursion involving water exploration has an adult who is focused on that child alone.

> *From Julie:* We had an impulsive child in our program. When we went on walks, he was likely to run off when he saw something interesting. One strategy that worked well was asking him if he could walk by himself or wanted to hold the hand of an adult. He often said he wanted to walk by himself but then would again start to run off. Through my working to develop a close relationship with him, he learned to build self-regulation because he wanted to do what I, his beloved teacher, wanted from him. One day I said to him, "When you run off, I am afraid you will be hurt, and I don't want anything bad to happen to you!" He responded, "I love you, Julie," and took my hand. He still forgot sometimes, but it got easier. Focusing on building trust by starting each walk with a choice, rather than assuming he would run off and needed to hold the hand of the teacher was key.

RESOURCES

Author Favorites

- **Julie's favorite:** *Be Good to Eddie Lee* by Virginia Fleming. 1993. New York: Philomel Books. This beautifully illustrated story tells the story of three children playing near a pond. One child (Eddie Lee) has Down syndrome. He is picked on by another boy, but Eddie Lee's understanding of nature helps the children out of a bad situation.

- **Sheila's favorite:** *Tough Boris* by Mem Fox. 1998. New York: Houghton Mifflin Harcourt. This book helps readers see people as unique individuals when they take the opportunity to get to know others. It also demonstrates the special relationship that animals have in our lives.

Resource Books for Adults

- *Practical Solutions to Practically Every Problem* by Steffen Saifer. 2003. St. Paul, MN: Redleaf Press. This book has ideas for just about any challenge you can think of in just a couple of pages. Strategies for dealing with general issues, including challenging behavior, parental concerns, and health concerns, can be useful when venturing into nature education.

- *Black and Brown Faces in America's Wild Places: African Americans Making Nature and the Environment a Part of Their Everyday Lives* by Dudley Edmondson. 2006.

Cambridge, MN: Adventure Publications. This book highlights the experiences of several African American individuals around the country with a deep connection to the natural world and is an inspiration for others to join in the adventure.

Materials for Children with Disabilities

Free and Collectible Materials

- **Standing tables, support chairs, and walkers.** This equipment should be available for individual children through grants or their public school to support their individual education plans (IEPs). Having the correct equipment to ensure involvement in all activities is important. If children with special physical needs are only provided activities at a special table away from the group, they don't benefit from the interaction of or with their peers.

Best Indoor Materials to Purchase If You Have Limited Funds

- **Wagons with sides.** A wagon will help bring children who have limited mobility, limited energy, or limited pulmonary function on walks and field trips. Pulling or pushing the wagon is a way to keep other children with you who might be likely to run away, teaches responsibility, and builds strength, so it is win-win for the whole group.

- **Sleds.** If you live in a snowy area, sleds have the same benefits as wagons.

Extras If You Have More Funds

- **Shade screens.** Keeping children who are photosensitive due to medication or other reasons cool and safe from sunrays is important.

- **Accessible water tables.** Water tables come in a variety of sizes and heights. If the height of your table is not adjustable, you can cut the legs.

- **Accessible raised-bed gardens.** Raised beds can be purchased or built to meet the needs of your program.

- **Strong magnifying glasses, lighted magnifiers, and binoculars.** These are very helpful for children with limited vision.

- **Personal sound amplifiers.** These are very helpful for children with limited hearing.

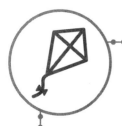

LET'S GET OUTSIDE TOGETHER!

Dear Families,

Whether your family enjoys walking around the neighborhood, biking around a nearby lake, flying kites, hiking in a mountain area, or exploring in a nearby park, we encourage you to make nature accessible for your family. Contact other families from school and venture out together. This can be a great time for your child to form social connections while building community and learning together in nature. There are opportunities in our community to take advantage of experiences in nature that are free or low cost. Please check with your city or county parks and recreation department or your local nature center or preserve to find out about opportunities near your home.

If your child has difficulty staying near you or tends to be impulsive on outdoor explorations, please be sure to consistently enforce rules about staying nearby, especially around bodies of water. Giving the option that he or she can either stay near you or hold your hand can help, as well as presenting points of interest as stopping points so your child knows he or she can run ahead a little but not a lot. Giving instructions like "Let's meet at that big tree" can also help. You can also have your child carry his or her own supplies, such as water, snacks, and tools for exploration, in a backpack, which will help slow your child down a little.

Here are several helpful resources:

- *Adventuring with Children: The Complete Manual for Family Adventure Travel* by Nan Jeffrey. 1990. New York: Avalon.

- *100 Places That Can Change Your Child's Life: From Your Backyard to the Ends of the Earth* by Keith Bellows. 2013. Washington, DC: National Geographic.

- "Accessible Outdoors: Kids with Social, Emotional and Physical Disabilities Go Outside!" by Kathy Ambrosini. 2014. *The New Nature Movement* (blog). See note #8. December 17, 2014.

- Natural Families: Nature Clubs and More (www.childrenandnature.org /initiatives/families/)

- www.outdoorafro.com

- http://latinooutdoors.org

- www.hechoonline.org

CHAPTER 3

TAMING THE WILD

Nature-Based Experiences in Your Indoor Environment

Although having the children in your program outdoors every day is valuable, many great nature experiences do not require access to the outdoors. There are wonderful ways we can support nature-based learning in our classrooms, and often they give children an opportunity to connect with plants, animals, and each other in unique ways. For example, the "pond in a jar" in the classroom allows children to watch the life of the pond in an intimate way. A pond in a jar is very different from looking at the pond, or even pouring out a little pond water into a bucket to observe for a few moments. The daily connection, seeing change and watching elements like duckweed multiply, can lead to wonderful discoveries.

This chapter is intended to help you think about your indoor environment and steps you can take to provide great nature activities indoors. "Night" is one topic in nature that can be explored more easily in the classroom during the school day. Creating spaces to bring to life experiences children will have outside of the school day helps build the community connection and helps children continue to construct their understanding.

From Sheila: Including animals in our indoor environment was an important connection for our program. A few years ago, we had a classroom guinea pig named Pumpkin. Over a school break he went home with a family, and when he returned he seemed fine, but a few days later he started to limp and drag his back legs. We assumed that perhaps he had an injury during the visit or transit, but when we took him to the vet and started to learn more about guinea pig care, we found that this sometimes happens due to a lack of important nutrients. We engaged the children right away in the research and care. In the evenings, I took Pumpkin home with me to continue vitamin doses and leg massages, and he was back to normal in a few days. This was a scary event, but the children were deeply engaged in caring for their class pet, and our community learned a lot about proper guinea pig care. Since that incident, anytime we consider getting a new pet, we research the animal's habitat and nutritional needs and post basic information on its enclosures. We also share a care sheet and emergency information with any families who take animals home over the break just in case an animal were to become ill while in their care.

DIPPING YOUR TOE IN

A good place to start is moving away from the model of a "museum table" to embedding nature experiences throughout the classroom. By "museum table," we are referring to the typical science table that has a magnifying glass, some natural items like seashells, and maybe a book. This approach is too stagnant to engage children for the long term. The following suggestions will help you engage the children in your classroom by bringing the outdoors in.

Provide new nature-related items to examine often. Change the nature-based components of your classroom often to make the learning experience more exciting. Include resource books and hands-on activities that will engage children in making discoveries. For example, if you live in a place where the leaves change colors, bring in fresh leaves each day along with paint colors that children can mix to help create or match colors. Add a field guide about tree species for children who are interested in exploring where the leaves originated.

Look for opportunities to include nature experiences in a variety of centers or areas of the classroom. Because most children have a favorite center, by including nature experiences in many centers, you will engage children who might not gravitate to science experiences. Future chapters will provide ideas for using centers to investigate different topics.

Examine your classroom to see how the arrangement supports nature investigations. Sometimes rearranging the classroom makes a huge difference. Noticing mica in rocks is hard if the science center is in a dark corner. Spend at least some of your bulletin board space on documentation of children's work related to nature studies. Documentation is an important form of communication between you, your children, and their families. Having photos, quotes, and explanations of what children are exploring in your program makes their learning more visible for the adults and affirms their work. If your bulletin boards are filled with identical artwork or motivational quotes that children cannot read, you are losing the opportunity to use the classroom to engage children in understanding nature. Posting documentation demonstrates to parents that you value the nature education portion of your curriculum.

WADING IN

Provide display space for items that can be handled as well as items that need protection from children. Small bulletin boards, random shelves, and Lucite boxes can bring natural items into more parts of your classroom. Moving away from displaying natural items only in the "science center" can bring attention to nature. A bulletin board in the block area with photos of houses made from stone may inspire children. Placing a Lucite box with a fish skeleton in the book corner displayed with books about fish brings more understanding of fish while protecting the delicate bones. A small shelf in the art center with a flower arrangement may inspire paintings of flowers.

Replace plastic and brightly colored furnishings with as many natural materials as possible. Too often preschool classrooms are overly stimulating with bright, primary colored furnishings, rugs with the alphabet or some other "lesson," and cartoonlike decorations. Not only are these environments overwhelming to many children, but they are lost opportunities to bring nature into the classroom. In *Creating Effective Learning Environments* by Karyn Wellhousen and Ingrid Crowther, the authors explain this issue. "Bright, primary colors serve to stimulate and excite. Pale, warm colors cause the opposite effect—they are calming, soothing and relaxing, and early childhood environments need to balance both components. It is important to remember that children's creative efforts are often bright and colorful. Displaying these creative efforts in an environment that is already highly stimulating in terms of the use of color can cause a very unsettling, overwhelming effect" (2003, 32). To further understand this idea, books from Reggio Emilia or Waldorf programs can provide more background on the importance of the environment. Furnishings made of wood, stone, woven grass, and other natural elements allow children to revel in the beauty of nature even when they are indoors.

DIVING IN

Let the outdoors in by providing the best access to outdoors that your building and ecosystem allow. Windows that open need screens so you can leave them open as much as possible. Use natural light and place nature-related activities closest to windows that provide light. If access to natural light is limited during certain times of the year, lamps can be used in place of harsh overhead lighting.

Reduce the amount of carpeted flooring. In many parts of the country, preschool classrooms tend to be half carpeted and half tiled. This discourages innovative classroom arrangements and too often causes adults to discourage wet and messy activities. If you have any control over flooring, consider eco-friendly flooring that can be easily dried and cleaned, and use area rugs to provide padding in certain areas.

Improve access to water. Water, especially plumbed-in water, brings opportunities for nature education throughout the classroom. One of our favorite features at Dodge Nature Preschool is the plumbed water tables! These water tables have their own plumbing, just like a sink or bathtub, including a faucet and a drain that is directly connected to the building plumbing, which makes setup and cleanup much more efficient.

Include things that are alive throughout the classroom. Plants and pets can be included in most centers. Patty Born Selly's book *Connecting Animals and Children in Early Childhood* has many examples of wonderful classroom pets as well as guidelines for choosing the right companion for your program.

CULTURAL CONSIDERATIONS

Make sure you are responding to natural items in a culturally appropriate manner, including the cultures that are native to your part of the country and the cultures of the families in the program. The following are some cultural issues to consider as you incorporate nature into your classroom.

- **Collecting items.** In some parts of the country, taking rocks from one area and carrying them into the classroom for display would be considered disrespectful.

- **Treatment of bones and animal carcasses.** Some indigenous groups believe that the bodies of animals continue to hold their spirits and they should be treated with respect.

- **Taking feathers.** Taking certain feathers can be illegal, as well as considered a sign of disrespect. Federal laws prohibit the collection of eagle and migratory bird feathers and other body parts.

HEALTH, SAFETY, AND GUIDANCE ISSUES

One of the challenges of providing nature experiences indoors is that you will need to limit how many children take part at one time. A popular water activity can cause children to squabble over turns. Here are some suggestions for setting limits indoors:

- **Allow the environment to provide a limit if possible.** A small water table may not accommodate more than three or four children without crowding. Environmental cues, such as having a certain number of smocks available or bath rugs to stand on, can give a clear message regarding how many children can take part.

- **Resist the urge to limit the amount of time each child can spend with the activity.** If children are limited to five or ten minutes, the depth of their discoveries will be limited. Instead, make sure the same activity is available for enough days or weeks to give each child enough time making discoveries. Creating lists for who is waiting for a turn expands to literacy and social opportunities as well.

RESOURCES

Author Favorites

- Julie's favorite: *Designs for Living and Learning* by Deb Curtis and Margie Carter. 2003. St. Paul, MN: Redleaf Press. This book is full of photos and ideas for making improvements to indoor spaces. It includes lots of natural touches.

- Sheila's favorite: *Inspiring Spaces for Young Children* by Jessica DeViney, Sandra Duncan, Sara Harris, Mary Ann Rody, and Lois Rosenberry. 2010. Lewisville, NC: Gryphon House. This book has helped me gain inspiration and ideas for improving our spaces at school.

Materials to Enhance the Indoor Environment

Free and Collectible Materials

- **Books from the public library.** It is nearly impossible to own all the children's books you will want to support nature education. Taking the time to make a book list and using a system to easily track it will save time in the long run and allow you to search the library efficiently.

- **X-ray prints.** You can ask veterinarians or families in your community to donate X-rays; they are also available for purchase through science catalogs like *Acorn Naturalists*. X-rays help children see bones and other parts of bodies.

- **Lite-Brite.** Lite-Brite is a light-up toy that includes a small board that lights up from behind and many multicolored pegs that can be placed in the holes. A Lite-Brite allows children to explore light and color and can be found at donation centers or at thrift stores. When you make it available, don't include the picture to follow so that children must use their imaginations.

From Julie: One of my favorite X-rays showed a penny inside a child's stomach. It led to lots of discussions about what was safe to put into our mouths!

Best Materials to Purchase If You Have Limited Funds

- **Tubs, tables, or other systems.** A variety of different-sized tubs and materials can help make the most of your indoor space. A small tub allows an individual child to explore water, sand, soil, or other substances without having to share it with others. Clear plastic tubs allow children to see substances from all angles. A sturdy, hard plastic sensory table can withstand the weight of large rocks. Having a variety of containers will allow you to make natural substances available even when other activities are taking up space indoors.

- **Flashlights.** Flashlights are helpful for exploring dark and light.

- **Overhead projector.** Overhead projectors allow children to create shadows on the wall and explore light and color.

- **Dark or blackout fabric.** Blackout fabric and similar materials will allow you to create a space in your classroom to explore light and dark.

Extras If You Have More Funds

- **Specimens.** Early childhood resource catalogs have specimens of insects, plant parts, and so on encased in clear plastic for purchase. Children can carefully examine the item without damaging it or themselves.

- **Replicas.** You can purchase replicas of animal scat, foot-/hoofprints, and bones from early childhood resource catalogs.

- **Light tables.** Light tables can be used to examine X-rays and experiment with light.

- **Nature posters.** Decorative posters can add to displays. A poster of flowers brings attention to a wider variety of flowers than you may have available in live specimens. A poster of the life cycle of a butterfly helps children hold the images in their minds of what caterpillars looked like before they were transformed into chrysalises on display.

- **Nature items used for pretend play.** Fabric that looks like animal fur, plastic animals to use in the block area or sand table, and other related items will allow children to put what they are learning into pretend play and thus understand it better.

CURRICULUM EXPLORATION

Dear Families,

We often share examples in our documentation about what children are experiencing in the classroom. Sometimes it is hard to know exactly what your child is interested in, especially if he or she doesn't share it with you. If you have time, look around during pickup or drop-off and ask your child to tell you about what is interesting. If that won't work for you, we invite you to come in while we are outside on the playground to look around the classroom and explore what your child is learning about nature. The classroom is usually a little messy around this time, but we are happy to have you in the room, using the magnifying glasses to look inside our pond in a jar or watching the classroom fish. You can explore the track replicas or the animal mounts and read your child's nature journal.

We know that some of us did not have an opportunity to explore nature at school when we were children, and we would like to welcome you to explore this wonderful world with us. Please stop by, and if you also happen to have a chance to recap a few markers, put dirt back into a plant that was tipped over, or tidy up the classroom, that would also be appreciated but not expected. Our goal is to invite you to be a part of the learning process and to help make the experiences that your child is having at school clear for you and your family. Thank you.

CHAPTER 4

TAKE THAT OUTSIDE

Making the Most of Your Outdoor Environment

A natural space allows for children to be more creative and challenged by the changing environment. In any region, each day in a natural environment will be a little different from the day before. For example, in the desert the wind can smooth over tracks, a rainstorm can add new paths in the dirt, or a cloudy day can add shade and allow for a longer exploration into large open spaces. On playgrounds where the ground, climbing structures, and play elements are all manufactured, they will stay the same from day to day, and children will seek out challenges in other ways that may be more disruptive or dangerous. The novelty that the natural environment offers from day to day will allow for more variety in play with young children.

Many outdoor features can present unique challenges and opportunities. For example, firepits can have many benefits as well as safety considerations. When you have access to a firepit, you can cook snacks, gain warmth in the winter, and explore the elements of fire. Of course, having fires with children near requires comprehensive supervision and planning for fire building, fire maintenance, and extinguishing the fire properly. Water features also present benefits and challenges. Water is a joy for children to interact with, and it is a wonderful medium for learning about the principles of elements and sensory experiences. However, water features can be dangerous because they provide a risk of drowning and require close supervision at all times. If, how, and when you add these features will depend on your environment, your population of children and families, your licensing regulations, and your own comfort level.

Some outdoor play areas are accessible to the neighborhood outside of school hours. This can add many meaningful community benefits but also some challenges. Sometimes a few signs inviting others into the space but also stating the rules can be a helpful reminder. If you deal with vandalism of the space, having carts of natural materials that can be brought in each day can save your materials for use with your children. We also recommend that you make a safety tour of this shared space each day before children have access to it to remove any unsafe debris.

Stories from the Field

Taking children outside does not always come easy. Working at three different nature centers in the Midwest for more than twenty years, I saw many instances when teachers had issues taking children outside. One was at the Nature Center at Shaker Lakes in Cleveland, Ohio. As the early childhood environmental educator, I had the opportunity to work with a Head Start class twice a month (one program at the nature center and one at the Head Start location) for nine months. The lead teacher agreed to the program because she would not have to plan twice a month. She made it clear that she didn't really like to go outside but was willing to do whatever I asked of her. After nine months (eighteen programs) the teacher told me that she realized that she really liked this "nature stuff" and wondered how she could do what I do. She told me that she had figured out how to dress for the cold weather (in layers) and now knew how to help her children be warm during winter excursions.

Fear of taking children outdoors with wild animals stems from a lack of knowledge and experience being in natural habitats (during different seasons) and interacting with different types of animals. Overcoming these fears can be difficult. Animals (especially wild ones) tend to elicit strong emotions (positive and/or negative) from children and teachers. When I was the director of the Schlitz Audubon Nature Preschool in Milwaukee, Wisconsin, we had a grant-funded program that allowed urban child care centers to visit the nature center. On one such visit (with three- and four-year-olds and their teachers), we brought out one of our fox snakes. Immediately two of the teachers stepped back and were visibly afraid of the snake. However, one of the three-year-old nonverbal children, upon meeting the snake, spoke for the first time in front of the teachers. The teachers were so surprised and happy that one of them decided she would try and overcome her fear and touch the snake too.

Both stories illustrate the necessity for positive experiences outdoors and with animals facilitated by an experienced naturalist or nature-based educator. Over time, as teachers become more comfortable in natural environments and with familiar animals, they can provide these positive experiences for the children in their classes. —**Patti Bailie**, PhD, assistant professor of early childhood education, University of Maine at Farmington, Farmington, Maine

• • •

When we walked into the play space at the arboretum, Greta paused at the gate and turned to me. "Can we just . . . go play?" she asked. "Yep," I said. And that was all it took—she and the other children were off and running. The play space at the arboretum is spacious and stocked with open-ended, nature-based play materials. Our preschool children were particularly interested in the sand and water play space. Littered with branches, wooden troughs, PVC pipe, and rope, the area was spacious and unstructured. There were several water sources, and a group of children immediately began to share ideas about how they could use the materials to build a waterfall. "I can't get this to stay," yelled Josiah, trying to hold two branches together. "We could tie it up, maybe," said Greta, running over with a rope. From the other side of the sand area I had seen Josiah struggling with the branches and had immediately started to walk over to intervene and offer support. I knew Josiah as someone who was easily frustrated; he often displayed big feelings when confronted with seemingly minor inconveniences like a hard-to-open juice box or a crayon breaking in the middle of a coloring project. When I heard his voice rise and saw him struggling with the branches, I sensed another meltdown coming on and approached him, ready to help him collect his feelings and regain some control.

When Greta came running over with her rope, though, I held back and just observed. Tom looked at her and said, "Yeah, tie it up so the water goes to this part." As Greta and Josiah began to wrap the rope around the branches, another child came over to help. "I could bring the water," she said and ran away to find a bucket. As the afternoon went on, more and more children joined in on the project. I watched the children negotiate materials, share ideas, and collaborate as they attempted to construct a waterway that would stretch across the sand. These skills that we had struggled to model and construct in the classroom, the children were exhibiting here in this unstructured, open, child-directed free play experience. It was humbling to step back and give up that sense of control and see how wildly successful the children were when we trusted them and allowed them the space and freedom to take matters into their own hands. —**Marie Lister**, MEd, preschool teacher and instructor, Shirley G. Moore Lab School at the University of Minnesota Twin Cities, Minneapolis, Minnesota

• • •

When I accepted a teaching job on the Upper West Side of Manhattan, I wasn't sure how easy it would be for me to bring my love of nature and the outdoors into the classroom. In the past, I would step outside my door, and the environment provided everything I needed to support my passion. The school I taught at in New York had a rooftop playground. The only signs of nature were pigeons and raised gardens. Luckily, we had Riverside Park just a block away, which we frequently visited. During one of our many trips to the park, we discovered an orb spider. I explained to the children that it was possible for us to bring her back to the classroom and create a habitat for her. Of course they were thrilled at the idea of caring for a spider, but we agreed that we would need to do a lot of research first. We had read that spiders need at least two sticks or stems to make a web. We decided to make a spider tree with a Y-shaped stick, an ice cream bucket, and plaster of Paris. At the end of the day, we placed her on the tree and were excited to see what would take place overnight.

The next morning, we were devastated to discover she had escaped. We thoroughly checked all the shelves and areas we thought she might be hiding but could not find her. Later that day, I heard a child yell with excitement, "I found her! Here she is!" In the corner of one of the far windows was a large, intricate web with our spider sitting patiently in the middle. After reading a couple of books on spiders, we knew she was waiting for her prey. We carefully placed a cricket on her web and watched as she injected venom and wrapped the cricket in silk. When she was done, we added another. News quickly spread through the school that the four/fives were caring for a spider in their classroom. Older grades came by to feed and watch our spider. After two weeks of our caring for her, she died. We buried her in one of the raised gardens outside the classroom and spent the rest of the fall searching for more spiders. —**Natalie Gilmore**, MEd, preschool teacher, St. John the Baptist Catholic School, Jordan, Minnesota

DIPPING YOUR TOE IN

If the space you currently have is completely manufactured and resources for a large change are not available, small changes can make a big difference.

- **Add a garden.** A couple of raised-bed gardens can add a new area of interest to the outdoors and help foster your nutrition curriculum.

- **Add an outdoor sensory table.** Each day you can fill an outdoor sensory table with water or natural items like leaves, sand, and rocks, or sticks and mud from the local area for further investigations.

- **Add a dedicated play space for classroom pets outdoors.** Whether your pet is a rabbit, guinea pig, or turtle, it will enjoy some time outside.

WADING IN

- **Add a digging space/mud pit.** If the ground is not covered in manufactured flooring, adding a place for digging with good-quality shovels can add a lot of large-motor possibilities and space to explore what lives below the ground.

- **Create a mud kitchen.** Mud kitchens allow children to make mud pies, soups, and much, much more. They can be created by adding materials like old muffin tins, spoons, and funnels to a muddy area on your playground and can grow to include kitchen furniture, tools, and more. There are many resources online for building mud kitchens that will engage children of all ages.

- **Plant a tree.** Depending on your area, adding a few plants or trees can add depth to play outdoors. Plan more routine activities outdoors that have traditionally been indoors.

- **Eating outdoors is often more pleasant.** Noise is easier to handle, cleanup is easier, and smells are less bothersome. You can wash hands inside and head right out to a picnic spot.

- **Circle time outdoors is also very enjoyable.** Circle time outdoors works especially well with activities that take up space, such as movement or noisy activities like using musical instruments.

- **Napping outdoors is done every day in many countries.** Children are less likely to spread germs through coughing in their sleep when the germs are dispersed outdoors. Another advantage is that when some children have woken and others are still sleeping, the early risers can play without waking others.

DIVING IN

Create a nature-based playscape. This area is created using natural materials with the goals of providing a variety of spaces for children to engage in open-ended and creative play outdoors. Many great resources for converting your traditional playground into an outdoor classroom or learning environment can be found at the Nature Explore website, www.earthplay.net, and even Pinterest. Include some wild space; if you have a natural space adjacent to your program, consider putting in a gate directly from your playground so you can visit it more readily.

Including families in the outdoor spaces can be very meaningful for your community. Whether it is constructing a raised-bed garden, building picnic tables, or planting a living willow hut, families can share their talents and their time with your program and build skills within their community as well as make a meaningful contribution to their child's education. Although sometimes this will require evening or weekend work for a teacher or school administrator to coordinate the project, having one day for many projects to be happening at once can help pool resources. At my school, we have an Earth Day event where some families help with the gardens and fixing broken things on the playground while others coordinate the children's involvement in cleaning up litter around the school, moving rocks or sticks back to their designated spaces, and enjoying time to play together.

INCLUSION OF ALL CHILDREN

Accessibility is an important consideration in outdoor spaces. Children should find a good balance of opportunities to work with others and alone to do things they are familiar with and comfortable doing and others that will challenge them. A play space with open-ended opportunities will allow access to children of all abilities and levels of development. Please refer back to chapter 2 on individualized needs for more details.

CULTURAL CONSIDERATIONS

Some families, especially those who live in dense cities, may be uncomfortable with their child being outdoors for a variety of reasons. Sometimes it is about their child getting messy or the need to provide extra clothes or a variety of outdoor gear. Other times it is about their child being exposed to bugs, animals, or the elements, or just a general discomfort or unfamiliarity with exploring outdoors. Inviting families to be a part of their child's exploration and sharing information and photos that demonstrate the learning and joy that their child experiences outdoors can create collective ownership in the community and connect children and nature through increased time outdoors.

RESOURCES

Author Favorites

- **Julie's favorite:** *Umbrella* by Tarō Yashima. 1958. New York: Viking. This book takes place in Japan. A girl has received an umbrella for her birthday and eagerly waits for rain so she can use it. It describes rain as something to be desired.

- **Sheila's favorite:** *Where the Wild Things Are* by Maurice Sendak. 1963. New York: Harper & Row. This classic book has brought the joy of imagination and exploration to my home and to the homes of many others.

Resources for Adults

- *Loose Parts: Inspiring Play with Infants and Toddlers* and *Loose Parts 2* by Lisa Daly and Miriam Beloglovsky. 2016. St. Paul, MN: Redleaf Press. These books are full of ideas for ways to bring excitement to your outdoor space without spending a lot or money or committing to permanent changes to your playground.

- *Natural Playscapes: Creating Outdoor Play Environments for the Soul* by Rusty Keeler. 2008. Lincoln, NE: Exchange Press. This wonderful resource highlights nature-based play areas for young children and how to implement some of the playground improvements utilizing your community.

Materials to Enhance the Outdoor Environment

Free and Collectible Materials

- **Loose parts.** Tires, stones, pieces of wood that aren't too splintery, tubs, buckets, rope, and other collected materials allow children to use their imagination, experiment, and test theories in nature.

- **Old beach or patio umbrellas.** When families upgrade, ask them for their old umbrellas. They can be used to create shady areas, allow children to notice the movement of the sun, and provide a variety of outdoor play experiences during light rain.

- **Wood pallets.** Pallets can be used to store outdoor equipment, create water and sand areas, and more.

Best Materials to Purchase If You Have Limited Funds

- **Gutters, plastic tubing, and other materials for moving water.** These items are often on sale after the summer season at hardware stores.

- **Sandboxes with covers.** If cats have access to your play yard, toxoplasmosis is a concern. Sandboxes can be constructed, and tarps can be used as covers. Covering and uncovering the sandbox makes for an authentic "job" for children.

- **Real metal shovels.** If you can't find the child-sized metal shovels, you can cut the handles down from a small standard shovel to a good height for your children. Not only will this add to their involvement with nature, but shovels also provide great motor development, including strength, motor planning, and coordination.

- **Wooden or metal wheelbarrows.** Use functional, sturdy wheelbarrows with big tires and a well-balanced wheelbase. Using a wheelbarrow helps children with balance and motor planning as they learn to keep it from tipping over and the contents from spilling out. Children appreciate the "real work" they can do with a wheelbarrow.

From Julie: We needed to constantly replace sand on the playground in my school in Tucson due to erosion and the sand getting packed down after monsoons. We had the contractors dump the sand over the fence, and it was the children's job to move the sand from the fence to where it was needed. Moving the sand took days, and the children took great pride in their accomplishment.

Extras If You Have More Funds

- **Good outdoor storage.** Finding a program that has enough storage and storage that is arranged for easy access is rare. Depending on your environment, this could be a homemade shed made of wood, a premade metal or wooden shed, or several smaller storage containers. You may find these on sale at the end of summer at hardware stores. You are most likely to offer good outdoor experiences if you have materials accessible and you are most likely to respond to children's spontaneous nature interests (finding insects, hearing a new bird, noticing a spiderweb) if you have easy access to the materials that will take their interests to the next stage of exploration.

- **Outlast Blocks by Community Playthings.** These outdoor hollow blocks are made to withstand the elements.

- **Firepit.** If your program is ready to add fire to your outdoor spaces, a firepit can be constructed with bricks or rocks. Keep in mind any safety regulations in your area around fires on the playground, and build the firepit with a cover so that it does not become a tripping hazard. Also consider any local regulations regarding firepits. Make sure to create plenty of space for children and adults to sit around the fire together, sing, and occasionally roast an apple or marshmallows.

OUTDOOR EXPLORATION

Dear Families,

Throughout the year, we will have many opportunities for outdoor exploration. To help keep children both safe and comfortable during these times, we ask that you send them prepared for the weather each day. We will have extra clothing and outdoor gear available when needed, but our supply is limited.

Here are some examples of the gear we would like you to provide:

Gear for general exploration:

- hiking shoes with covered toes

- hiking sandals for warm weather

- waterproof boots for marshy area exploration

Gear for rain:

- galoshes/boots/wellies

- waterproof jackets with hoods

- waterproof pants

Gear for sun:

- sunglasses
- hats with chin straps

Gear for snow:

- waterproof mittens (Mittens keep children's hands warmer than gloves and are easier for children to put on independently, and mittens with higher arm cuffs will help keep snow from going down their sleeves.)

- neck warmers or gaiters

- snow pants (either coverall style or pants-only work well)

- warm socks

- warm, waterproof boots

- In temperatures below zero, an additional layer such as thermal liners underneath pants and mittens can be helpful as well.

You can find these items after the season at secondhand stores, discount stores like Target, or outdoor gear stores like REI. You can also donate what your children have outgrown for our school supply. You will find that you use these items more often than you think!

CHAPTER 5

IT'S RAINING, IT'S POURING

Getting Outdoors in Any Weather

Take them out in this?

Many teachers seem hesitant to take children outdoors when the weather isn't perfect. This robs children of many learning opportunities and is based on myths and misconceptions. We offer some myths versus facts to help you base your practice on current facts about weather. As the saying goes, "There is no such thing as bad weather, only unsuitable clothing."

Myth #1: Being out in cold weather makes people sick.

Fact: While it is true that people have colds and flu more often during winter months, according to the American Academy of Pediatrics (AAP), this is not due to the cold weather. The increase in illness is due to people staying indoors close together and passing germs to one another. Also, because people use heaters during cold weather, sinuses get dried out and become more susceptible to germs. Getting children outdoors more often will reduce these challenges. Many children are more susceptible to runny noses in the winter. This is not usually related to a cold or virus but due to the nose producing more moisture during the cold and dry winter. Keeping a scarf and tissues handy helps.

Myth #2: Children will get sick if they are out in the rain.

Fact: Getting wet will not make you sick. If you stay wet and cold long enough to lower your body temperature, your immune system can be affected, but that is easily remedied by changing out of wet clothes.

From Julie: I ask folks in warm climates, "Which is colder, the ocean (or the swimming pool or lake) or the rain falling from the sky? Which makes you wetter? Why would we avoid rain but not avoid bodies of water?" One of the advantages of rain is that we can wear rain gear that will keep us dry.

Myth # 3: Being out in the wind will make you sick.
Fact: While allergies might act up if pollen is swirling around in the wind, the learning opportunities outweigh the risks unless you have children with severe health problems. You may also need to take steps to protect children's eyes.

Myth #4: You shouldn't take children outdoors in sunny climates between 10:00 a.m. and 2:00 p.m.
Fact: While this is when people are most at risk for exposure to damage from the sun, precautions are easy to take. The best solution is ample shade either through planting trees or erecting shade screens and canopies. Children should be in the habit of wearing sunscreen and hats. If you don't take them outside during the prime hours of your program, how will you include nature activities as a core to your curriculum?

Myth #5: Parents won't tolerate us taking children out in less-than-perfect weather.
Fact: While some parents may be influenced by myths, it is our job to provide a safe and appropriate curriculum, and this involves getting children outside. Taking time to educate ourselves and our families about the facts of weather-related risks is an important part of our community engagement. See chapter 15, which includes ideas for educating parents with information and common experiences.

WHAT PRESCHOOLERS ARE READY TO UNDERSTAND

Thunder is not dangerous. Lightning is. Some children are very frightened by thunder, so this can be helpful information. A story like *Thunder Cake* by Patricia Polacco can be helpful to read during a thunderstorm (see appendix 2).

Hail is inherently interesting to children, and they can understand its properties when they have an opportunity to handle it. Even though hail is frozen, it doesn't have to be cold out for hail to form. Avoid having children outdoors in hail, because it can be dangerous. It is fun to watch from indoors and collect outdoors when the storm is over. If you know it may hail, place a few buckets outside to collect it and bring it into the classroom for further study.

WHAT IS TOO ABSTRACT FOR PRESCHOOLERS TO UNDERSTAND

Weather they have not experienced. Children in Hawaii do not understand snow unless they have visited a snowy climate or have been to a summit on Maui or Hawaii Island with snow on top. Some programs in warm climates buy "instant snow" from catalogs. While children enjoy playing with the substance, it is confusing and gives them misinformation. This "instant snow" is a polymer similar to what is inside of diapers. It expands when wet. It does not feel like snow and is unrelated to weather. Another concept that is too abstract for young children is weather that they experienced in the past. Instead, focus activities on the weather they are experiencing now. Children are also too young to understand the difference between weather and climate. Weather is what we experience day to day and climate is the compilation of weather patterns over long periods of time.

ISSUES FOR DIFFERENT ECOSYSTEMS

Whatever your ecosystem, some weather will influence your activities. Current weather patterns may be different from what you or the parents of children in your program remember in your region. For example, many adults in Minnesota remember winters that were colder and longer, or in the Southwest they don't remember so many hot days during the summer. Whether you are in the mountains, valleys, or plains, you will have opportunities to engage in your place. We will explore some of the options for common weather that is generally safe to explore with children. Later in this chapter we will address severe and hazardous weather as well. Below is a list of various weather elements children should experience.

- **Rain.** Rain is a gift from nature. It sustains life and is appealing to young children.

- **Fog.** Fog can be magical. Some ecosystems see it often, but for others it is a rare treat. Play hide-and-seek and other games in the fog.

- **Snow.** People living in parts of the country that have snow for months at a time may easily become annoyed by it. Remember that preschoolers have few memories of the last year's snow. Playing outdoors in the snow provides children who live in these ecosystems with joyful memories and skills that will last a lifetime.

- **Sun.** When it is sunny, it is a perfect time to play and enjoy the sunshine, but there are also many opportunities to use the solar power the sun provides to have some educational fun. Building solar ovens and trying to cook outdoors, melting crayons for art, or painting on dry surfaces with water and watching your drawings quickly disappear can be wonderful science for young children to engage in on sunny days.

- **Wind.** Try living in an ecosystem that does not have wind very often and you will miss it! Wind is magical for young children because it is invisible, and yet they can see the results. Activities including making simple kites and wind socks, and dancing outdoors with scarves all help children develop understanding of and appreciation for wind.

- **Frost.** Although scraping car windows early in the morning may keep adults from loving frost, there is something magical about the coating on the trees and blades of grass early in the morning. Frost coats the playground equipment and makes the slide a little slippery and wet, but it also allows children to write with their finger on almost any flat surface. Have a few scrapers on the playground for children to have a chance to do some scraping of their own.

If you live where there are four seasons, each season can provide a wealth of experiences. Think of this as replacing the holiday-based units of study that have been the staple of so many preschools. You can provide activities that help children learn about weather-related changes for each season as it impacts plants, animals, and insects of your area, as well as changing temperatures. You will find related information in the chapters that follow.

If you do not live where there are four seasons, don't focus on experiences children do not share. Your environment has plenty to offer. Most environments have several seasons—be they fall/winter/spring/summer, rainy/dry, winter/deep winter/still winter, or hot/not that hot. Our home ecosystems are complex and can vary not only by season but also by day and, with climate change, by the year. It is important to think about weather as an opportunity to learn about our home—its capabilities, its dangers, and its magic.

If you live in the mountains, the most dramatic change is the coming of snow and the melting of snow. Activities that help children learn about and love snow can be a focus for months at a time. As snow melts and "mud season" arrives, embrace mud rather than avoiding it. You will find more information about mud in chapter 7.

If you live in the desert, focus on the weather-related changes that come with seasons, including dropping or rising temperatures, monsoon season, and the effect of long, dry times on plants, animals, and insects. You will find more related information in the chapters that follow.

If you live near the sea, focus on the weather-related changes that come with seasons, including changes to the tides, temperatures, and precipitation.

If you live near the woods, focus on how plants change in different weather throughout the year. Trees change color and lose their leaves in the fall. In the spring sap flows and buds are forming, and some trees even flower before they have leaves. You can also take advantage of sprouts and compare the types of trees that stay green year-round while others go through many changes. Areas near the woods vary throughout the country. Some states experience snow and cold (such as Minnesota) while others do not (such as Mississippi), but their woods have a lot in common.

If you live in a prairie or on plains, focus on weather and watching the sky, which can be seen for miles around. You will have the opportunity to observe the four seasons in most prairie areas. Areas with tall grasses can be easily compared to the heights of the children.

Stories from the Field

"Why don't we just go to the gym?" This was a question I had heard several times from my assistant teachers. It was winter. And worse, it was winter in Minnesota. It meant snow pants, hats, boots, and gloves. It meant dedicating a large chunk of our daily schedule to the process of getting ready for outdoor play. It meant venturing into the hallway to the children's lockers and helping them dress while also monitoring that nobody slipped off to parts unknown in the relatively open area. And, most importantly, it meant adding a lengthy and multistepped transition into a routine for the four-year-olds in my emotional-behavioral disorder classroom. Anyone who works with young children, especially those who are challenged by impulse control and emotion regulation, knows to minimize transitions to ensure success.

So, on an almost daily basis, from December to April, the question was raised: "Why don't we just go to the gym?" Some days it seemed like we were the only classroom who braved the dressing adventure and the bitter cold. We often emerged from the building to the white winterscape to behold a completely untouched outdoor play space. The absence of foot-prints meant that no other children and teachers had stepped outside that day. And thus, the recurring question, "Why don't we just go to the gym?"

And yet day after day I watched children encounter snow, icicles, wind, animal tracks, and evergreen branches with a joyful exuberance that could never be replicated in the gym. It meant that children who struggled to process their big feelings in the classroom could find space to be mindfully alone and to, quite literally, place their boot prints on the world with pride and power. It meant that children who normally could not bear any infringe-ment on their personal space would sit on the laps of peers as they created a multiperson "train" down a snow-covered slide and tumbled into a laughing pile, their speedy exit from the slide aided by a combination of ice and slippery snow pants. Peaceful was not a word that I used very frequently to describe our school days. However, as the children hunkered down to mold, melt, and taste the snow, the mind-body connection led into a special serenity that was beautiful to behold.

When I think back on those preschoolers of many years ago, I think first of those glorious winter days. I treasure those days when the chil-dren (to paraphrase Vygotsky) stood several heads taller than themselves as monarchs of a frosty kingdom, with a sense of pride and control that eluded them in so many other settings. And when I think of them, I am so very happy that we didn't just go to the gym. **—Elizabeth Criswell, MEd, instructor, University of Minnesota Twin Cities, Minneapolis, Minnesota**

From Sheila: It was my two-year-old niece Kiara's first time on an airplane and her first time visiting Minnesota from her home in Las Vegas. She was excited to spend the holidays with her cousins on the farm. When she arrived at the airport, she was ready to go. I picked her up in the car and she just stared out of the window and said, "Grandpa, can I play in the sandbox?" My dad told her, "Of course," wondering why she was asking about the park but assuming she was probably just tired. Then, more excited than the time before, "Grandpa, can we stop and play in the sandbox?" As he looked at her in the rearview mirror, he put it together and understood what she was so excited about. The vast snow that covered everything along the streets was what she was anxious to visit. He explained, "That's snow, but you can play in it later." As I parked the car and unbuckled her car seat, Kiara jumped and put both of her hands right into the "sandbox." Then with a look of slight pain and betrayal, she started to scream, "The sand is so cold!" On this ten degree day, it was indeed cold, and she was unprepared but also now more curious than ever. For the next week, we played in the snow, made snow angels, snow people, and snow forts, and of course brought out snow shovels and pails. The seemingly unending "snow box" of Minnesota became a playground for the girl visiting from the desert.

DIPPING YOUR TOE IN

Skip the "weather report" at circle time. Too many programs rely on "weather reporter" as a job for a child on their job charts. In ecosystems that have weather that does not change often, this is a dreary waste of time. There is a saying in the mountains, "If you don't like the weather, just wait ten minutes and it will change." Have props ready to take advantage of interesting weather. If you have these in readily accessible bins or boxes, you can grab them when the opportunity arises.

Windy days fascinate young children. Include a book about the wind, such as *The Wind Blew* by Pat Hutchins, a wind sock, and scarves. None of these take a lot of preparation or knowledge on the part of the children. One of the simplest activities to do on a windy day is to go on a hunt for things that have blown to a new place on the playground. You can make sure there are lightweight items outdoors for children to discover.

Rainy days provide endless possibilities and excite young children. Include a book about rain, such as *Rain* by Robert Kalan. Have rain gear available to take children outdoors to play on rainy days. One of the simplest and most satisfying experiences is letting children jump in mud puddles. You can begin with lots of limits (must have rubber boots on, only in shallow puddles) and widen the opportunity as you become more comfortable. Using items such as coffee cans to collect rain allow children to bring the rain indoors to play with later.

Sunny days can be great for experiencing light and shade. Include a book such as *Shadows and Reflections* by Tana Hoban. Talk to children about shadows and have chalk available to outline shadows.

Snowy days are wonderful days to go outside and experience the beauty of snow. Include a book such as *The Snowy Day* by Ezra Jack Keats. Have snow gear available for children to be warm and dry. Teach children to make snow angels, and have buckets and shovels ready for them to collect snow. Bringing snow indoors to use in the water table is very satisfying, especially if you have mittens for children to use.

Start getting children out in weather you might have resisted before. Delay running indoors when it starts to sprinkle.

WADING IN

Take small groups out for "weather walks." You can begin as soon as you have enough all-weather clothing for a small group. Start by asking children what they think they will hear, see, smell, and touch. You can invite them to tell other children about it when they return, and this may encourage resistant children to venture out in different weather. Carefully ask inquiry-based questions but try to refrain from making the walk a quiz. Children can be scaffolded through thoughtful questions, but too many or ones that are too focused, can make them disinterested.

Commit to take children out every day for some portion of time unless the weather is dangerous. By making a commitment to yourself, your children, and their families, children will arrive at school better prepared and will have the opportunity for hands-on exploration in a variety of weather conditions. You will also have the chance to see them build understanding for how to prepare their bodies for safe exploration and build resiliency.

Teach children to put on their own weather gear. One of the reasons cited for keeping children indoors is the drudgery of dressing and undressing them. Learning to put on your own bathing suit, snow pants, mittens, rain jacket, and so on helps to build a sense of competence, and parents will appreciate it too. When children are given opportunities to explore outside daily, the reasons for the weather gear become apparent. You won't have to have as many arguments about putting on proper clothing, because children will begin to see the value of waterproof mittens, bathing suits, and rain jackets.

DIVING IN

Add elements to the environment to learn about weather changes. These can include a sundial, solar cells, an ice auger for measuring depth of ice in a pond, and even a windmill. If you have the funds and space, adding solar power to your school can be a wonderful way to save resources and money and to teach about renewable energy sources in an authentic manner that children will be able to see each day. Build a snow fort (page 188). This activity can quickly turn into a snow village and can include snow tunnels and snow slides as well.

INCLUSION OF ALL CHILDREN

Including children with health problems in different weather can be especially challenging, but it is often possible. In our Minnesota program, we had a child who developed leukemia during her first winter with us. The chemotherapy made her too weak to walk for periods of time. To make sure she was included in walks through the snow, the adults placed her on a sled and the children took turns pulling the sled through the snow. It helped them develop empathy, built their strength and stamina, and helped them understand the functionality of a sled. During warm weather months, she was pulled in a wagon when she was unable to walk.

CULTURAL CONSIDERATIONS

Some families have superstitions, traditional beliefs, and old sayings about being out in the rain or cold. How many times have you heard someone say, "Don't go out in the rain or you'll catch a cold," or "If you don't wear a coat you'll get sick"? Viruses and bacteria cause colds. Being wet or cold alone does not make a person sick, although it can stress your immune system over time and make it easier for a virus to spread. Spending time outdoors in very cold weather can lead to hypothermia, and that can make a person more susceptible to infection. During the winter, people are often more susceptible to colds because they tend to be less physically active and spend more time indoors. Getting outdoors for fresh air and regular exercise can make you healthier during the winter. When preparing children to be outdoors in any weather, make sure children are safe and comfortable to get the most positive experience. For example, light pants are important in the summer in many different regions because they protect the skin from sun, hot sand, sharp grasses, ticks, and mosquitoes.

Working with families to get children outdoors in a variety of weather begins with establishing credibility and trust, as well as having resources available so all children have access to the clothing needed for a positive experience. For example, let families know that you will not go outside in dangerous weather, such as high winds in a heavily wooded area because of the risk of falling branches, lightning or thunder, or pouring rains because they can produce flash flooding. Also, provide resources; for example, waterproof mittens and neck warmers are very important staples for positive experiences in subzero temperatures.

From Sheila: I was a mom who spent all day every Sunday for many years braiding hair for my four daughters, and I couldn't have unbraided, washed, and rebraided again in the same week if I wanted to. So, when taking young children with kinky or tightly curled hair outdoors in the rain, sand, and mud, I usually put braids into a ponytail and just have them wear a regular knit hat. If it is over fifty degrees, then a scarf will do just fine. At the beginning of the year, I ask families, "How do you feel about your child getting mud, sand, paint, etc., in their hair?" I also ask at drop-off if they have something to do after school so we can help clean their children up a little when necessary. Water and rain generally don't matter quite as much unless their hair is straightened. It is best to ask parents if they want their child's hair to stay straight, and if so, to be sure they have a rain jacket with a good hood.

HEALTH AND SAFETY ISSUES

The health and safety of children is the most important consideration in early childhood education. Considering their physical and emotional well-being helps us keep them safe and builds trust between children, families, teachers, and other caregivers. Every type of weather comes with its own considerations. We will explore some of the extremes, but be sure that your environment has spaces that allow for shade, shelter, and access to water.

How Cold is Too Cold?

Keeping children safe and comfortable in the winter is important to encourage play and learning. Determining how cold is too cold has more to do with the wind and weather gear that the children and teachers wear than just a temperature gauge. If children and adults are wearing several layers, water- and windproof outerwear, warm wool socks, warm hats with earflaps, insulated boots, and water- and windproof mittens, then they should be safe and comfortable in most temperatures. When the wind chill starts to dip below zero, make sure that children have additional warm gear like neck gaiters or scarves that can help cover their noses and mouths. During this weather, the ice becomes crunchy, and walking in the deeper snow becomes hard work, so it is also important to be sure children don't get overheated. Observation and communication with children while outdoors is key in figuring out if they may need to shed a layer or two or add another. For example, even at days that are twenty degrees below zero, if we are building a quinzhee or snow fort, and shoveling piles of snow, playing tag, or hiking up a sledding hill repeatedly, it is possible that children may need to shed heavy coats and wear just their under layers that usually comprise a thermal layer, a shirt, and a sweater or jacket liner.

Keeping children safe when it is cold

- **Hydrate!** Winter is a dry season, and it is important to make sure children are drinking plenty of water.

- **Pay attention to children who are not active.** When children and teachers are standing still in very cold temperatures, they can quickly become uncomfortable and may be more likely to get frostbite.

- **Pay attention to children who may be wet from snow play.** Wet clothing can quickly get extremely cold. Making sure children have warm and dry clothing is critical.

- **Watch the wind.** The biting wind chill is often the part of the wintery weather that is the most uncomfortable. Be sure to have spaces that offer shelter from the wind. Venturing into wooded spaces or building a fort can offer a place for play during the winter.

- **Listen to children.** When a child says "I'm cold" instead of saying "Okay, let's go inside" or "You're fine," ask questions and find out why they are feeling cold. Probing questions like "what part of your body is feeling cold?" can give you more information and create a teachable moment about preparation for the outdoors. Often it is a mitten or sock issue that when remedied can make their experience outdoors much more enjoyable.

How Hot Is Too Hot?

Hot is relative to humidity, hydration, sun exposure, and activity level. In dry desert climates, it would not be possible to always keep children indoors when it is above 100 degrees because much of the summer is this temperature. In hot, humid climates, our bodies can't use sweat as a "cooling system" as well as in dry climates, so temperatures above 100 degrees become reason for concern.

Keeping children safe when it is hot

- **Hydrate, hydrate, hydrate!** Most people don't naturally drink enough water, and children are even less likely to drink enough due to their focus on play. Make water available in a manner that encourages enough hydration. Standard drinking fountains do not work well for children. They require dexterity to turn the handle at the same time as bending into an unnatural position. Either children put their mouths on the faucet or most of the water goes up their noses and all over their faces. The best solution is individual water bottles. They should each look very different so that children grab the correct bottle. Don't forget to ask families to label the lid and the bottle with the child's name, because once they are in the dishwasher, it can be impossible to match them all. They need to be cleaned out every day to reduce bacteria. This also allows adults to monitor water intake. Enforced water drinking breaks are more important than enforced bathroom break time.

- **Pay attention to children who are not urinating.** If children become dehydrated, they will urinate less.

- **Take advantage of times of the day with less direct sun.** This may mean re-arranging your schedule, which can breathe life into a stale program. While the 10:00–2:00 time frame shouldn't be banned, look to spend more time outdoors earlier and later in the day.

- **Ensure shade.** Trees take a long time to grow, and shade screens are expensive, but both are critical for programs. Place popular activities in the shade.

- **Teach children to wear hats.** A hat that fits well is more likely to get used. Parents can benefit from specific ideas for hats rather than just letting their children pick hats they like but that don't fit well or provide enough protection. Children will grow accustomed to wearing hats in time, especially if adults model this behavior. Make sure the brim is large enough to provide protection to eyes. The more sun exposure, the more likelihood of developing cataracts later in life.

- **Use sunscreen.** You need to learn what the rules are regarding application of sunscreen for your area. All children—not just light-skinned children—need sunscreen or protective clothing.

- **Use water play to keep children's body temperature down.** Children are drawn to water play, and it is an easy way to keep them cool. Find ideas for water play in chapter 6.

How Do We Avoid Bug Bites?

Each ecosystem has its own insects, and some children are especially sensitive to bites. A combination of protective clothing and insect repellent can minimize this problem. There are now non-DEET insect repellents that provide the same level of protection without the concerns about DEET. For a deeper look into repellents like DEET and picaridin, see the Consumer Report at www.consumerreports.org/insect-repellent/how-safe-is-deet-insect-repellent-safety/.

Danger Signs to Watch For in Different Weather

Frostbite occurs when children have exposed skin in cold temperatures. Especially watch for children's cheeks getting extremely red or shiny, or skin that is hard to the touch. These are signs that the exposed skin may be getting frostbitten.

Hypothermia occurs when your core temperature drops below a safe level. This can happen with wet and/or cold conditions. To reduce the risk of hypothermia, be sure children and adults have the proper outdoor gear for the weather. You can usually find extras to keep on hand at thrift stores for very low prices.

Heat exhaustion and heatstroke occur when your core temperature rises above a safe level. This can happen with hot conditions in any setting. Staying hydrated and providing areas for shade on sunny days is critical.

Lightning is a different risk for different ecosystems. In the mountains and prairie areas, children and families are accustomed to lightning and are more likely to have safety habits in place. Lightning is somewhat predictable and somewhat related to the formula of a mile away for each second between the lightning strike and the sound of thunder, but it can change quickly, so don't count on this. In Hawaii and other areas with very few thunderstorms, children may panic easily when they hear thunder. Avoid being outdoors, as children's fear may cause them to take part in unsafe behavior.

Dangerously high winds are not the same as the risks on a breezy day. While being outdoors on a breezy day provides great learning opportunities, avoid being outdoors with high winds. Broken tree branches and other flying objects can be dangerous. High winds can be especially dangerous when there is a high fire risk.

Dehydration comes before the physical desire to drink. Young children are especially disinclined to stop play to drink water. Drinking fountains are difficult for young children to use to get enough water and are likely to pass germs. Provide individual water bottles that are cleaned daily to reduce the growth of bacteria.

Sunburns are a true danger for children. Bad sunburns from a young age have a cumulative effect on skin damage and are correlated with skin cancer later in life. It is a myth that only light-skinned people are at risk for sunburn—it's just easier to see them! Dr. Aletha Maybank in *Ebony* magazine shared that "people of African descent can have a natural sun protection factor (SPF) of up to 13 as compared to 3–4 for Whites. This does protect us from ultraviolet (UV) sunrays, thereby decreasing our risk for skin cancer and aging early. However, it does not provide complete protection from either" (Maybank 2013). Taking precautions against sunburn even when it is cloudy out and during winter months is essential. High altitude also increases sun exposure, so this is especially important in mountainous areas. A combination of protective clothing and sunscreen is key.

Smog and vog should be monitored. When the air is full of contaminates, it is dangerous for children. This can be natural, like volcanic smog known as "vog" in Hawaii, or human-made, like smog. It is especially a problem for children who have asthma. Pay attention to air quality and avoid taking children outdoors when air quality is bad.

Flash floods are a danger in some parts of the country. Flash floods can happen with little warning and can have devastating consequences. Make sure that families are aware of this danger.

Create emergency plans for changing weather specific to your ecosystem. Redleaf Press has an easy-to-use book to plan for emergencies: *Disaster Planning and Preparedness in Early Childhood and School-Age Care Settings* by Charlotte Hendricks (see appendix 3).

GUIDANCE ISSUES

Do you notice children's behavior changing when the weather changes? There can be many causes.

Some of them are physical. You may find children with pollen allergies reacting to wind. The reaction may be directly related to the wind or may be related to antihistamines. You can support these children by understanding mood changes, providing relief from winds, and encouraging them to wash their faces and hands when returning indoors.

Some are due to excitement. If you grew up with snow, do you remember the first snowy day of the year? It tends to be met with great excitement. Sometimes the excitement is followed by frustration of how cold and wet the snow is to play in. Keep in mind that very young children are less likely to have clear memories of playing in the snow. You can help children manage these feelings by resisting the temptation to build up unrealistic expectations about the fun of snow, providing warm, dry clothes to change into, and accepting that some children will need time to "warm" to the idea.

Some are due to fear. Weather changes may frighten children. Keep in mind that children who are fearful may behave in ways that make their behavior difficult to read. They may get overly active, aggressive, withdraw, and so on. Trying to "jolly" them out of their fears is not likely to help. Several things that have a positive impact on unreasonable fears are information, empathy, and giving children a sense of control. Children really benefit from the message that they might not always feel this way.

Behavioral Issues Related to Weather

- **Keep group sizes small when going outside for complex activities.** This will allow you to respond quickly to any unsafe behavior.

- **Keep children's hands free.** Don't use umbrellas. They are distracting and can cause accidents, and children may squabble over the use of the umbrellas.

- **Make expectations clear.** Children won't automatically know what you want them to do outdoors. If you don't want them to jump in mud puddles, let them know. If a child forgets and breaks a rule, remind her and give another chance. This is how children build self-regulation skills.

- **Return to the classroom if behavior is unsafe.** Avoid making punishing statements such as, "I guess we all need to go back indoors because Tommy isn't listening." This has a detrimental effect on relationships. Instead, say, "It seems too hard for us to be outside safely right now. Friends are getting bumped, and I am afraid someone will be hurt. We are going back inside, and we can try again later."

RESOURCES

Author Favorites

- **Julie's favorite:** *The Mitten* by Jan Brett. 1989. New York: G.P. Putnam's Sons. This is a folktale about a boy who drops his mitten and the animals that claim it as their home. It is an inviting story, has beautiful illustrations, and provides a great plot to dramatize. Jan Brett has written similar books that are set in different ecosystems, including *The Umbrella* and *The Hat*.

- **Sheila's favorites:** *The Snowy Day* by Ezra Jack Keats. 1962. New York: Viking. This is a simply beautiful story of a young boy and a big snowfall in a big city and his explorations with the snow. Because I grew up in the desert, this was a book that I have only known as an adult. I have experienced the joy of reading it with children in Minnesota, and it feels like a meaningful reflection of the awe and wonder they feel around our snowy days.

  My second favorite is *Sun and Rain: Exploring Seasons in Hawaii* by Stephanie Feeney. 2008. Honolulu: University of Hawai'i Press. I have two favorites for the wintery books because "winter" as we know it looks very different depending on where you live. This engaging story of the dry and wet season in Hawaii resonates with children and adults who experience seasonal changes.

Songs and Chants

- "It's Raining, It's Pouring," traditional song

- "Five Little Snowmen Standing in a Row," traditional song

- "Rain Is Falling," traditional song

- "Snow Is Falling," traditional song

- "The Mitten Song" by Wayne Potash

- "John Had Great Big Waterproof Boots On," chant by A. A. Milne

Materials to Enhance Going Outside in Different Weather

Free and Collectible Materials

- **Real snow shovels.** Plastic toys are limiting. Find child-sized metal snow shovels or cut the handles down on regular-sized snow shovels so children can easily use them. Ask families to donate shovels if they move or upgrade.

- **Buckets, sand toys, Jell-o molds.** Make sure to dispose of these items when they become broken and potentially unsafe.

- **Kite-making materials.** Be prepared for a windy day by having a tub of light-weight fabric, paper (lightweight or transparent are great options), tape, staplers, sticks, yarn, ribbons, streamers, and other kite-making materials. You can also add stickers and have crayons or markers available to add decorations. Do not use plastic bags; these are unsafe for children and not good for the environment if they blow away.

Best Materials to Purchase If You Have Limited Funds

- **Books.** You can find weather-related books at the library, but they can be hard to find during specific seasons, and you may want a book quickly with unexpected weather. Watch at yard sales and thrift stores to ensure you have a good stock of books about rain, snow (even if you are in an area that only occasionally gets snow, you will want the book handy if it happens!), wind, clouds, ice, and heat.

- **Rain gauges.** These allow children to have an accurate reading of the amount it has rained.

- **Gear for safe exploration outdoors.** Investing in outerwear for children is money well spent. It is worth doing a fundraiser or asking a local charity to donate. Good outdoor gear for the children in your program will have a greater impact on your ability to take advantage of nature.

  For rain: Invest in galoshes/boots/wellies, waterproof jackets with hoods, and waterproof pants. You can find these items after the season at secondhand and discount stores like Goodwill or Target. You can also ask families to donate what their children have outgrown. You will find that you use these items more often than you think you will! Companies that offer great rain gear include Oakiwear, Tuffo, REI, and Columbia.

  For snow: Waterproof mittens, neck warmers or gaiters, snow pants, warm socks, and warm waterproof boots are essential when exploring in below freezing temperatures and snow. In temperatures below zero, an additional layer such as thermal liners underneath pants and gloves can be helpful as well. In the snow and cold weather, it is also important to keep an eye on the little details of children's outdoor gear, such as that elastic band on the inside of snow pants. Children seem to find it most comfortable if that is inside of the boot or, if the boots have two layers, between the two. It can also be helpful to keep out snow when they are actively playing, so it really is about figuring out which way they prefer. Be sure to have children hold on to their middle layer jacket or sweater with their hands while they put on their outer jacket; this assures that the middle layer won't bunch up and they will be much more comfortable.

  For sun: Sunglasses help protect children's eyes. The lighter color the eyes, the more susceptible to cataracts later in life. Hats with chin straps help shade children's faces.

Extras If You Have More Funds

- **Weather station.** Being able to track temperatures and other weather issues from indoors using a weather station is helpful.

- **Shade screens.** If you live in a sunny climate, having good shade on your playground will have a huge impact on your ability to enjoy the outdoors.

- **Outdoor equipment.** Snowshoes, children's skis, kicksleds, misters for a small area of the playground, inner tubes for rainy puddles, and a Slip 'N Slide can help you make the most of any weather.

- **Washer and dryer.** You will win the support of parents if you can send children home in clean clothes.

From Julie: I learned this the hard way. At our nature-based preschool, we allowed children to play in the mud. Afterward we had them change into their spare clothes and put their muddy clothes in a garbage bag to go home. We had a family say they were withdrawing their child from our school because they didn't think she was learning enough. At the exit interview, we learned that the family did not have their own washing machine, and the mother was spending every other night at the Laundromat. Because this school had primarily middle-class families, she felt ashamed to tell us. Once we learned, we began laundering children's clothing during naptime. Children loved putting on clothes warm from the dryer, and learning to fold clothing was an excellent fine-motor skill for the children.

PLAYING IN THE RAIN

Dear Families,

We wanted to let you know that if it is not too cold and there is no hail or lightning, we will take advantage of rain as a learning experience for your children. We can teach children scientific facts, but when they have firsthand experiences with nature, they can understand and remember those facts more easily.

What Can Children Learn from Playing in the Rain?

- **The joy of nature.** One of our goals is to engender a joy of nature in your children. Most children are drawn to puddles, and when they are allowed to play in the rain, they may learn to love, enjoy, and protect nature.

- **To navigate on slippery terrain.** We work to build good motor skills in children in this program, including balance. The experience of playing outdoors in the rain helps children learn to test slippery paths before stepping on them, avoid deep puddles and take advantage of shallower puddles, and keep their balance in different types of shoes.

- **To learn through their senses.** You know that scent that tells you that rain is on its way? It provides a deep sense of pleasure for most of us. The sound of the rain against different surfaces, the touch of raindrops of different sizes and frequency, and the taste of rain dripping into your mouth are all opportunities to awaken the senses.

- **To learn about rain through firsthand experience.** If the only water you experience comes from a hose or faucet, you don't know much about water. Playing in the rain gives children an opportunity to learn about where the water we use comes from, that rain comes at different rates of intensity, that wind affects the direction of rain, that water seeks its own level, which causes puddles to collect in holes and slanted ground, and so on.

- **To learn about properties of water and interaction with other parts of nature.** This includes how soil absorbs rain at different rates depending on its dryness and density, that plants exposed to rain grow in different ways, that sun exposure affects evaporation, that rocks do not absorb rain, and so on.

- **To use scientific equipment.** When children see a rain gauge filling up, they understand it and other scientific tools more easily.

- **A healthy respect for the power of nature and weather.** When children experience the difference between drizzling rain and torrential rain, they will make better decisions about what is safe. Trying to play with hard-driving rain in their eyes helps them understand the concentration their adults need when driving in the rain.

- **Responsibility for toys, equipment, and belongings that get wet in the rain.** We want to provide many opportunities for children to grow in their independence and responsibility. Playing in the rain provides meaningful chores, including moving items that can be ruined by rain to dry areas, placing rain gear to dry after play, and wiping up muddy tracks when coming indoors after playing in the rain.

Have you played in the rain lately? Trust us, it's good for you!

CHAPTER 6

SPLISH-SPLASH

The Joys of Water

Water is essential for all life on earth. Most children respond with joy at opportunities to learn about and in water. The context of each program's ecosystem is important to lead these activities and discoveries. If water is scarce in your area, you will need to be especially sensitive to its use and waste when planning activities.

WHAT PRESCHOOLERS ARE READY TO UNDERSTAND

- **Water is wet.** Water can be compared to other wet substances.

- **Water dries.** It takes some children a lot of firsthand experience with getting their clothes wet to believe that water will dry.

- **When water is frozen, it is hard and is ice.** This seems obvious, but even if children learn to say the words, they need firsthand experiences to truly understand the transformation.

- **Frozen water melts.** Children in ecosystems that regularly drop below freezing learn this transformation more quickly.

WHAT IS TOO ABSTRACT FOR PRESCHOOLERS TO UNDERSTAND

- **Understandings about water that are learned other than through hands-on experiences.** For example, in Tucson, children learn that water seeks its own level much later than children who live in wetter ecosystems and have opportunities to see rain more often.

- **Transformations that are hard to follow (steam, vapor, fog, etc.)** It is clear to adults that steam, vapor, and fog are forms of water, but young children struggle with these "invisible" transformations. Even absorption is challenging for pre-schoolers to understand, but they enjoy experimenting with wet sponges or other materials.

TOPICS FOR DIFFERENT ECOSYSTEMS

Topics for water should be connected to the environment children experience. Consider both what children experience daily and what are typical background experiences for the children in your program. Is your program in the desert but many of your families take trips to the beach? Is your program in the city but many of your families go to the lake? A survey to your families should supply useful information. A good rule of thumb for focusing on water-related learning is to listen to children's questions ("Can we walk on the ice without it breaking?") and theories ("It will snow because it is almost Christmas."). Examples of a few water-related activities can be found in appendix 1.

Rain

Most children experience rain, but some ecosystems have seasons that tend to be wetter. Save rain activities for the times that children can experience rain firsthand.

Snow

If your ecosystem doesn't experience snow, skip this. Children can learn about snow theoretically when they are older. On the other hand, be prepared for the unexpected snowfall. It occasionally snows in high deserts, and dropping any plans you have to enjoy the snow is just magical.

From Julie: When I was in second grade, my mother wrote the following excuse for school: "Julie missed school yesterday because it was snowing and she needed to play." Pretty progressive for a mom in the early 1960s! Occasionally, it snows on top of Haleakala in Maui and programs rush to arrange field trips so children can experience the snow. Skip the artificial "snow" that can be purchased in catalogs. It gives misinformation to children and confuses their scientific understanding. The exploration of how polymers found in artificial snow expand with water can be interesting to watch but is unrelated to real snow.

Ice

If children experience very cold temperatures, they can have wonderful experiences with ice. Ice can be brought into the classroom and placed in the water table. You can make molds out of old Bundt pans, sand toys, or even balloons. Add salt with small spoons to melt and experiment with the ice. Adding watercolor can add increased interest in the ice table. Outdoors, be careful walking on ice. Always be sure it has been measured for safety, and never venture onto a frozen pond or lake without two adults. When walking on frozen puddles, be sure to check children's boots for wetness if they break through the shallow ice to be sure they won't be susceptible to frostbite.

Salt Water

If your children have opportunities with oceans or saltwater lakes, experiencing the difference between salt water and freshwater is interesting. Experiencing the differences in buoyancy, taste, and texture are some examples of learning opportunities.

Water Sports in Your Ecosystem

What do the families who attend your program take part in? What do children see others doing when they go to a body of water? Opportunities to better understand these sports, even if the children are too young to participate, will add to their understanding of water.

- **Swimming.** In most parts of the country, children participate in swimming at least some time during the year. Water safety needs to be taught in the context of being in the water—otherwise it is just a bunch of rules that will never be remembered.

- **Boating.** If your program is near a body of water of significant size, your children are likely to observe or participate in boating. Some children have annual trips to a lake in the woods, a lake in a very warm area such as the Southeast or Southwest, rivers, or the ocean. Pretend play opportunities can build understanding. A real boat on your playground with life vests allows children to play some of the scenarios they witness.

- **Surfing, kayaking, and stand-up paddling.** These sports are not only popular in coastal communities, but we see stand-up paddling on lakes and kayaking on rivers. Pretend play and movement experiences can help children build understanding. You can provide real boards or just pieces of cardboard indoors or out and use the language and moves of these sports.

- **Arroyos (natural ditches), ditches, and irrigation systems.** Understanding of natural and human-made areas that are sometimes dry and sometimes full of water is important both for understanding water and staying safe. A field trip to see these as well as the opportunity to recreate them in the sand area builds knowledge.

Stories from the Field

Hiking across the pond boardwalk on a cool November morning, we noticed the changing seasons and lack of rain had exposed a muddy area that had previously been underwater. Suddenly we had access to a small island that had been surrounded by water all spring and summer. Crossing over the damp, exposed muck to explore the island proved irresistible to the children—especially to one child. Jack was an intensely physical and well-coordinated child who thrived on challenges. He was the first one across and quickly launched himself up onto a tree branch. As I approached to "spot" his climb, I saw that the branch extended from the trunk over the other side of the pond, which was still covered in water. I held Jack at bay while I tested the depth, but he was a child who did not respond well to being deterred. It seemed shallow enough to go with him as he moved along the branch, so I continued to move under him. His classmates watched in admiration.

Unfortunately, my initial "testing" did not fully account for the silty quality of the pond bottom. With each step I took, my boots sank a little deeper. I described what was happening to the group, and they became engaged in my struggle to keep myself from sinking. We kept moving along together until he made it to the turning point. Luckily for us all, Jack accomplished his climb, turned and worked his way back across the branch and down. For me it took a little longer, as with each step my boots were filling with cold water and I had to work hard to pull each foot free of the sucking mud. The children cheered me back to dry land, and we all headed back to school. Jack's climb and my being soaked to the hips in near freezing water was a shared experience that became part of our class folklore that year. In the experience, I found common ground with a particularly strong, independent child that strengthened the trust and bond between us. The risk was well worth the reward. —**Kris Rollwagen**, MEd, educator, Mendota Heights, Minnesota

From Sheila: When my daughters were young, we used to visit Yosemite National Park each summer. We would spend hours hiking, climbing, exploring, watching stars, and especially playing in the water. The Merced River provides many wonderful shallow spaces for exploring in the valley. My daughters Hailey and Olivia were especially interested in collecting rocks and stacking them on the shore. At the time, they were eight and three, and would work together, exploring how to make small rivers and dams and setting traps for minnows. The cool river water was the perfect place to safely explore the water while marveling at how powerful the water can be in shaping an area like Yosemite over millions of years. This play helps set the foundation for children to be able to learn about larger concepts like geologic land formation over time.

DIPPING YOUR TOE IN

Take advantage of teachable moments about water. When a child spills water, skip the lecture on being careful and join the child in watching how the water moves or what cleaning tool has more absorbency. Involve children in wiping rain or dew off playground equipment and encourage them to think about where the water came from, why there is more in some places than others, and how long it takes to evaporate. Take time to notice steam when involved in a cooking project, and encourage theory-making about what it is and where it came from.

Increase water activities. Move away from the idea of "water day" or "swimsuit day" toward offering water activities often. If you currently only offer water play outdoors, add indoor experience and vice versa.

Save rainwater in buckets. This is easy to do and provides firsthand experience for children. The water can be used for water play, watering plants, and so on. We caution you to make sure to keep the buckets off the ground to ensure that children won't fall into them. A visiting toddler could venture into the area and drown quickly. Also, be sure to empty buckets frequently so mosquitoes won't be able to breed.

Provide water table activities. Change the available equipment and tools to encourage intentional activity rather than just pouring or splashing. Providing map tubes with golf balls and Ping-Pong balls will encourage children to experiment with floating and sinking as they watch the balls move differently when they pour water in the tubes and turn them over. Separate containers of water with different food coloring added to each encourages children to experiment with color mixing.

Provide individual water activities. A simple tray with a pitcher and water for pouring, painting with water, and color mixing will invite children who may feel intimidated by highly active water play.

Make water available outdoors on a regular basis. The sandbox is a good place for regular water use. Wet sand and dry sand are very different to work with.

Add daily chores involving water. Watering gardens and other plants, providing clean water to pets, pouring water into pitchers for meals, and washing items help children understand the functions of water in human life.

WADING IN

Make water play an everyday activity. Once you experience the benefits of increased water play, you are likely to want to offer it as a staple activity alongside activities such as block play and dramatic play. Find a permanent area in the classroom for water-related experiences. Add water play as a block to be filled in when you write lesson plans to keep it on your radar. If you plan using units of study, include water-related studies to ensure that you are including all areas of development in learning about water. Purchase sprinklers, if possible, and add them to your playground for water enjoyment in warm weather.

DIVING IN

Water can become a permanent part of your learning environment. Add water features that are accessible for young children. Hand pumps for water are a great addition to a playscape. Children can move water from a trough through a hand pump to gain access to water. This type of system is especially appropriate in areas with limited water supplies, because children have freedom of access while adults control how much water is available each day. Rain barrels and other water play items can add hours of enjoyment and spark an interest in science, physics, and engineering. A few examples can be found at www.earthplay.net/tag/water-play.

Taking field trips with the children can be another way to immerse everyone in water. Taking children on excursions to streams, creeks, and other bodies of water can be a wonderful way to explore water in depth, take samples, and see changes over time. Visiting these spaces also involves safety precautions.

IDEAS FOR IMPROVING WATER EXPERIENCES

You are more likely to offer water experiences if you don't dread the setup, cleanup, or children's actions during the activity itself. Make a plan beforehand, taking into consideration materials needed, choices, limits, and supervision.

Where is the best location for the activity? If weather and your facility permit, outdoors is usually the best location for water experiences. The outdoors allows water to dry more easily, allows for noise and activity without disturbing others, and makes it easy to include more natural elements in water play. If providing the activity outdoors isn't viable, create a space for water play in the classroom. The late author, instructor, and founder of the Child Care Design Institute, Anita Rui Olds, talked about dividing the classroom into separate wet and dry areas. Designated dry areas protect books and other materials. Having carpet in dry areas encourages children to work on the floor as well as at tables. Wet areas should have hard-surface flooring and be near a water source.

How many children can take part in the activity? Decide how many children will be invited to take part in the activity. This will reduce conflict because you can plan to have enough space and materials/equipment for the number of children.

How much material/equipment is the optimal amount to support discovery without overwhelming children? There are two possible mistakes with how much equipment and material you make available. Providing very limited materials is often done with the assumption of a learning outcome. Examples include "sink or float" activities and pouring activities. We have found that teachers who have such a limited outcome expectation end up discouraging children from their own investigations and work to get the children "back on track." These limitations will cause children to spend less time at the activity. Setting up an experience that will only hold children's attention for five to ten minutes is too much trouble, and you will find yourself feeling like water play activities are not worth the effort. The other mistake is offering too many materials. When the setting is crowded with equipment, it is much harder for children to see the results of their actions, and they learn less from the experience. On the DVD *Discoveries with Water*, there is an excellent short video that shows play getting chaotic when too many materials are available. With experience and getting to know the individual children in your program, you will find the sweet spot of enough materials/equipment to encourage experimentation without overwhelming children.

How easily can children use the bathroom while playing with water? A physiological issue is that getting wet brings awareness of needing to empty one's bladder. Even if we suggest or insist that children use the toilet before engaging in water play, some children will have to "go" in the middle of play. The best way to limit accidents and encourage prolonged engagement in water discovery is to make it easy for children to stop play to use the toilet and then return. A system for saving a child's place at the water activity can include a backward chair or a sign.

How will you clean up after the activity? Water play requires cleanup, including emptying and disinfecting tubs, tables, and equipment daily. As stated below in the section on safety, water conducts germs with ease, and we keep children healthiest when water is changed often. Cleanup will be easier for you and provide learning experiences for the children if you involve them in the process.

Do you have the support of families for water play? You and the children will have the best experiences in water play if the children's families understand its value. When parents are on board, they will be more tolerant of wet clothing and excited about the learning experiences their children are having. At the end of this chapter, you will find a reproducible letter for families on the value of water play.

INCLUSION OF ALL CHILDREN

Indoor water tables can be adjusted to be accessible for all children. Outdoor water features can be a little more difficult to make inclusive because they are often built into the landscape or may come at a standard height. When designing water features for play, remember all code and licensing guidelines as well as the ages of children in your program. Since standing water is generally not allowed on playgrounds, be sure to design appropriate drainage. Water features like rain barrels can have larger knobs to make them easier for children to turn on, and extending the handle on a hand pump can make it more accessible and help children be more successful.

CULTURAL CONSIDERATIONS

During outdoor water play, children will often change into swim clothes. Depending on the families in your community, you may notice a wide variety of what families are comfortable with their children wearing and where they are comfortable with them getting dressed and undressed. Before the water play season begins, ask your families about their preferences and address any concerns. In addition to asking what they would like their children to wear, also ask if they are comfortable with them changing in front of other children or outdoors. During water play it is not unusual for children of both genders to go shirtless or to change in the classroom or outdoors in the same space as other children. Be sure to have spaces available for children or families who request privacy, and listen for any words that may be "othering" children who wear more or less clothing, words that signify gender stereotypes, or anything else concerning.

HEALTH AND SAFETY ISSUES

Water tables can be a wonderful place for exploring the properties of water and the world around us, including gravity, buoyancy, transparency, density, mathematical concepts like measurement and volume, and physical properties like motion and flow. When you introduce water in other states like snow or ice, or add some soap into the mix, they can also learn chemical and physical properties about water. However, water is also an ideal environment for the multiplication and transference of germs—like bacteria and viruses. Emptying the water table between groups of children and sanitizing the table, as well as any tools used in the table, is essential. Children often put the water and tools into their mouths and can be exposed to germs if the table and tools are not cleaned regularly.

GUIDANCE ISSUES

Before making a water experience available, know what limits you want to enforce and make those limits clear to children.

How wet are children allowed to get with this activity? Have a clear picture in your mind. If children are allowed to get drenched, make sure all the adults agree, or children will receive conflicting messages. If there are limits, make them clear to children. You can offer them waterproof smocks or tell them, "The water needs to stay in the. . . ." If children exceed the limit you have set, give a clear message that they will no longer be able to stay at the activity. Worded positively, you can say, "It seems like it is hard for you to play here without soaking your clothes. Let's find another activity for you, and you can try again later." Make sure you give the child the opportunity to use the water activity as soon as they ask again. It takes children time to learn how to respond to adult limits, and they need lots of practice. If they are barred from the activity for the day, they won't have a chance to figure out how to comply.

Are they allowed to get other children wet? This should be clear to both the children who want to get others wet and those who don't want to be splashed. If the activity is designed for splashing, make sure all the children know they are going to get wet. Some children might think they are okay with it, but when they start to experience getting splashed, they may object. Reprimanding children with comments such as, "I told you you'd get wet" is not helpful. We need to support children changing their minds as they get new information. A more helpful comment might be, "Getting splashed doesn't seem fun for you right now." Notice that the comment is set in the present. We want children to feel open to new experiences, and if we say, "You don't like to be splashed," then we have made it a permanent preference. If children are not allowed to make others wet, make that rule clear as well. If a child is splashing another, you can assume positive intent even if it is obvious that the child is doing so intentionally—this keeps blaming and discipline from taking over the experience. Children need practice at self-correction. You can say, "When you splash with the cup, you are getting water on Sally. Remember we are keeping the water in the table." If you don't want to set a limit beforehand and would rather allow the limit to develop from the desires of the group that is using the activity at one time, you can check in with children as they are getting each other wet. "John, you don't look happy. Are you okay with Lauren splashing you?" This becomes a teachable moment for learning social-emotional skills.

Plan for children taking responsibility for splashes. Be prepared with towels, changes of clothing, and even mops and buckets for activities with a large volume of water.

Is using waterproof smocks a choice? Some programs make smocks available. Others require children to use them. We recommend that you do not require smocks. You may choose to offer smocks; however, putting on a smock is a form of commitment to an activity. Children who may feel unsure about taking part in water play are less likely to give it a try if they are required to put on a smock. Some children do not like putting on smocks, and that is enough to keep them from taking part. Lastly, smocks don't tend to work particularly well, and children will often get wet anyway.

RESOURCES

Author Favorites

- Julie's favorite: *Jump, Frog, Jump!* by Robert Kalan. 1989. New York: Greenwillow Books. I love this book because it includes so many creatures that live in and around water. I encourage children to dramatize the story both by taking the role of one of the creatures and through providing plastic replicas of a frog, insect, fish, snake, netting, and a basket.

- Sheila's favorite: *A Cool Drink of Water* by Barbara Kerley. 2002. Washington, DC: National Geographic Society. This beautiful book highlights the common theme of water in the lives of children around the world.

Songs and Chants

- "It's Raining, It's Pouring," traditional song

- "Listen to the Water," by Bob Schneider

- "My Bonnie Lies over the Ocean," traditional song

- "Row, Row, Row Your Boat," traditional song

- "A Sailor Went to Sea, Sea, Sea," traditional song

Materials to Learn About Water

Free and Collectible Materials

- **Natural materials.** Bamboo, leaves, driftwood, and rocks all add to water play.

- **Waterproof buckets and containers.** It is hard to have enough containers, especially when they need to be clear, which will allow children to be able to view objects in water from several vantage points. Big-box stores often sell popcorn, candy, and other items in big, clear, waterproof containers. Containers from food like peanut butter should be well cleaned to avoid contamination.

Best Materials to Purchase If You Have Limited Funds

- **Items from hardware and discount stores.** Gutters, funnels, basters, eyedroppers, and the like, can be used to move and transfer water.

- **Liquid food coloring.** Liquid food coloring can be purchased in large containers from school supply catalogs and allows you to add some color to water, which can make it easier for children to track. It is much cheaper than food coloring at grocery stores.

- **Rain gauges.** You can make your own, but a sturdy plastic rain gauge is preferable. You can find rain gauges at hardware stores, garden stores, and in catalogs. They are tubes that collect water with inches marked off, so it is easy to measure how many inches it rained.

Extras If You Have More Funds

- **Variety of water tables.** If you can afford it, having water tables that are clear, some that have different compartments, some for groups of children, and some for children to work in alone will add to learning about water. At Dodge Nature Preschool we had the ultimate—built-in water tables with faucets and drains in each classroom. They made it easy to assure clean water for each group.

SPLISH-SPLASH

Learning through Water Play

Dear Families,

We know that many children enjoy splashing around in water. Sometimes they like to wash their hands for a very long time or jump into puddles, even without their rain boots. We also know that water play can get a little messy. We would like to share some of the benefits of this messy play and offer a few ideas to make it a little easier at home.

At school we have areas dedicated to water play—like our sensory table in the classroom or the water feature on the playground. We know that at home this can look different. Sometimes just a little extra bath time is all that is needed to give your child time to play in the water. You can also offer water play while you are cooking by having a small tub of water in the kitchen with some small scoops for pouring (empty food containers or funnels) and spoons.

When children are given time to play with water, they learn so much about its properties and our world's properties. Things like gravity, buoyancy, transparency, density, mathematical concepts like measurement and volume, and physical properties like motion and flow can all be learned through water play. When you introduce a few ice cubes or some soap into the mix, children can also learn about the chemical and physical properties of water.

Always be sure to supervise children closely when interacting with water, and happy exploring!

CHAPTER 7

BENEATH OUR FEET

Sand, Soil, Mud, and Rocks

Sand, soil, mud, and rocks are a good place to start with adding nature studies to your class. They are available in every ecosystem, are not weather dependent, and are inherently interesting to children. How many times do you hear adults telling children to put rocks down, or to get out of the mud or sandbox because it's time to go? Sand, soil, mud, and rocks are easy to cover in your classroom because most children have some knowledge base about these topics.

WHAT PRESCHOOLERS ARE READY TO UNDERSTAND

- **There are many kinds of rocks.** You can't always tell what kind of rock it is from just looking at the outside. A perfect example is a geode, which looks like most other rocks until you break it open and find crystals inside.

- **Rocks come in many sizes.** Children can climb on boulders, collect rocks, and measure pebbles.

- **Rocks can change forms.** Rocks can be smoothed by movement in water or by a rock polisher. Stonecutters can change the shape of rocks to use in building. Jewelers can cut rocks to change the way they look and let light shine through the gem.

- **Rocks can be moved and handled.** Children are fascinated by large machinery moving and breaking up boulders. Rocks can fit into different sizes and shapes of containers, and this is a concrete way for children to explore the mathematical concepts of shape and space.

- **People use rocks.** Walls, buildings, stepping-stones, jewelry, and tools made of rocks are all interesting discoveries.

- **You can't tell how heavy a rock is by looking at it.** Experiences with pumice stone, iron, and other minerals allows children to learn more about the difference between size and weight in a hands-on manner.

- **Sand can be very fine or very coarse.** Investigating different coarseness of sand can be done through a variety of hands-on experiences.

- **Soil changes when it is wet.** Adding water to sand, dirt, and clay helps children learn more about its properties.

WHAT IS TOO ABSTRACT FOR PRESCHOOLERS TO UNDERSTAND

- **The moon and other celestial bodies are rocks.** Space is a very abstract concept for young children, and trying to make sense of something being so large that looks so small is best understood in elementary grades.

- **Rocks are millions of years old.** As said before, time is a difficult concept for young children, and this is a topic best studied later.

- **The detailed differences between types of sediment.** Waiting until children are older and have had experiences with several different types of sediment is best.

TOPICS FOR DIFFERENT ECOSYSTEMS

Earthquakes. Children who live in regions that experience earthquakes can benefit from learning more about them. Earthquakes are both exciting and scary, and understanding can help ease fears.

Rock formations. Look at the rock formations in your region. Mountainous areas are full of potential experiences with boulders. Provide a hands-on experience rather than looking at photos of famous formations.

Sand. Sand is essentially crushed rock, usually quartz; calcium carbonate (made from shells and skeletons of marine life); or volcanic materials. Coastal communities can provide many hands-on experiences. In the desert, you can find sand with different levels of fineness.

From Julie: In one school I worked in, we had families who traveled a lot, and we always asked them to bring back a small sand sample from different places.

Soil and mud. Soil and mud will vary by ecosystem. Some soil will be sandy and reddish, gray, or brown and light, while some will be dark brown and heavy. Many areas also have layers of different soil, so encouraging children to dig will help give them opportunities to see different types of soil occurring naturally.

Volcanoes. Volcanoes can be found throughout the world, and they can be exciting to study. Although most children will not have access to a live volcano, many live near a place where a volcano lies dormant or has erupted in the not-too-distant past. Learning about volcanoes does not mean a baking soda volcano! These replicas are flashy but don't add to children's understanding. Looking at the rocks and soil and what does or does not grow around a dormant volcano is much more useful.

Tucson's giant Gem, Mineral & Fossil Showcase is a highlight of snowbird season. It's the cue for me to pull out some amazing rocks from my classroom collection to connect with preschoolers who may have visited the vendors who pop up all over town for about three weeks. Children are eager to share cool crystals, fossils, or geodes they've chosen to buy. They add them to the specimens on the "interesting table" or compare them with smooth sorting stones on the carpet. We talk about the "lava rocks," the "trees that turned to stone," the rocks that feel like sand. My friend K. shows me her rock family, "Mommy, Daddy, and me."

Some children pore over rock field guides, the illustrations from the Gem, Mineral & Fossil Showcase program, or *Everybody Needs a Rock*. Children lift the rocks—the largest is the lightest, how can that be? We put rocks in water, what happens? How are these the same? How are these different? We try drawing with chalk on old-style slate. Because winter is a wonderful time to be outside, we find our own rocks and build collections. We sift sand from our yard through sifters, a screen, or a pool net. We collect a tub of the soft, smooth sand and run our fingers through it. What happens when we stir the sand with a magnet wand? We're lucky to live in a place where building blocks of the earth are so visible! **—Cheryl Lazaroff,** retired teacher from Tucson Community School, Tucson, Arizona

From Sheila: When my daughter Sierra was nine, our family was fortunate enough to visit Maui, Hawaii. There were so many wonderful natural spaces to explore, and we tried to visit as many beaches as possible. On one beach, filled with red sand, we found some amazing shells that were surrounded by rock. Sierra was in love with these rocks and really wanted to take them home. Our friend (Julie) from the island reminded Sierra that it was not a good idea to remove any rocks from the island and that leaving them will make sure that many others can enjoy them in the future. This was not an easy sell to a curious nine-year-old, but we took many pictures and even made a book about them when we returned home so we could meet her needs to have a piece of the rock with her as well as respect the land and the cultural beliefs of the people who lived on the island we were fortunate enough to visit.

DIPPING YOUR TOE IN

- **Take advantage of teachable moments with rocks.** Take time to notice rocks on walks. Look up the names of different types of minerals that children discover.

- **Add water to soil.** Mixing water and soil can be done outdoors or indoors.

- **Share a rock collection.** Find a rock hound in your area to share his or her rock collection with the children.

- **Substitute clay for play dough.** Clay is a natural substance that is more flexible than prepared play dough.

WADING IN

- **Invite a guest teacher.** Ask a local expert to bring in different types of rocks to help children learn more about rocks.

- **Break a geode.** Seeing the crystals inside of a geode is magical.

- **Use a rock tumbler.** Be sure to read all the instructions for a rock tumbler and give children an understanding of how long the rock will take to change its appearance.

- **Start a sand collection.** Different sand samples can be provided in a sensory table to allow children to experiment with different substrates.

- **Celebrate International Mud Day.** June 29 each year is a celebration of childhood, the earth, and the joys of getting messy. Plan a variety of activities, such as painting with mud, making mud in the sensory table, buying a few bags of topsoil to add to the playground just for making mud, or constructing a mud slide.

DIVING IN

- **Build a rock wall.** This is an activity that teaches cooperation and builds gross-motor skills and mathematical knowledge as children find rocks that will balance, fill spaces, and so on. Building a rock wall also provides a hands-on activity to learn about the properties of rocks.

- **Include a playground element that is related to rocks.** Have a professional create a boulder-climbing area or another element for daily use. At Dodge Nature Pre-school, we had a cement tunnel with rock walls built into a hill for pretend play.

- **Visit a jeweler.** If you find the right jeweler, he or she will show children the process of selecting stones to create jewelry.

- **Make adobe bricks.** This allows children to see how straw, water, and soil work together to make a building material.

From Julie: At Tucson Community School, kindergarteners added to an adobe structure on the playground every year for years.

INCLUSION OF ALL CHILDREN

Exploring rocky places with young children can be difficult, especially if they experience limited mobility or have low muscle tone. Planning ahead of time to be sure there are wide varieties of climbing opportunities and having enough adults to scaffold individual children when needed is important for success. For children who are deaf or hearing impaired, knowing when to be alert to moving rocks is essential. In these explorations, a high number of adults is necessary.

CULTURAL CONSIDERATIONS

Find out about the beliefs of your families. Two areas may come up when studying rocks and minerals.

- **Are rocks alive?** We often tell children that rocks are inanimate. This is inconsistent with some cultural beliefs, including those of many American Indians and Native Hawaiians.

- **How old are fossils?** While time is a difficult concept for preschoolers, studying fossils adds to the confusion. Some Christian religions believe that the earth is much younger than science supports, and this is a topic that may be best avoided with young children.

HEALTH AND SAFETY ISSUES

Make sure to supervise children around rocks, stones, and pebbles. Rocks come in a variety of sizes and can represent a choking hazard for children under three and children who still are likely to put things in their mouths. Also, be aware of sharp edges, especially with larger rocks or when climbing on rocks. When walking on unstable rocky areas, be sure to have plenty of adults nearby to help children, climb only on the rocks in dry weather, and have your first aid kit nearby for any slips or falls. When discovering with soil, children can often find ants or other biting insects, so be sure they know what to look for in the soil. When exploring in mud, some may be very sticky—we call that boot-sucking mud. Be ready to help retrieve shoes and make sure children have well-fitting shoes or are barefoot when in the mud.

GUIDANCE ISSUES

Throwing rocks occasionally becomes an interest for young children. The temptation of most people is to toss a rock to see how far it will go. Allowing young children to throw rocks is dangerous. They don't have an accurate aim and are unlikely to understand the consequences of hitting someone with a rock. Set clear limits. You can also provide an area to throw mud clods at a target, a safer activity that is likely to satisfy the desire to throw rocks.

Limit the number and/or size of rocks children collect. While it can be exciting to pick up every rock on the playground, remind children that some rocks need to stay at school so that other people and the bugs can enjoy them. As a group, come up with a number of rocks that seems to work. Consider having a shelf in the classroom where children can temporarily display their favorite rock of the week. This way you are showing the child that you value their interests and that eventually natural items need to be returned to nature.

From Julie: Children may find limiting the number of rocks they pick up to keep difficult. When Sheila's family visited me in Telluride, her rock hound daughter filled her pockets so full she struggled to walk! Limiting how many rocks a child can keep is an opportunity to develop self-regulation in a relatively painless manner.

RESOURCES

Author Favorites

- **Julie's favorite:** *Everybody Needs a Rock* by Byrd Baylor. 1985. New York: Aladdin Paperbacks. This story is told from the perspective of a child in the desert. The author demonstrates respect for children's serious investigation, and the book provides a wonderful jumping-off point for a rock-hunting activity.

- **Sheila's favorite:** *One Duck Stuck* by Phyllis Root. 1998. Somerville, MA: Candlewick Press. This is a story of a duck stuck in the muck and other animals who try to help. It is especially fun after celebrating International Mud Day when children have enjoyed the experience of being stuck in the mud and having others help them.

Songs and Chants

- "I Love Mud" by Rick Charette
- "Ooey Gooey Mud" by Sweetly Spun Music
- "Dirt Dirt Dirt" by Sesame Street
- "Soil, Water, and Sun" by Heroes of the City

Materials to Support Rock Investigations

Free and Collectible Materials

- **Books.** Look for books about rocks, gems, and minerals. You will find reference books with clear, full-color photographs in the adult section of the library.

- **Jewelry.** Put the word out to families, and chances are they will have some items that are out of fashion or are missing stones and so are not used.

- **Old kitchen supplies.** Whether you are making a mud kitchen or a sand exploration area, it can be created with all previously used materials. Collect old spoons, ladles, funnels, colanders, bowls, and so on.

Best Materials to Purchase If You Have Limited Funds

- **Clean gravel.** Gravel from a parking lot is too likely to be contaminated by oil, antifreeze, and other dangerous substances. Instead of scooping some, you can purchase large bags of gravel at a home improvement store.

- **Tools for exploration.** Good magnifying glasses, magnets to detect iron, and iron filings are all useful.

- **A variety of rocks, gems, and minerals.** Avoid the boxed sets with tiny samples that are typically sold. Most towns have a store with minerals for sale. You can also alert jewelers in your area that you are interested in gems that are not suitable for their use due to breakage or another reason. They may even give them to you!

Extras If You have more funds

- **Drills for rocks.** Being able to open a geode or see inside of other types of rocks can be highly engaging for children.

- **Variety of rocks in different states.** Polished, unpolished, slate, and so on, can allow children to better understand minerals. Examples of minerals that look very different in varied states include pyrite, quartz, and mica.

- **A kiln.** Using clay can be enhanced when it is fired in a kiln and can build a connection with the clay that children may find while digging outside.

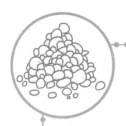

ROCKS ROCK

Dear Families,

We know that children have a fascination with empty boxes, sticks, rocks, cabinet doors, and wooden spoons; they love the simple things! They can play with a piece of fabric or an empty container for hours. That love of simple items can lead to a lifelong fascination with rocks.

Rocks are more varied than boxes and easier to put in a pocket or arrange on a log. They can be used as currency, food for dolls, building structures, and more. The possibilities with rocks are endless. We also know as adults that we have deemed some rocks more special than others throughout our history—marble, granite, gold, diamonds, and other gems. Children have not begun yet to discriminate between rubies and river rock, but they clearly see the beauty in all of them. We have a variety of rocks in the classroom and around the playground for children to investigate and use in play.

We do not encourage children to take rocks home, but we do not prohibit the collection of a special rock here and there and will replenish our playground streambed with river rock as needed. We also encourage you to share in children's love of rocks and help them create a place to display, sort, and explore the properties of rocks at home or while out in the community. With a little imagination and care, those gems and treasures often become an important part of their childhood.

LET'S GET GROWING

Flowers, Trees, Fruits, and Vegetables

In any environment, children have opportunities to interact with plants. Sometimes the plants are in deep, lush forests or wide-open prairies, and sometimes they are thriving in the desert or fighting to grow through the cracks in the sidewalk. Gardening with children is a wonderful way to help introduce children to the process of planting, caring for, and harvesting plants.

WHAT PRESCHOOLERS ARE READY TO UNDERSTAND

- **Plants start from seeds or bulbs.** Preschoolers can closely observe this change over the period of several classes indoors or by watching trees and plants in their outdoor spaces.

- **Fruits and vegetables come from plants.** Help children see the connection by pointing out stems, roots, and other parts.

- **Plants grow and change throughout the seasons.** Children can take pleasure in studying the changes of a plant or tree over time or watching a bulb grow in the classroom and bloom.

- **We can eat some plants, like herbs, lettuces, fruits, and vegetables, but some plants are not good or safe to eat.** Therefore all adults need to know which plants that grow in your space or are brought into the classroom are safe and which are not.

WHAT IS TOO ABSTRACT FOR PRESCHOOLERS TO UNDERSTAND

- **Botanical rules** (such as, is a tomato a fruit or a vegetable). It is hard enough for adults to keep them straight, and they really don't matter.

- **Names of each stage of the plant cycle.** It is more important for preschoolers to track the different stages through observation than to name them.

- **Health benefits of organic fruits and vegetables.** Preschoolers don't have control over the food their families buy. Organic versus nonorganic is a topic best left to elementary school.

- **Difference between a weed and a flower.** The main difference between a weed and a flower is the opinion of the people living in the ecosystem, so there is no reason to spend precious time on this idea.

TOPICS FOR DIFFERENT ECOSYSTEMS

Depending on your region, you may have the opportunity to observe and experiment with plants or foods from the grocery store, grow things inside your classroom, plant things on an outdoor patio, or garden in a larger space. Wherever you are, you can take advantage of the spaces available for hands-on experiences with plants. Simple investigations and experiments with seeds, fruits, and leaves can help foster a sense of wonder around how things grow and their life cycles.

Learning about Local Plants

One of the most important kinds of knowledge young children need is about their own environment. Knowing about and becoming interested in the plant growth they see every day will connect them to nature. Resist focusing on types of trees and other plants just because there are lots of books, games, and equipment you can use. An example of what we consider inappropriate is focusing on maple leaves and other trees that change color in autumn if you live in the desert. Remember that children have a whole lifetime to learn, and starting with what is most relevant to their lives fits the expectations of developmentally appropriate practice.

Topics to consider regarding local flora:

- **Trees.** What trees grow naturally in your area? What type of trees do people tend to plant? What trees can be seen from your classroom? Investigating the trunks, branches, leaves or needles, and the animals that make these trees their homes provides a wealth of discoveries for children.

- **Bushes, vines, cacti, and other smaller growth.** What is native and what do people tend to plant? Do they produce berries or other fruit? Are the branches and leaves soft or prickly? Do insects live in them or use them?

- **Flowers.** Some parts of the country have flowers for short periods of time. If this is true in your region, don't miss the best time to learn about them in favor of topics that are less time sensitive. Help children learn to appreciate flowers that are subtler and less likely to be sold in flower stores.

Indoor Growing

Indoor planting is a good alternative for programs that have limited space, share space, or are in a region with a very short growing season. Move beyond the science activities you remember from your childhood, such as celery in colored water, and instead focus on opportunities for children to learn about the whole life cycles of plants.

- **Edibles.** Many vegetables can be grown indoors. Sprouting seeds is a quick and satisfying experience. You can grow a variety of spouts from spicy radish sprouts to mild alfalfa sprouts.

- **Herbs.** You can stimulate children's senses by growing herbs. The scent of different herbs will remind children of different kinds of food. Herbs can be enjoyed alone or used in cooking such as in homemade pizza or hummus.

- **Flowers.** Children can help to select the flowers to grow. We suggest that you offer only seed packages of flowers that are likely to grow successfully in your classroom environment. Making pictorial directions and calendars for the care of individual flowerpots will help children see that plants have individual requirements.

- **Changing leaves.** If you live in a region that has deciduous trees, take advantage of the beautiful season when the leaves change color and drop.

From Julie: In Minnesota we used to collect maple leaves, and children mixed tempera paint to try to match the color of the leaves. This is so much more authentic than cutting leaf shapes out of colored construction paper. One of my favorite quotes is from Dr. Lillian Katz, professor emerita at the University of Illinois Urbana–Champaign and former president of NAEYC, who described watching children take part in such an activity and say to each other, "This is really dumb, but my mum is going to love it!" (NAEYC conference 2013). In up-country Maui, our jacaranda trees bloom with purple flowers that fall to the ground, making large piles of purple in the springtime. Too many teachers don't take advantage of this lesson material because they schedule lessons on trees only in autumn.

- **Cactus study.** If you live where there are cacti, children should learn about them before trees. They can learn which have sharp needles and require caution, which have flowers and how they each look, how they hold water, and more. Cacti are beautiful, and children who live in the desert will learn to appreciate them when exposed to positive attitudes from adults. Even if your area has trees, they are less likely to be indigenous to the area, and children are more likely to hear negative comments about cacti. We know attitudes about nature are formed at a very young age.

- **Farms.** What grows on farms in your area? Too often we focus on stereotypical farming found in songs about animal farms, when in reality many farms are centered on the growth of plants for food. In many areas of the country, children can explore certain crops—like corn in the Midwest, pecans in the South, and citrus fruits in the West and the Southeast.

In my visits to more than a hundred school gardens in many different states and climate zones, I have observed that most of them have compost piles or bins (Williams and Brown 2012). Compost serves as a marvelous entry point to teach children of all ages about decomposition and soil. Art, science, math, and language arts (including poetry) come into play as profound learning experiences emerge. I watch young kindergarteners fascinated by the myriad soil critters they discover in the compost as they squeal with excitement; no educator can draw them away easily from their new discoveries. I notice second graders excited to identify ants, earthworms, potato bugs, millipedes, slugs, and spiders as they turn the compost; they are enamored by the varying legs and movement. In the classroom, they create an art mural of soil as their teacher integrates the "decomposition" experience in the garden. It is fun for children to learn about FBI—fungi, bacteria, and insects—that convert their compost to soil. They also learn about the "big four": browns (e.g., leaves, straw), greens (e.g., grass clippings, food waste), air, and water, and how to layer and mix these proportionately. They check the temperature with thermometers stuck in the hot pile as they ask questions and learn about the biological processes that enable life-sustaining soil.

In countless ways, compost captivates children as they learn about the dance of decay, birth, and life affecting texture, smell, porosity, and color of soil. When adults allow children the space to explore, children do so naturally. Beyond the distant outdoor field trips, children can connect to their own locale and the human-biotic community in the learning gardens on school grounds. School gardens invite children into kinship with life. Students question, wonder, marvel, and make connections as they get their own hands and feet soiled. **—Dilafruz Williams**, PhD, professor, Portland State University, Portland, Oregon

DIPPING YOUR TOE IN

Take time for teachable moments with plants. Start a discussion about plant-based foods at mealtime. Stop to notice changes to plants outdoors. Comment on pictures of plants in books.

Include a live plant in your classroom. Live plants are good for classrooms! Select a plant that will thrive in your classroom environment. If your classroom tends to have dry air, a cactus or succulent might work well. If it is more humid, think about a fern.

WADING IN

Provide planting and growing activities. Resource books with planting activities are abundant. The trick for making them meaningful is focusing on what is observable rather than abstract concepts.

Offer cooking and food preparation activities. Food preparation activities have a great influence on what children are willing to eat. If your state regulations limit your cooking activities in the classroom, talk to a licensing specialist to find solutions. If no solutions are possible, you can send activities home with children, including a bag of ingredients and recipes.

Take trips to farms, community gardens, and flower gardens. Most communities will have some space for growing things that you can visit. Plan to visit when you can see equipment, people tending plants, and plants at different stages of development.

DIVING IN

Start a family garden. If your center is a dedicated space, find a location that has a variety of sun exposure, enough space to avoid overcrowding, access to water, and access for families outside of school hours. If your center has shared space with another organization (church, public housing, elementary school, etc.) work with others to find a space that will accommodate a large enough garden for many to use.

Provide in-depth curriculum units on topics related to plants. The topic web in chapter 1 offers an example of a plant-based unit topic. Select a topic that includes a type of plant that you have easy access to, that is interesting to children (they tend to like plants they can eat), and is appropriate for your ecosystem.

INCLUSION OF ALL CHILDREN

Raised-bed gardens are beneficial when you have the space for them in your outdoor environment, but planters can also be a wonderful way to include plants, flowers, fruits, and vegetables in your space. When planning raised-bed gardens, be sure to choose a height that is accessible for young children and for children and families in wheelchairs. Also, be sure to plan enough room between the garden beds for people in wheelchairs to access them.

CULTURAL CONSIDERATIONS

Plants are present in every habitat—dandelions growing through the cracks in the cement, tumbleweeds in the deserts, tall sequoias on the coast, and many more. There are plants to be enjoyed, protected, and propagated everywhere. Growing food is a big part of many cultures, and being mindful of the families in your program can bring a rich diversity to your garden and to your snacks and meals. When planning your outdoor gardens, invite the children and their families to share some of their favorites from their gardens or tables.

Using edibles for art activities or sensory experiences continues to be controversial in our field. While a sliced bell pepper provides a perfect print for a butterfly, it is now a pepper that cannot be eaten. Rice is considered a staple of substances to use in a sensory table, but many worry about the message it sends when so many people are food insecure. This is especially distressing in programs that serve low-income families or employ low-income workers. One alternative is to use food items that can be reused. Pinto beans provide a nice substance for a sensory table as they are a satisfying texture, make an interesting sound when poured, and are easily handled. They can be washed after play and cooked for dog treats. Another alternative is using birdseed. The birds won't mind the germs!

HEALTH AND SAFETY ISSUES

When exploring around plants, it is important to know if any are dangerous or may irritate skin if someone touches them, like poison ivy or stinging nettle. Knowing which plants to look out for and teaching children rules like "Leaves of three, let it be," or helping children search for stinging nettle to make nettle tea or nettle soup can help them learn to identify it and understand its hazards and its potential usage.

Since children learn with all their senses, some might try to put dangerous plants in their mouths, such as nonedible berries, mushrooms, oleander, and burdock leaves. Be sure to help children learn to identify what is edible, but remember that it is up to the adults to keep children safe and be sure that they do not eat anything poisonous.

In your program, it is likely that children will have the opportunity to learn about food that grows in your area. Grape tendrils are a popular item to taste and are found on wild and domestic grapes. Children enjoy chewing on them for a little sour grape taste. Wood sorrel is also popular; it has three heart-shaped leaves and small yellow flowers. These plants have a lemony taste and grow in many areas. In Hawaii nasturtiums grow just about everywhere, and their blossoms are both beautiful and tasty.

Here are some rules about eating food, whether it is prepared in a kitchen, fresh from the garden, or found on a walk, that you can add to your program:

1. Always ask a grown-up each time you are interested in eating something. This is a safety concern at home and at school because we don't want children actively playing and eating, and want to prevent choking.

2. Even if you are sure that something is edible, ask an adult each time.

3. Don't pick from places where people or dogs could have walked on it. Other rules come up depending on the situation—especially if herbicides or pesticides are used in the area.

Great resources are available for many other wonderful treats that we may enjoy throughout the year, including dandelions, raspberries, and other items from our gardens. Information can be found at www.foraging.com and your local library.

GUIDANCE ISSUES

There are many schools of thought on how much, when, and where children should be able to pick flowers, fruits, and vegetables. Ultimately, the decision is an important one to consider within your specific community. If you plant flowers, fruits, or vegetables in a garden, you may need to limit picking to be sure there is enough for all your children to have an opportunity to plant and harvest. This happens on our playground with the raspberry plants. We try to give both our morning and afternoon programs opportunities to pick and enjoy the fruit in other spaces, such as prairies, meadows, or along sidewalks. Allowing children to pick until they are content may be appropriate or even beneficial. However, be sure children do not pick all of a certain fruit but leave some for pollinators that may rely on the plants in the area.

RESOURCES

Author Favorites

- **Julie's favorite:** *Sunflower House* by Eve Bunting. 1997. New York: Scholastic. I love to provide activities involving sunflowers because they are so dramatic and easy to grow. This story describes how children pretend with sunflowers.

- **Sheila's favorite:** *Rah, Rah, Radishes! A Vegetable Chant* by April Pulley Sayre. 2011. New York: Simon and Schuster. This beautifully photographed book celebrates the beauty of vegetables with new vocabulary and can build interest in trying many new foods found at farmers' markets or grocery stores.

Songs and Chants

- "The Green Grass Grew All Around," traditional song (easy song to use with sign language)

- "Carrots Grow from Carrot Seeds" by Ruth Krauss (it goes with the book *The Carrot Seed*)

- "Here Is a Seed So Soft and Round," traditional fingerplay

- "Oats, Peas, Beans, and Barley Grow," traditional folk song

- "Dig a Little Dirt" by Mary Godfrey

- "The Compost Bin" by Hap Palmer

- "Growing" by Hap Palmer

- "Many Pretty Trees All Around the World" by Ella Jenkins

- "Apples and Bananas" by Raffi

- "Way Up High in the Apple Tree," traditional finger play

Materials to Support Learning about Plants

Free and Collectible Materials

- **Expired and used seed packets.** The packaging from expired or used seeds can be used for making games and labeling plants. Expired seeds can be used in collages or experiments.

- **Natural materials.** Leaves, stumps, sticks, bark, cones, and pods from trees in your ecosystem. These can be used in sensory activities, the block area, pretend play, and so on.

- **Discarded flowers from florists.** Flowers can be used for investigations.

Best Materials to Purchase If You Have Limited Funds

- **Fresh seeds for plants.** Find plants that will grow successfully in your ecosystem. Connect with a master gardener in your area for advice.

- **Soil.** Good plant soil will make a huge difference in how much you are able to grow.

Extras If You Have More Funds

- **Wooden furniture and play equipment.** If you have any control over these types of purchases, furniture and equipment that has visible wood grain, veins of color through real stone, or metal that isn't painted makes a visual connection to nature.

- **Tree blocks.** These free-form blocks can be purchased in catalogs and add an element to the block area that encourages micro-sociodramatic play about nature.

- **Flower press.** You can always use books, but a real flower press is very satisfying.

WILD EDIBLES

Dear Families,

Young children are naturally curious about the world around them and eager to explore with all their senses. Children often will want to put things in their mouths, so it is important that we are conscious of any safety hazards. One item to be especially conscious of is what is safe to eat and what is not.

Occasionally on our playground or on hikes around the area, children will have the opportunity to learn a little bit about food that grows in our surroundings. Grape tendrils are a popular item to taste near our school. These are found on the wild and domestic grapes, and the children enjoy chewing on them for a little sour grape taste. Wood sorrel is also popular. It has three heart-shaped leaves and small yellow flowers. These have a lemony taste and grow in most yards in our area. On our recent hike, we also enjoyed mulberries that grow along the road. We held out a sheet and shook the tree to enjoy the dark purple berries.

Throughout our tasting experiences, we continue to let children know the rules about eating food, whether it is prepared in a kitchen, fresh from the garden, or found on a walk.

1. Always ask a grown-up each time you are interested in eating something. This is a safety concern at home and at school because we don't want children actively playing and eating, and want to prevent choking.

2. Even if you are sure that something is edible, ask an adult each time.

3. Don't pick from places where people or dogs could have walked on it. Other rules come up depending on the situation—especially if herbicides or pesticides are used in the area.

Great resources are available for many other wonderful treats that we may enjoy throughout the year, including dandelions, raspberries, and other items from our gardens. Information can be found at www.foraging.com and your local library.

CHAPTER 9

POLLINATORS, PREDATORS, AND DECOMPOSERS

Insects, Spiders, and Worms

Attitudes about creepy-crawlies begin at an early age. If you ask a group of adults about insects, spiders, and worms, they are likely to start by telling you what they hate or fear the most. When we model these fears and distastes, children are watching. Children see if we respond with yelling and killing insects, spiders, and worms, or if we observe with fascination.

WHAT PRESCHOOLERS ARE READY TO UNDERSTAND

- **These critters are alive and are part of the animal kingdom.** Children are, at times, unaware that bugs are "real" and have senses. By helping children learn to be gentle with these small and vulnerable creatures, we give them opportunities to develop empathy and understand how to treat all living things. Without this understanding, they will be confused by admonishments to treat them gently.

- **Some ways that insects, spiders, and worms help us.** There are many hands-on ways to help children understand the positive role these creatures play in our lives. A wonderful example is composting with worms. Another is to notice the insects caught in a spiderweb to see how spiders are natural pest control.

- **What is safe to approach and what we need to keep distance from.** Children can even learn to identify a biting ant from one that does not bite people.

- **How to treat insects gently.** Treating critters gently needs to be a consistent message at school, but we cannot control the behavior of families. One way to keep from sending negative messages to children about their family's behavior is to frame differences by beginning with, "*At school* we move bugs outdoors. . . ."

WHAT IS TOO ABSTRACT FOR PRESCHOOLERS TO UNDERSTAND

- **The anatomical parts of insects.** While it is an easy thing to teach children to memorize, it does not generally add to their appreciation or understanding of insects.

- **Complex information about pollination.** This is too abstract a concept to focus on and should be saved for when children are older.

> *Stories from the Field*
>
> Some of the children in our class this spring discovered that bugs loved to hide under the logs. One child, Zadie, was curious about bugs but never voluntarily attempted to touch them. She often looked under the log with a teacher and observed from a slight distance. Her peer, Lydia, is quite comfortable with bugs. She picks them up gently, moves them around her fingers, and thinks about whether the bug is lost and needs a new home to live in the ground or the trees. One day Lydia found a small bug crawling near a log, so she picked it up and observed it gliding through her fingers and the palm of her hands. She giggled and said, "It tickles." Zadie noticed Lydia's movement and came closer and asked, "Can I see?" After a while, Zadie asked further, "Can I try?" As the bug crawled around her fingers and hand, she looked at Lydia. They giggled together, and Zadie squealed, "It tickles!" They were sharing a moment, noticing the bug and its many feathery legs and laughing together. They found a new home for the bug and continued to observe its movement throughout the morning. —**Ayuko Boomer**, MEd, toddler and preschool teacher, Shirley G. Moore Laboratory School, University of Minnesota Twin Cities, Minneapolis, Minnesota

From Sheila: When I was a parent of a kindergartener, the teacher asked me about my ideas for having a classroom pet. The problem was that the school district did not widely support reptiles or mammals in the classroom, and she needed something that would not need weekend attention. She also didn't have much pet experience outside of dogs and cats, and she didn't want something that would take a lot of time to clean up after or create a "smell" in the room. After some consideration, I thought mealworms would be a good choice. She immediately said no to the idea of handling worms. I told her I would lead a small group with a few children and she could see what she thought about it. I was a classroom volunteer once per week, so the next week I brought in eight mealworms, eight strawberries, and eight small, empty, clear containers (I chose baby food jars, but any small empty container with a lid would work well). I took a small group and showed them the different life cycles of the mealworms. We played with them, named them, and read a book. Then I asked the children to tell Ms. Stone what they thought about their new pets, what they knew about them, and what they still had questions about. She was sold. She held an adult mealworm beetle, a squiggling pupa, and eventually even the mealworm larva. I ran into her about five years later, and she told me all about her classroom pets—now hundreds of mealworms that she uses to talk to children about life cycles, care, overcoming fear, and even composting.

TOPICS FOR DIFFERENT ECOSYSTEMS

What is poisonous, what is not. Insects with the same name may not be equally venomous. Centipedes in Minnesota are very shy and usually do not bite. Centipedes in Hawaii have a nasty sting, and some people have dramatic allergic reactions to the venom. Focus on what is safe to touch and what should be viewed from a distance that is specific to your ecosystem.

Worms make a great first discovery into nature that you can hold in your hand. Different regions have different kinds of worms. Some things we call worms are not actually worms, like mealworms or inchworms.

Learn which spiders are native to your ecosystem. Most spiders are nonvenomous. Learn the difference so you can safely enjoy observing spiders. Some children are interested in learning to identify a spider from its web or may even be comfortable handling spiders.

From Julie: In one school I worked in, we had a pet tarantula named Flower. She made a great pet, and the children could handle her if they were gentle. The advantage of a tarantula is that they are large enough for children to see their body parts well.

Learn which ants have painful bites and which are safe to observe closely. We have lots of myths about how to tell which ants are safe (that red ants bite and black ants don't is not true, nor is the size of the ant a determinant). There is no easy way to tell which ants are likely to bite, but insect guides can be a great tool for discovering which are safer to explore. The habitats used by different types of ants can be very interesting to children, as can watching how ants work as a community.

Beetles come in many kinds—from ladybird beetles (ladybugs) to green June beetles (June bugs) to mealworm beetles. Children who don't like bugs are more likely to enjoy ladybird beetles than other insects. While fireflies (glowworms, lightning bugs) might be children's favorite kind of beetle, they do not make for the best study for children who live in regions that do not have them.

From Julie: Growing up in Tucson, I never saw fireflies until a trip to the Midwest as an adult. I grew up thinking they were imaginary like fairies!

DIPPING YOUR TOE IN

Bring magnifying glasses to the playground. This will give children an object to focus their attention and help them stay still while observing. They are also less likely to stomp on a creepy-crawly if they are busy observing. On sunny days, ensure that children are not directing too much heat through the magnifying glass to keep creatures safe.

Take advantage of teachable moments. One of the most important lessons for children to learn early is to respect insects, spiders, and all living creatures. Stop children from killing insects. They may have this modeled at home, so word directions to avoid conflicting with messages from home. Examples include, "At school we care for living things. I will move the spider outside." Or "Move your feet so you don't hurt the ants. Let's watch them and see where they go."

Read books about insects, spiders, or worms. Read simple stories and give children lots of time to converse about the topic. This is where you will learn children's interests and fears.

Examine spiderwebs. Different types of spiders make different types of webs. As children observe these differences, they will develop more respect for them. A lovely, but somewhat long, book called *Be Nice to Spiders* by Margaret Bloy Graham tells what happens at a zoo when the staff clears out all the spiderwebs.

WADING IN

Provide a temporary bug pet. Bringing an insect in for a short period of time allows children to carefully observe it without disturbing it too much.

Visit an apiary. Some apiaries (places where collections of beehives or colonies are kept) are outfitted with areas for children to watch safely.

DIVING IN

Create insect habitats. Insect habitats can be indoors or outdoors and can range from a worm bin to a pollinator garden.

Take part in butterfly tagging. A great place to find information on monarch migration and ways to be involved in tagging and habitat preservation is www.monarchwatch.org.

INCLUSION OF ALL CHILDREN

When exploring bugs, remembering that some children may be allergic to bees or other stinging/biting insects is vital. When children are very young, their families may not yet know that they have an allergy. Be prepared for any reactions to bites by having a way to contact other adults and emergency support for help when exploring outside. If you know a child or adult has a life-threatening insect allergy, always travel with the medication needed to respond to the emergency. Make sure all adults have been trained in the use of EpiPens.

CULTURAL CONSIDERATIONS

Sharing our indoor spaces with bugs can be inconvenient when they get into our flour or crawl across the floor and surprise us. Most bugs are harmless, and modeling respectful treatment of living things can be meaningful for children's development. Cultural and individual attitudes toward some bugs like roaches, ants, or spiders can make exploring bugs in your program challenging. Some bugs are considered pests while others can mean good fortune or can signify a spiritual encounter. It is important to consider all the views of those in your community when designing your curriculum around bugs. Although freeze-dried mealworms or deep-fried crickets are not a part of our diets, historically and throughout the world today they are a sustainable and healthy food source. A wonderful resource is https://ed.ted.com/lessons/should-we-eat-bugs-emma-bryce, which highlights that even if bugs are not something that many of us eat regularly, they may be a part of a sustainable and healthy future for our children.

HEALTH AND SAFETY ISSUES

Throughout the country insects and arachnids exist that can transmit serious diseases or that can cause harm to adults and especially children. Several precautions can be taken to keep children and adults safe in areas with mosquitoes and ticks, poisonous spiders or scorpions, bees and wasps, fleas, kissing bugs, fire ants, and even poisonous caterpillars.

The first step is to do an assessment and find out which potentially dangerous bugs may live in your area. Once you know what the hazards are, it is much easier to teach children what to look for and how to avoid creating spaces that invite those bugs. For example, black widow spiders can be found throughout the Southwest and prefer to live in dark sheds, on the underside of ledges, logs, wood planks, or rocks, or around debris. This makes keeping your outdoor storage areas open and cleaned often imperative. It is also important to remember that cold weather or drought may drive some of these insects into buildings, especially garages, basements, closets, and cluttered areas.

In addition to the hazards that the bugs can bring, some children and adults may have allergic reactions to some bites, especially bees. Keeping supplies needed to treat someone having an allergic reaction on hand is crucial.

From Sheila: Understanding bugs of all kinds can help children build an appreciation for their role in our habitats. Often adults bring their own fears into the classroom and avoid pursuing learning opportunities with certain bugs. For example, spiders have always frightened me. I grew up in areas with black widows and brown recluse spiders, and even understanding they are not likely to hurt me and would rather be far away from me doesn't make my reaction when I see one any less surprising. Recently I was refilling a paint cup at our outdoor easel and looked up to see a large spider sitting at the top. I let out a small gasp and then smiled at the children and said, "Wow, that spider surprised me. I wasn't expecting to see it on our easel." I wanted the children to know my authentic feelings but didn't want to transfer my fears.

We decided to leave it on the easel so it could watch the painting and enjoy the sunny day.

Occasionally children may be interested in taking an insect back to the classroom to watch it more closely and care for it over a few days, and this can be a great opportunity to learn more and develop a deeper understanding. It is best to leave bugs where you find them, but if you have the time to observe in the classroom and research the best ways to care for the particular bug, bringing it back to the school may be a good choice. Be sure to provide a safe and secure habitat and provide for the bug's food needs. One of the most popular bug guests are caterpillars so that children can watch their growth and metamorphosis. Finding fresh food for specific breeds of caterpillars can be a challenge, so having a pollinator garden on the playground can add a food source that is easier to access.

From Julie: I have lived many places and have a healthy sense of caution with creepy-crawlies. Growing up in Tucson, I knew which scorpions were more dangerous (the small ones) and how to avoid mistakenly touching one. I learned the different webs of spiders, both dangerous and not. One of the rules I always had for teachers was, "Don't kill things in front of children." We carefully moved things that were not safe in the classroom outdoors. The other important lesson we had for children was "Grown-ups know which creatures are safe and which are not." This kept children safe from stinging and biting insects and spiders as well as teaching a healthy appreciation for the natural world.

RESOURCES

Author Favorites

- **Julie's favorite:** *Yucky Worms* by Vivian French. 2010. Somerville, MA: Candlewick Press. This engaging book tells a story while sharing information about worms in a manner that will win children over to worms as pets.

- **Sheila's favorite:** *Mealworms: Raise Them, Watch Them, See Them Change* by Adrienne Mason. 2001. Toronto: Kids Can Press. This book is a wonderful resource to have in the classroom so children can follow along with the growth of their own mealworms, learn to use a book to find information, and gain interest in the changes that occur with this beetle's development.

Songs and Chants

- "Incy Wincy Spider" or "Eensy Weensy Spider" or "Itsy Bitsy Spider," traditional song

- "Spider on the Floor" by Raffi

- "The Ants Go Marching," traditional song
- "Herman the Worm," traditional song
- "Walter the Waltzing Worm" by Hap Palmer
- "Snails' Trails," chant by Glenda Mac Naughton
- "Slimy Worm," chant by Susie Davies

Materials to Support Learning about Insects, Spiders, and Worms

Free and Collectible Materials

- **Bug containers.** Collect clear plastic containers of different types. We do not recommend using glass as bug containers because they are not safe for young children.
- **Butterfly habitats.** Butterfly habitats can be built out of wood or a plastic tote and screen to provide a safe place to raise caterpillars and watch their metamorphosis from caterpillars to butterflies.

Best Materials to Purchase If You Have Limited Funds

- **Realistic replicas of bugs and spiders.** Replace your plastic bugs of random sizes, inaccurate colors, and human faces with realistic-looking insects.
- **Replicas of butterflies in life-cycle stages.** Purchase resin-encased butterflies at different stages (egg, caterpillar, chrysalis, butterfly).
- **Honeycomb and refined honey.** Seeing and tasting honey in different states helps to develop appreciation for bees. If possible, use honey from your area.

Extras If You Have More Funds

- **Plants that attract butterflies.** Specific plants attract butterflies, and the results can mean stunning access to butterflies. Research to find out what will be best in your environment
- **Butterfly nets.** These can be made or purchased in a toy section of a store, but high-quality butterfly nets will work best.

From Julie: At Dodge Nature Center, we had many monarchs that stopped on their way to Mexico at the beginning of every school year. That meant that our children knew a lot about butterflies. The first time I read *The Very Hungry Caterpillar* to my class and asked what the hungry caterpillar would eat, the children yelled, "Milkweed!"

CREEPY-CRAWLIES

Learning through Interactions with Bugs

Dear Families,

If your children's first reaction when they see a bug is to scream, ask someone to kill it, or attempt to kill it themselves, it is important to give them experiences with bugs to help build their understanding and empathy.

Helping children learn gentleness with nature and being respectful of bugs and other animals in nature can be exciting and a learning experience for everyone. You can begin with experiences with bugs that are usually considered friendly, like ladybugs, worms, or beetles. You can also set an example by catching bugs that enter your home and releasing them outside. You can also read stories with your children. Some favorites from your own childhood might include *Be Nice to Spiders* or *The Very Hungry Caterpillar.* Talking with your children about the lives of these bugs in real life may be a good way to help extend their understanding.

We will always consider some bugs to be pests, and it may be hard not to spray or smash that spider with the long legs in your home or swat those mosquitoes. Talking with your child about the lives of bugs is a good way to expand their understanding of the complex communities we live in together.

CHAPTER 10

THE EGG IS ONLY THE BEGINNING

Learning about Birds

All ecosystems have birds. Some teachers avoid a study of birds because birds are so mobile that they are hard to observe. When children do learn about birds at school, it tends to be domestic birds. In this chapter, we will focus on both domestic and wild birds.

WHAT PRESCHOOLERS ARE READY TO UNDERSTAND

- **What makes a bird a bird?** Children are interested in learning how birds are different from other animals. If you ask preschoolers what birds are like, they are most likely to mention that they fly. A challenge to that notion can be a great conversation!

- **You can tell what kind of bird lays specific eggs.** When children learn to identify eggs, it gives them the opportunity to observe nature without disturbing it. Peeking in the nests they have watched birds sit on will help children learn the colors and sizes of different types of eggs.

- **The process of laying eggs.** This is something we can make visible to children. The birthing process of any species tends to be a taboo topic, and yet it is something children want to understand.

- **There are many kinds of nests.** Each type of bird creates or finds a place for eggs. Young children can understand some of the issues that go into nest building and consequences of those choices.

- **Bird feathers can be identified.** Too often children have only seen dyed bird feathers. Most birds in North America don't have brightly colored feathers, and we can help children learn to appreciate and notice subtler differences. They can be collected from the ground (if cleaned) or purchased from a nature catalog.

- **Birds can carry diseases that are not safe for humans.** This will be important information to keep children safe. We can model safe practices of handling birds and nests.

- **Fun fact.** Birds don't crash into each other, they always veer to the right. We should spread the word to humans! (Curiosity.com 2016)

- **People eat some birds but not others.** Teachers will need to decide if it is appropriate to broach this topic in their educational environment.

- **Migration can be difficult to understand.** You can decide if your classroom community is ready for this topic. If children can see migrating birds easily (like Canada geese) the topic is more meaningful.

- **Some people keep birds as pets.** Children find the specific issues of pet birds interesting. They may ask questions such as "How do you keep them from pooping all over the place?" and "How can they fly?"

- **Birds eat with different kinds of beaks.** The shape of a bird's beak is directly related to the type of food they eat.

- **Color difference between males and females.** Ducks, peacocks/peahens, cardinals, and many other birds have stark differences in coloring between genders that children may find interesting.

WHAT IS TOO ABSTRACT FOR PRESCHOOLERS TO UNDERSTAND

- **That dinosaurs are the precursors to birds.** Extinction is bound in an understanding of the past, including before children were alive. This is beyond their understanding. Children are fascinated with the idea of the size and power of dinosaurs, but preschoolers struggle with understanding time they experience, let alone what happened millions of years ago. Dinosaurs are generally a more appropriate topic for kindergarten and elementary school-aged children. Other investigations with and about dinosaurs may be appropriate, but trying to relate them to birds may feel abstract to most preschoolers.

- **Detailed information about their anatomy.** Birds have qualities unique to their bodies, such as light/hollow bones that will be more appropriate to study when chidren are older. Because we don't generally look inside of our bones, the notion of hollow bones versus bones filled with marrow is better for older grades.

Stories from the Field

Our class pet, Miss Chick, had a unique and natural ability to connect children with nature. Freely roaming the classroom and playground, she was the children's constant companion. She took dirt baths in potted plants and in the sandbox, she would catch insects and toads for a snack, and her eggs were used for classroom cooking projects. Miss Chick also spent a lot of time in the garden. She set a good example for healthy eating as she snacked on tomatoes, peas, and beans. However, it was her love for compost that brought most of the children together. Miss Chick learned quickly that when the shovel cabinet opened, it meant children would be digging in either the sandbox or the compost. She would come out from under her favorite bush and wait to see which direction the children were headed. If they walked toward the hill, she would run as fast as she could and follow them into the compost. The children would use their shovels to unearth and cover the decomposing vegetables. Miss Chick would work side by side with them, using her feet and beak to turn up the soil. When worms or bugs were discovered, the children would yell, "Miss Chick, here's a worm!" Miss Chick would quickly run to the hole and gobble it up. She would stay close to the hole, bobbing her head in and out, as the children continued to dig deeper into the earth. When Miss Chick had had her fill of insects and other critters, she headed up the hill to the classroom door. She would hop up to the windowsill and peck on the glass to let the teachers and children know she wanted to come in. After a long time of digging in the compost, Miss Chick would settle into her cage for a late morning nap. —**Natalie Gilmore, MEd,** preschool teacher, former Dodge Nature Preschool teacher, Chaska, Minnesota

• • •

I grew up in a world without eagles. The prolific DDT usage of my parents' childhoods relegated these birds to a realm approaching myth, and during my formative years in New England I was taught that the eagles were well on a path toward extinction. Back then, the only eagles I saw, the only eagles I expected ever to see, were the fierce creatures on a dollar bill or perched atop a flagpole. So I am even more impressed, many years and many miles from that childhood, by the eagles that now preside over my forest classroom in the Pacific Northwest. Even from a distance their enormity is compelling. A female bald eagle can grow to thirty-seven inches, tall enough to look a three-year-old in the eye. These creatures capture the excitement and imagination of our little community and won't let go.

It is late January, and the children are soaring through the classroom like the birds that fly overhead; pounding out a rhythm in the forest floor that echoes the beat of the wings above them. The children's energy this morning is bound to the flight of our magnificent neighbors. They are our resident nesting pair, and whenever we hear their strange warbling peal resound, the dichotomy of teacher and student, adult and child, breaks, and we become simply a group of humans enthralled by the call of a creature that knows no bounds.

In the classroom, this excitement and energy builds each time the eagles dip in and out of view. The children know instinctively that there is something special about this day, and their energy grows wings and swells to a high point as they laugh and tumble and call to one another. We are in the midst of some particularly fantastic imaginative play when suddenly the grove descends into silence. At the loud crack of a branch, one of the children points to the big-leaf maple in the center of our grove. And there, thirty feet above the ground, perches the larger of the pair—the female, I'll later learn. We pause in the sunlight at the base of the tree, catching on to the drama that is playing out before us. Before we even truly process what is happening, the second eagle descends, and suddenly it becomes quite clear that the eagles are mating in the tree. In that split second, I am overwhelmed by the thread connecting my eagle-less childhood to this moment now, where I am a teacher in a classroom in which eagles land and mate overhead. And just as a thousand teacher-ly questions fill my thoughts— "What on earth should I say? How do I respond?"—the moment passes; the eagles shake their wings, and the larger one departs. I look to the children in awe. How can I possibly capture and reflect this moment in a way that is not only suitably meaningful but also developmentally appropriate? Lost in the world of the teacher, I am momentarily speechless.

But of course, the children are one step ahead of me. They look to each other ponderously, and I hold my breath. A five-year-old boy, one of the oldest in the group, puts his hand on his hip, cocks his head, and declares with finality, "Ah, I think she's going to go lay an egg now!" The others nod solemnly in agreement and they are off, screeching and soaring once again through the classroom. Just another day in the forest grove. —**Kit Harrington**, MA, director/teacher, Fiddleheads Forest School, Seattle, Washington

• • •

In the fall, we were studying trees since they are particularly interesting in Minnesota when the leaves change color. After the leaves had fallen, the children were able to clearly see nests up high in the branches. They began looking around at every tree, counting to see which tree had the most. I was pretty sure they were squirrel nests, so I encouraged the children to watch closely so they could identify what type of animal or bird might live there. The children would watch for brief moments each day on the playground. After about a week, no one had seen any visitors to the nests, so I asked if they had any ideas about how we could attract birds. They shared ideas, such as providing food and nesting materials. After making bird feeders and scattering seed around on the playground, the children became far more interested in birds than nests. I added a bird feeder outside our classroom window and a bird-watching station inside. The children watched the birds all winter long. We investigated feathers and nests in our science center. The children marveled at the way the birds could make nests "without any hands!" They tried weaving their own nests and found it very challenging; their respect for and admiration of birds grew. In the spring, they hoped to welcome birds home from the South by making nests for them on the playground. They gathered string and sticks and used plenty of springtime mud to hold them together. They were thrilled when they saw their first robin of spring. —**Amy Vavricka**, MEd, preschool teacher, Shirley G. Moore Laboratory School, University of Minnesota Twin Cities, Minneapolis, Minnesota

TOPICS FOR DIFFERENT ECOSYSTEMS

What birds are in your area? Focus on the birds that are in your environment rather than flashy tropical birds like parrots or peacocks.

What birds in your area eat. Children can learn a lot about birds by learning about what they eat. It will be easier to see the connection between the birds that are drawn to your ecosystem and the plants and insects that are available. Examining scat can provide some clues for children. Experiments with which types of food disappear when left out and which do not is another. Children can see that the size of birds impacts what they eat (have you ever seen a seagull pick up a whole bag of potato chips at the beach?) as well as the shape of their beaks (children tend to think woodpeckers eat wood rather than that they are drilling into the wood to get access to insects).

Where birds nest. Nests are more accessible than birds for children to examine. Depending on your ecosystem, birds may nest on the ground, in cacti, in trees, or on human-made structures.

What birds in your area use to build nests. Extend your lessons from where birds nest to what they use for the nests. This helps children connect birds to the rest of your ecosystem.

DIPPING YOUR TOE IN

Take time to watch birds that come nearby. We can help children develop the habit of stopping action to pay attention to nature. Take advantage of teachable moments with birds. Stop to notice nests or part of nests that the wind blows out of trees. Notice bird droppings and talk about what you can tell about the birds from looking at their poop (you may be able to see seeds and colors of food they have eaten). Keep windows to the classroom open whenever possible to be able to hear bird activity. A change of focus takes place when you move from creating noise in a classroom through constant recorded music to allowing the sounds of children's play and nature to take over.

WADING IN

Create a bird-feeding station. Select an area outside a window that children have easy access to and set up a bird-feeding station. Select bird feeders and birdhouses that are appropriate for the kinds of birds in your ecosystem (refer to the websites in appendix 4). Keep the bird feeders filled with appropriate birdseed. This can be a wonderful "job" for children. Set up an observation station at the window facing the bird feeders. Binoculars (real ones, not taped together paper towel rolls), bird identification posters, and checklists with small photos of the types of birds that frequent the bird feeders all add to children's experiences.

Contribute items for birds to use in their nests. Once you learn where birds are building nests, you can encourage children to leave a piece of shiny tinsel or otherwise easily identifiable pieces of string or yarn. You can then walk to find the "presents" in nearby nests.

DIVING IN

Visit an aviary. Find out if there is an aviary at your local zoo, nature center, or conservatory. A trip to an aviary allows children to see a wide variety of birds in a setting where they can observe birds at leisure.

Keep birds as classroom pets. First make sure that your area doesn't have licensing restrictions on birds in classrooms.

Incubate eggs. You will find directions in the "Incubating Chicks" lesson on page 176.

Dissect owl pellets. As disgusting as it sounds, owl pellets are the undigested bones, fur, and other parts of prey that they spit up. Children can learn a lot about birds of prey from taking these apart with tweezers. You can purchase presanitized owl pellets and appropriate tweezers from nature catalogs. Be sure to have children wash hands and disinfect tables afterward to avoid exposure to salmonella.

INCLUSION OF ALL CHILDREN

Having a bird visit the classroom can be an exciting event. If a child in your classroom has a bird for a pet, they may have experience with handling, feeding, and caring for a bird and can share that experience with the community. For children with sensitivity to sound or sudden movements, a bird can be frightening and disruptive.

CULTURAL CONSIDERATIONS

Many families have strong and varied opinions about hunting and eating birds, and about some birds as pets or pests. It is important to keep the families in your program in mind when planning curriculum and classroom visits, adding pets, or having discussions about birds. For example, some people see pigeons or seagulls as pest animals, while others marvel at their coos and calls, their grace in flight, and other abilities.

HEALTH AND SAFETY ISSUES

Salmonella is a possible safety concern when cooking with eggs or handling birds. The danger of salmonella is increased for children younger than five, especially because they are less likely to have good hand-washing routines and still may put things in their mouths.

Below are several guidelines you can follow to keep young children safe when interacting with birds or bird items like feathers, eggs, or pellets (the coughed-up nuggets from owls):

- The most important is good hand washing every time children touch an animal.

- Do not allow birds in the same spaces where children eat, and make sure to disinfect every surface that animals touch.

- Do not allow children to touch the inside of animal habitats.

- Be sure that any staff interacting with pets in the classroom understands the importance of following proper hand-washing routines after every animal interaction for the children and teachers.

- If you have chickens in the classroom or on the playground, be sure to clean up any chicken waste immediately and disinfect the area.

  Guidelines for cooking with eggs:

- Use brown eggs if you can, or if you use white eggs, use a metal bowl so it is easier to find shells.

- Make sure children wash their hands after cracking eggs.

- Do not allow children to taste any food before it is fully cooked.

- Disinfect the cooking area immediately after cooking in the space, including the table, chairs, and sink faucets.

GUIDANCE ISSUES

Hatching chicks in the classroom can be a wonderful experience for young children. The "Incubating Chicks" lesson on page 176 explains how to hatch chicks in your classroom. Once the chicks have hatched, providing supervision and guidance anytime the chicks are accessible is essential. Cover their habitat to be sure that children can't access the chicks except when a teacher is supervising. A good beginning rule is touching with two fingers and not picking up the chicks until they are about a week old.

RESOURCES

Author Favorites

- **Julie's favorite:** *Angus and the Ducks* by Marjorie Flack. 1930. New York: Doubleday. Even though this is a very old book, it provides the right blend of realism and a story told from a perspective to which a child can relate. Angus is a Scottie dog who meets ducks. Each animal acts according to reality, but the narrator provides insight into Angus's version of his experience in a manner that will delight children.

- **Sheila's favorite:** *Birds, Nests and Eggs* by Mel Boring. 1996. Minocqua, WI: NorthWord Press. This is one of a series of *Take-Along Guides* that are a wonderful resource for the classroom. They encourage children to explore and learn more about the animals they see in their community.

Songs and Chants

- "Six Little Ducks Went Out One Day," traditional song (great for dramatizing)
- "Who Fed the Chickens?" by Ella Jenkins
- "Amazing" by Hap Palmer
- "I Had a Rooster" by Pete Seeger

Materials for Learning about Birds

Free and Collectable Materials

- **Abandoned birds' nests.** Find nests and place them in clear plastic containers to protect the nest and protect children from possible parasites.
- **Bird feathers.** Special feathers can be saved for examination, and common feathers can be saved for artwork. If these are found outdoors, you can clean them by spraying them on both sides with your classroom disinfectant.
- **Bird song CD.** This can be borrowed from a library or listened to online.
- **Handmade bird feeders and birdhouses.** This can be a good project for a family member. You can find directions online.

Best Materials to Purchase If You Have Limited Funds

- **Apps for recognizing bird sounds.** You will find a list of both free and for-purchase apps in appendix 4.
- **Good-quality bird feeders.** Look for a bird feeder that is sturdy, easy for children to fill, and if you live in squirrel/chipmunk country, resistant to climbing creatures.
- **Birdseed specific to local birds.** Birds' diets matter. Also, if you have children with peanut or tree nut sensitivities, read labels to avoid allergens.

Extras If You Have More Funds

- **Bird egg replicas.** You can purchase egg replicas that are specific to the birds in your environment. These are sturdier than real eggs.
- **Bird mounts.** Real bird mounts or replicas can be purchased.
- **Bird feathers.** High-quality feathers can be purchased for displays and examination. Less expensive feathers can be purchased for artwork.
- **Birdcalls.** These whistles make the sound of specific birds and are often used by bird hunters. These can be purchased through catalogs or outdoor equipment stores. They should be used by the adults to avoid germ transmission.

THIS IS FOR THE BIRDS AND FOR THE CHILDREN

Dear Families,

Whether you have seagulls, cardinals, chickens, crows, pigeons, wild turkeys, road-runners, or hummingbirds in your community, there are always birds to explore with children. Birds bring new sounds and songs, are continuously busy, and can provide hours of enjoyment. My children and I have spent hours watching little sandpipers fishing on the beach or checking robin nests for little blue eggs.

Children enjoy caring for birds by building or painting houses for them, building or filling bird feeders, and exploring nests. At school we will have opportunities for children to care for the birds we have around our school and would welcome any donations of peanut free birdseed. At home you can continue to foster interest in birds by taking time to notice the birds near your home.

Children are often interested in where birds live, what they eat, and where they go when it is rainy or cold. You don't need to know any of the answers; just be curious and help them figure out the answers. You can help them investigate these questions by heading up to the roof of your apartment to see if there are nesting birds, walking to a park and looking for birds' nests, taking a walk to a nature center, or attending a class at a park that is focused on exploring birds in your area.

If your child is showing an interest in birds and wants to know more, wonderful children's field guides are available as well as websites that share their birdcalls and songs with audio clips. Here are a few resources for your explorations:

- www.allaboutbirds.org/how-to-learn-bird-songs-and-calls

- www.almanac.com/topics/birding-fishing/bird-sounds

CHAPTER 11

SLITHER, HOP, JUMP, OR CRAWL?

Reptiles and Amphibians

Studying reptiles and amphibians can be rewarding for young children and their families. Interacting with reptiles both indoors and outdoors can be exciting and challenging. Indoors, reptiles can make great pets because they don't produce dander that some children and adults can have allergic reactions to, and they require care a little less often than mammals. Reptiles can have a variety of behaviors that allow children the opportunity to compare with their own reactions and behaviors, such as turtles that are shy and duck into their shells, or those turtles that walk or swim over to the habitat when children arrive, waiting for treats. Outdoors, amphibians are often easy to find by sight or sound in many diverse areas, especially those near water.

WHAT PRESCHOOLERS ARE READY TO UNDERSTAND

- **Basic similarities and differences between reptiles and amphibians.** Children easily learn the difference between a salamander and a snake, but the difference between a frog and a toad or a salamander and a lizard may be more difficult for them to categorize and take a little more time to learn.

- **Some hatch from eggs and some are born live.** Most reptiles and amphibians hatch from eggs, but a few are born alive and are cared for by their parents.

- **They move in many different ways.** The variety of ways that reptiles and amphibians move, sometimes without legs or arms, can be surprising for children and adults. Exploring the movements of hopping frogs, plodding turtles, and slithering snakes can be educational and exciting for children. This is a great opportunity to add movement to your activities for your bodily kinesthetic-intelligent children!

WHAT IS TOO ABSTRACT FOR PRESCHOOLERS TO UNDERSTAND

- **Identifying poisonous animals.** Young children cannot be responsible for identifying poisonous animals or remembering safety precautions when handling these animals (an adult must consistently provide supervision and follow-through). Young children should begin to identify danger, but safety must remain the responsibility of the adults.

- **The mechanics of how snakes move.** The complexity of muscle movement is interesting to investigate but better saved for the elementary years.

- **The difference between toads and frogs.** According to www.livescience.com, "You can tell most toads and frogs apart by the appearance of their skin and legs. Both amphibians make up the order Anura in the animal kingdom, but there are some key differences. Most frogs have long legs and smooth skins covered in mucus. Toads generally have shorter legs and rougher, thicker skins. And while toads generally lay their eggs in long strands, frogs lay their eggs in a cluster that resembles a bunch of grapes" (LiveScience 2013). As you can see, this is interesting, but identifying which animal laid which set of eggs or comparing leg lengths might be a little tough for preschoolers.

TOPICS FOR DIFFERENT ECOSYSTEMS

What is poisonous, what is not. Exploring what is safe and unsafe is complex and educational for children and adults—but is ultimately the role of the adults. Knowing this distinction can help families feel more confident exploring outdoors, help teachers feel better prepared when visiting natural areas, and help children gain confidence to explore the wonder of the world around them.

> *From Julie:* When I lived in the Tucson desert, I had several children in my classes who were bitten by rattlesnakes (none at school). They all made full recoveries, but it was scary and hard work to recover full function. The joy of moving to Minnesota where almost no snakes are poisonous meant I was picking up every snake I saw. It served me right when one urinated all over me!

Building appreciation for reptiles and amphibians. These are animals that are sometimes feared or revered depending on the cultures where they are found.

> *From Sheila:* When we found a salamander on the playground, it was exciting to know that they live in our area and can be found if you just look closely. For the rest of the year, every time we found a wet leaf pile, we were hoping to find another salamander. We found lots of frogs and worms, but we didn't see another salamander that year. Knowing how your families feel about certain animals can help you construct your curriculum.

Types of lizards in your local area. Many regions around the country have native lizards that can be interesting for children to study. Most lizards are safe to handle, although they tend to be tricky to catch.

From Sheila: I once caught a very fast lizard and was very proud, so I brought it home. As a defense mechanism, its tail broke off and it ran under the refrigerator. I was not able to catch it again. My mom was not too happy about me bringing lizards into the house and losing them.

Stories from the Field

While I was teaching preschool at the University of Chicago Laboratory Schools, we had a box turtle named Fred as a classroom pet. Fred was rescued from the backyard of a local tavern and came with the name. The children built him a wooden maze of rooms as a home, complete with furnishings and pictures and notes he might enjoy. Fred was taken on outings to a favorite grassy area and pond on the university campus, and the children discovered that despite what they had been told, box turtles do swim. The children enjoyed observing and learning about Fred and began to worry he might be lonely. They also wanted baby turtles and decided Fred needed a wife. A parent brought in a female turtle, and the children voted on a name. "Sparkly Dress" won hands down. Now there had to be a wedding. Many discussions resulted in the basic ingredients for a ceremony. The location would be Fred's campus swimming hole; and of course we needed a minister, pretty music, vows, and guests in fancy dress. The children measured the stone bridge crossing the pond and glued patches of colorful fabric together to make a carpet down the aisle. Several turtle pets (and their owners) from other classrooms were invited, as well as the families of our students. The children made a turtle cake, along with human refreshments, invited all to sign the guest book, sprinkled flower petals down the aisle, and performed the ceremony. The turtle pair arrived across the pond via homemade boat (baby bathtub festooned with streamers and flowers). Vows were simple; following the ceremony, "Happy Marriage to You" was sung to the tune of "Happy Birthday." Other classroom turtle guests were given rides on the wedding boat, as one of the pond's resident turtles looked on. —**Sarah Sivright**, MEd, director, All Seasons Preschool, Inver Grove Heights, Minnesota

From Sheila: A few years ago, a child named Carl asked, "How old is [our class snake] Ramona?" I answered, "She is probably about ten." With a confused look, he asked, "You don't know how old she is?" I explained that she hatched from an egg and a family adopted her, and when their child grew older and went to college the family gave Ramona to me, so I didn't know exactly how old she was. He was not satisfied with that answer. "If she had a birthday party, then it would be her birthday, and you would know how old she is." I couldn't disagree with that logic, so I said, "That makes sense." By now other children started to listen to the conversation. He said, "Let's have a birthday party for Ramona." The other children cheered with glee. We started a conversation about what a birthday party for a snake would look like. We continued the conversation, and it naturally turned to party planning during our large-group times. After a few days, the children set a date, wrote invitations, sent the invitations to the pets in other rooms, and invited their parents. We talked about the treats that Ramona and the other pets would like, made treats that the other animals would like (Ramona only eats mice, so we did not get her a treat), and decided to make a cake that looked like a ball python (the species of snake that Ramona is) for her party. On the day of the party, the children from the two classrooms arrived along with their class pets. Children enjoyed cake and gave their pets some of the treats. Then it was time for presents. Ramona received several foil snakes from one classroom and some handmade toys from the woodworking area of another classroom. One aunt who often knits scarves for her nephew brought Ramona a nice red scarf (her nephew thought Ramona, with her long body, could really use a scarf). We had a wonderful day, and through the process the children learned writing skills with the invitations, planning and organizing, thinking of others when planning for food and games, and choosing a gift that someone, even a snake, would truly enjoy. Also, now we know that Ramona was ten on that day!

DIPPING YOUR TOE IN

Focus on what reptiles and amphibians are native to your area and found wild around your program. Learn about what lives in your area. In desert areas, it is more likely to be reptiles. Wild tortoises should be watched from a distance, as they are fragile. Too many people have captured them and brought them home as pets instead of leaving them to their happy lives in nature. A wide variety of lizards are likely to live in your area. Be careful with endangered lizards such as Gila monsters. If they are moved beyond their territory (typically one mile), they may not survive.

From Julie: In my Tucson school, we had a Gila monster whose territory included our playground. When he wandered onto our playground, we came inside and watched until he wandered off again even if that meant that we didn't use the playground all day. The children learned, "He was here before our school was here." Some amphibians show up in puddles after rains; some, like the Colorado River toad, are poisonous.

Wooded areas with lakes, ponds, creeks, and streams can be teaming with amphibians. If you take one back to your classroom to observe, be sure to return it quickly.

In coastal areas, you can also find a variety of reptiles and amphibians. Jackson's chameleons are not indigenous to Hawaii but are now found almost everywhere. Newcomers to Hawaii are often frightened by them, but they are a very gentle lizard.

Challenge children's discomfort, disgust, or fear. Some children learn from adults and some are just a child's first reaction. Examples of ideas to challenge:

● **"Geckos are disgusting because they poop everywhere."** Help children learn about the role reptiles and amphibians play in pest reduction.

● **"Reptiles and amphibians make you sick."** While it is possible to pick up diseases, including salmonella, proper hand washing and washing of surfaces that these creatures have touched will keep children safe.

Take advantage of teachable moments. Notice droppings from reptiles and see where they lead. Read books about reptiles and amphibians. Some of our favorites are listed in the resources section of this chapter, and in appendix 2. Don't rely too heavily on nonfiction, as it can be less engaging for some children. Avoid too many anthropomorphic books, as they will not add to children's understanding.

WADING IN

Visit a zoo, college lab, pet store, or other site that has a variety of reptiles and amphibians. Research what is available in your area. If field trips are not an option, consider having a visitor from one of these organizations bring reptiles and amphibians to your classroom.

Visit a nature center. Many nature centers offer specific classes for school groups that focus on native wildlife, including many reptiles and amphibians.

DIVING IN

Offer an in-depth study of a type of amphibian or reptile. Watch for which interest your group of children the most and begin there. Get a reptile or amphibian for a pet. Check with your licensing agency before investing in a pet to be sure it is allowed. Jackson's chameleons, box turtles, and corn snakes are examples of pets that do well in classrooms. Involve children in researching the best habitats and food for your pet. Add pet care to children's jobs.

INCLUSION OF ALL CHILDREN

Experiences with reptiles can be very meaningful for children with special needs. Children who are experiencing visual difficulties will find the comparison between a furry cat and a reptile quite amazing. Snakes range in size and weight, and their smooth skin and long cylindrical bodies can be fascinating for many children.

From Sheila: Reptiles also vary widely in their temperaments, even animals of the same species. Our two box turtles at the Lab School are just one example. One is very outgoing, comes out to see children and adults when they walk in the room, is picky about her food, and will eat worms as fast as the children can dig them up for her. The other box turtle is more timid and often goes right into her shell when anyone approaches her habitat. When children can observe these differences, it helps them build understanding that we are all different, have our own likes and dislikes, and react very differently to the same stimuli in the world. If children are immuno-compromised it is important to keep their interaction with reptiles and amphibians, as well as all animals, limited to viewing only.

CULTURAL CONSIDERATIONS

Some families do not feel as though interacting with animals is safe, sanitary, or positive in general. Provide opportunities to help families gain comfort with animals and learn about their care and safety, as well as what some of the positive interactions might be. However, when a family has deep cultural or religious beliefs, it is best to reach a compromise about ways to make your classroom emotionally safe for the child and their family.

From Sheila: I had a family in my class who believed that snakes were evil creatures, and they did not want their child to be near one. We had a wonderful conversation before the school year began and reached a compromise that the snake would be moved out of a primary place in the classroom and covered on days that their child was in class. Listening and hearing this family's strong religious beliefs and incorporating their beliefs into our classroom community was important. As the year went on, some children became interested in the snake, and I again had a conversation with the family. They agreed that if their child did not interact with the snake, it was okay to have it uncovered. By the end of the year, the family and I worked together to be comfortable with having the snake out for small groups if their child wasn't in the room. This kind and respectful family was a joy to have in the classroom, and we gained a mutual respect and understanding for each other's cultures. We had much in common and were able to have a thriving relationship full of open dialogue and friendship. The second year was much smoother, and we even joked about the snake occasionally. Whether the difference is a cultural belief, a special need, or a behavior that requires a certain environment or intervention, there is always something we can do as educators to continue to expand our understanding as we build our classroom communities.

HEALTH AND SAFETY ISSUES

Reptiles and amphibians are both wide and varied groups of animals. Over 140 different species of reptiles and amphibians exist throughout the country, and many can provide beneficial learning experiences for young children and teachers alike. Although most are wonderful to interact with, a small few can be aggressive, toxic, or even dangerous, such as alligators, Gila monsters, poisonous snakes, or certain toads with toxic skin secretions. Because some species can be hazardous, learning about the species that are native to your area and taking appropriate precautions to avoid them when possible is critical.

Salmonella is also a possible safety concern when interacting with reptiles and amphibians, and early childhood environments should consider carefully adding them to their environment. Although most cases of salmonella are from food sources like eggs, dairy, and poultry, salmonella can also be transmitted by reptiles, amphibians, birds, cats, and humans. Salmonella is more of a concern for environments with children younger than five, especially because they are less likely to have good hand-washing routines and still may put things in their mouths. There are several guidelines you can follow to keep young children safe when interacting with reptiles and amphibians as well as any animal in the classroom, with the most important being good hand washing every time children touch an animal. Do not allow reptiles or amphibians in the same spaces as children eat, make sure to disinfect every surface that animals touch, do not allow children to touch the inside of aquariums or equipment, don't catch reptiles or amphibians from the wild to keep as pets, don't release reptiles or amphibians into natural areas, and be sure that any staff interacting with pets in the classroom understand the importance of following proper hand-washing routines after every animal interaction for both children and teachers.

GUIDANCE ISSUES

Two benefits of having a variety of animals for children to experience in early childhood are the formation of positive attitudes and the reduction of fears about reptiles and amphibians. Having clear rules about the interactions with the animals allows children to be successful and keeps both the children and the animals safe. Children should wash their hands before and after handling amphibians. These animals often have sensitive skin, and talking with children about that can help develop empathy for a vulnerable animal and lets children know their actions can help keep it safe. Other rules include always waiting for an adult to bring the animal to them, sitting when handling an animal in case it falls, being sensitive to their own eyes and face, and remembering to use quieter voices to avoid scaring or surprising the animal. Children may need reminders about these rules, but they will start to build an understanding about how to care for animals and the reasons why.

RESOURCES

Author Favorites

- **Julie's favorite:** *Hop Frog* by Rick Chrustowski. 2003. New York: Henry Holt. While this book has a lot of words, it also has beautiful illustrations and accurate information.

- **Sheila's favorite:** *Better Move On, Frog!* by Ron Maris. 1982. Livermore, CA: Discovery Toys. This fun, illustrated story explores where a frog may live and what other animals live in that space around a backyard. I have read this book hundreds of times to my own children as it was a favorite in our home.

Songs and Chants

- "Five Green and Speckled Frogs," traditional song

- "I Had a Little Turtle," traditional song

- "There Was a Little Turtle," traditional finger play

- "You Can't Make a Turtle Come Out" by Malvina Reynolds

- "My Turtle, Fred" by Tom Hunter

Materials for Supporting Learning about Reptiles and Amphibians

Free and Collectible Materials

- **Snakeskins.** Find a snake owner and ask him or her to save the skins as they are shed. You could laminate the skins to protect them.

- **Homemade temporary cages for collecting and observing.** Make sure not to use containers with remnants of food, detergents, or other substances that can harm creatures.

Best Materials to Purchase If You Have Limited Funds

- **Apps for recognizing sounds of different frogs and toads.** Free and for-purchase apps can be found in appendix 4.

- **Reptiles and amphibian pocket guides.** Find reptile and amphibian pocket guides for your specific region, which are handy to have on walks.

Extras If You Have More Funds

- **Set of metamorphosis models.** These models are encased in resin and help children pay attention to differences in the different stages of development from tadpole to frog.

- **Model turtles of different sizes and species.** Use turtle models specific to your ecosystem.

BUDDING HERPETOLOGISTS

Learning through Interactions with Reptiles and Amphibians

Dear Families,

Reptiles and amphibians—also known as herptiles—like frogs, salamanders, turtles, lizards, snakes, and alligators can be fascinating for young children. There are so many wonderfully beautiful species with amazing capabilities, much like your own children. We encourage you, as we will learn about reptiles and amphibians at our school soon, to try not to transfer your worries and fears, but to continue to help flame the spark of wonder that your child feels when investigating something new. We also ask that you speak with your children, as we do at school, about safety concerns with any interactions with wildlife or domestic animals. Our rules at school around pets include the following guidelines for animals at school from the Centers for Disease Control (CDC):

- Children will be closely supervised during contact with animals to discourage contact with manure and soiled bedding.

- Hand-to-mouth contact (e.g., thumb sucking) will be discouraged.

- Appropriate hand washing will be required after each interaction with an animal.

- Staff will be present to encourage appropriate human-animal interactions.

- If feeding animals, only food for that purpose will be allowed in the space with the animal present.

When interacting with wildlife, we also have closely followed guidelines that include the following:

- Adults and children will approach wildlife after a teacher has given the okay, especially around animals like frogs, toads, salamanders, snakes, and turtles.

- Adults and children will not approach wildlife that may become unsafe, such as deer, raccoons, geese, turkeys, alligators, and large predators.

- Wildlife will be treated with care and respect.

- Any wildlife handled will be returned to its natural habitat after the interaction—some exceptions can occur for tadpoles, turtles, etc., that may visit the classroom for a limited amount of time.

- We will not feed the wildlife directly but may place a bird feeder in a space to be able to observe birds eating.

- Staff will supervise all interactions with wildlife.

- Adults and children will wash hands or use hand sanitizer, depending on the place of the interaction, after handling any wildlife.

CHAPTER 12

GOT MILK?

Learning about Mammals

Mammals may be some of the animals that preschoolers are most familiar with in their classrooms, homes, and natural spaces. There are many mammals to explore, and our relationships with other mammals can vary greatly. Learning about mammals can also mirror what children understand about families, since humans are mammals and have a lot in common with our fellow members of the class Mammalia.

WHAT PRESCHOOLERS ARE READY TO UNDERSTAND

- **Mammals are a class of animals.** Mammals are the most common animals for children to refer to as just "animals," so learning this subset can be helpful.

- **Humans are mammals.** Understanding our place in the animal kingdom can be helpful to children.

- **Mammals nurse their young.** That mammals nurse can be useful for children to understand. When cows, horses, deer, and other mammals are nursing, it can look to children as if the baby has its mouth on the mother's genitals. If children have been fortunate enough to have seen a nursing human mom, this can provide a frame of reference.

- **Mammals come in many different sizes, with differing abilities and habitats.** Children are most likely to think of domesticated animals when they think of mammals.

- **Many of our pets are mammals.** Exploring pets can be a great place to start.

- **Mammals are born alive and breathing air (with only a few exceptions).** Children are fascinated by the birthing process, and witnessing the birth of a domestic mammal is magical for them.

- **Mammals all have some sort of hair.** Some mammals have fur while others have hair only in certain places.

WHAT IS TOO ABSTRACT FOR PRESCHOOLERS TO UNDERSTAND

- **Detailed anatomical differences between mammals.** For example, that cows have multiple stomachs.

- **The complexities of predator and prey relationships.** These can be difficult for young children to understand unless they come up spontaneously, such as when looking at scat.

- **Evolution and genetics.** These topics may bring up religious issues that cause concern in your community. However, the timeline and process of evolution is complex and may be difficult for young children to understand.

- **Reproduction.** Because families have a variety of views on how much and when to share reproductive information with their children, it is recommended that discussions regarding reproduction are saved for older children. We suggest answering children's questions without offering much additional information when animal mating is observed as it occurs naturally outdoors or with pets in the classroom.

TOPICS FOR DIFFERENT ECOSYSTEMS

Wild mammals in your region. Teachers tend to spend too much time on "flashy" mammals like zoo animals (and remember, no animal's natural habitat is a zoo). Children benefit from beginning with what is familiar and learning about mammals they are less likely to have contact with when they are older.

> *From Julie:* In Hawaii we have very few native mammals (bats and monk seals) and a few more mammals that were introduced (mongooses, rats, pigs, horses, cows, rabbits, pets). In Maui we do not have a zoo. However, for some reason, you will find books about zoo animals and toy zoo animals in most Maui preschool classrooms.

Farms and ranches. This is especially relevant for children who live in farming and ranching communities. Focus on what your specific group of children finds interesting. Is it the sheepdog? The saddles and tack used by ranch hands? Milking machines? Farm vehicles? Move from the glorified past vision of farms and ranches (e.g., milkmaids, cowboys playing the guitar by the fire) and build curiosity about what farms and ranches look like in your area today.

Ways mammals are used in your area to assist people. Children are constantly told not to bother "working animals," but they are interested in assistance animals. Invite a trainer or person who uses an assistance animal to visit your classroom.

Safe ways to approach domesticated animals. We tend to give children conflicting messages about approaching pets. Providing opportunities for children to share information about their pets at home and inviting some to visit can help children learn safe ways to approach new animals. During a large- or small-group experience, children could list rules they know about approaching animals and offer advice to their peers, such as moving slowly and touching gently.

From Julie: One of my college students in Telluride was concerned about the number of dog bites children experienced in this dog-friendly town. She had a friend bring a dog to her classroom to talk about a safe way to approach a dog you don't know. The children chanted on command, "Don't put your hand in the dog's face." After the talk was over, she invited the children to approach the dog. Most of them put their hands right in the dog's face! Children more easily understand a direction like, "Give the dog your paw (hand) to smell."

Stories from the Field

The lambs arrived at the farm, and they had an instant friend. At two and a half years old, Anderson was still learning how to be a part of a group of learners. He found gathering to share the plan for our afternoon overwhelming. His parents helped him to stay with the group during these gathering moments, but he was thrilled when he could go off to play with his friends: the lambs.

The two lambs were tied out on ropes so the children could easily pet and bottle-feed them. As children headed to the garden or waited to ride the pony, they'd stop to pet the lambs. Some would pause longer to give them a kiss or try hand-feeding them some food. Not Anderson, though. He spent most of his time with the lambs. Anderson was not one to make much eye contact with his peers and seemed easily perplexed by their behaviors. As the lambs played and moved, Anderson watched them intently. He was clearly trying to make sense of what they were doing. Gradually Anderson began moving his head to mimic the lambs' movements. A couple of times he attempted moving his head in different ways to see if the lambs would follow. It was unclear if the lambs were following or not, but Anderson soon went back to simply watching and following the lambs' actions.

Anderson's fascination and desire to be close to the lambs continued for the duration of the class sessions. He partook in other activities, but clearly his time with the lambs was the most rewarding to him. Anderson was back in my class again this past spring, now as a three-and-a-half-year-old. He still enjoyed the lambs but branched out to spending more of his time with the other animals and his classmates. The time Anderson had with the lambs was a unique experience in which he could make sense of the behavior of another without the interruptions that human-to-human interaction can have. He practiced socialization on a level that felt safe and not too overstimulating to him. The lambs met a developmental need that Anderson had at that time, which helped him to move forward in his social growth and eventually be able to observe and watch his peers in a way he hadn't been able to do prior to his time with the lambs. **—Jenny Hanlon, MEd, preschool teacher and author, Tamarack Nature Center, White Bear Township, Minnesota**

From Julie: One of the benefits of having mammals as classroom pets is giving children experience with living things that are more vulnerable than they are. They can offer life lessons that are easier to accept from an animal than from one's own family. These include birth, illness, and death. To really benefit from a class pet, children need to develop attachment to it. That means more pain if the pet dies, but also the special relationship that only happens with a pet they love. A side benefit of these attachments is children developing empathy for the experiences of others. We had a classroom rabbit that signaled children when she was overwhelmed by noise by putting her ears back. Instead of nagging the children about noise level, we focused as a class on whether it was too loud for Velvet.

DIPPING YOUR TOE IN

Take advantage of teachable moments about mammals. If children are involved in pretending to be mammals, ask questions or add props that help them understand mammals. For instance, if children are pretending to be kittens, you can offer them a toy mouse to play with or a bowl of pretend cat food, or ask if they are old enough to have their eyes open yet.

Have pictures of real mammals rather than cartoonlike animals. Too often classrooms are filled with "cute" pink, smiling giraffes and dogs wearing clothes and reading books. Children's understanding of fantasy versus reality takes time to develop, and we unintentionally provide misinformation.

Read realistic stories about mammals. Too many stories for preschoolers are anthropomorphic. Most children's understanding of bears is really of stuffed teddy bears. This is a disservice, especially for children who live in parts of the country with bears.

WADING IN

Add replicas of mammals to block play, sand play, and other areas. Pay attention to the scale of the sizes of these animals. Giving children plastic horses to play with that are smaller than dogs in the same toy set is confusing.

Plan field trips to places with mammals, including nature preserves, farms, ranches, zoos, and dog breeding kennels. Find out what is available in your area and whose tour guides are likely to speak at the right level for young children.

From Julie: I once suffered through a field trip to the University of Arizona's Experiment Station with a tour guide who was lecturing the children about artificial insemination. The bus couldn't return fast enough for us!

Introduce a pet mammal to your classroom "family." Animals that are awake in the daytime are better pets than nocturnal animals. Some of our favorites include guinea pigs, rabbits, and rats. Hamsters are more likely to bite than the listed pets and are mostly nocturnal.

Invite mammals to visit. In some regions, it is possible to get a horse, goat, or sheep owner to bring them to school for a visit.

DIVING IN

Plan in-depth studies on different mammals. Start with a new classroom pet or a mammal that one of the children has at his or her home. Discover with children what they already know (or think they know) about the animal. Children can make a list of their ideas and help you understand what areas they would like to learn more about. Continue to scaffold their learning by providing tools for investigation like magnifying lenses. Avoid studying animals that children can have no firsthand experience with, such as whales if you are in the Midwest or monkeys if your community doesn't have access to a monkey.

Create a mini-farm at your school. Farm schools show up in interesting places—inner cities, island communities, and mountain communities. As we have moved away from farm-based communities, children have less understanding of food sources, the life cycle, and the real responsibility that comes from taking care of vulnerable animals. Chickens and rabbits are great animals with which to begin a mini-farm. If you are ready to challenge yourself more, adding a goat can be exciting and gives children an opportunity to learn more about animals that have been domesticated and are seen as companions.

INCLUSION OF ALL CHILDREN

Classroom mammals can be a wonderful addition, but allergies to pet dander can affect some children and staff. When adding a pet, consider any allergies and have at least one classroom without mammals for children with allergies. Other pets such as insects and fish do not have dander and can help children gain all the positive benefits of caring for an animal in the classroom without the risk of allergies.

CULTURAL CONSIDERATIONS

Humans have enjoyed relationships with animals in various ways over thousands of years. For example, some animals have been domesticated, some are feared, some are marveled at, and some are eaten. Each culture and each individual has a unique perspective on their personal relationship with animals of all kinds. Whether a family believes an animal is revered, disease carrying, or spiritual can affect their child's experience in your classroom. When interacting with animals in your program, be sure to consider the relationship that your children and families may have with those animals and integrate that into your community. For example, if you have a family that sees rats as disease-carrying pests, you will want to begin a dialogue with the family and the children before adding a pet rat to your classroom. Some other cultural considerations include choosing to serve meat at snack, balancing the beliefs of families who hunt with those who believe it is wrong, choosing to visit a zoo or other place that holds wild animals captive, sharing information about the circus, or having dogs or other animals visit the classroom.

HEALTH AND SAFETY ISSUES

When choosing a pet for your classroom, key considerations are the age of the children, the time available to dedicate to pet care, and what animals you are most comfortable handling. The CDC offers guidelines for classroom safety around pets on their "Healthy Pets, Healthy People" website, available at www.cdc.gov/healthypets/index.html. Patty Born Selly, in her book *Connecting Animals and Children in Early Childhood*, discusses health and safety concerns and preventative measures around pathogens, injuries, allergies, and asthma associated with certain classroom pets.

From Julie: Another decision to make if you have a classroom pet is whether you will allow children to take turns taking the pet home to care for over weekends and holidays. While it provides a nice way to involve families in the life of the classroom, there are risks for the well-being of the pet. I once sent a classroom rabbit home with a family who did not provide proper supervision, and the rabbit was killed by our student's sibling during rough play.

GUIDANCE ISSUES

Teaching gentle treatment of classroom pets is an ongoing process and will vary depending on the animal and the age of the children. A good beginning rule is touching with two fingers. Although that can sometimes become a poke, it is much preferable to have a hamster poked than squeezed a little too tightly. Many small rodents that are common classroom pets, like guinea pigs or rats, will bite out of defense if squeezed hard. There are practical ways to set limits when children handle pets. For instance, we had children select a long blade of grass to feed to the guinea pig when holding her. This kept one of the child's hands busy, kept the guinea pig's mouth busy, made the guinea pig look forward to being held, and provided a natural time limit for holding the animal. Once children had a blade of grass, they would sit down on a log with a small piece of mattress pad on their laps before we placed the guinea pig in their arms. This protected the child from becoming the guinea pig's toilet and from the sharp nails of the animal. We taught the children to pet mammals' fur in the direction that it grows. This feels better to the animal, and so it is less likely to fidget, jump off the child's lap, or bite.

RESOURCES

Author Favorites

- **Julie's favorite:** *Blueberries for Sal* by Robert McCloskey. 1948. New York: Viking. This very old story by the author of *Make Way for Ducklings* is very engaging.

It tells the story from the perspective of both a child and her mom and a bear and her cub. Rather than anthropomorphizing bears, it provides information through a realistic story.

- **Sheila's favorite:** *Looking for a Moose* by Phyllis Root. 2006. Somerville, MA: Candlewick Press. This beautifully illustrated book tells the story of a group of children on a search for a moose. They talk in a child-friendly manner about preparing for exploring in different habitats.

Songs and Chants

- "Did You Feed My Cow?" by Ella Jenkins
- "Scamper" by Hap Palmer
- "Animal Action" by Greg Scelsa and Steve Millang
- "Gray Squirrel, Gray Squirrel," traditional song
- "All the Pretty Little Horses," traditional song
- "Mister Rabbit" by Pete Seeger

Materials to Support Learning about Mammals

Free and Collectable Materials

- **Borrowing mounts, skins, and other animal exhibits.** Check with local museums and nature centers to see if they have a lending program. By examining real mounts, skins, and other animal displays, children can explore wildlife specimens and learn about their bodies and adaptations, and ask important questions about skin, fur, life, and death. These hands-on learning opportunities are an important component of early childhood education and learning about the natural world.

- **Mammal skulls and other bones.** Boil them to make sure they are clean and simmer in hot water—use an old Crock-Pot overnight on medium or high. The high temperature of boiling is important for killing bacteria, and the simmering continues to clean the bones without a rolling boil, which could destroy the integrity of the bones.

Best Materials to Purchase If You Have Limited Funds

- **Realistic plastic mammal reproductions.** Children can use these toy mammals in pretend play in the block area, sand, or other areas to demonstrate what they are learning. We urge you to pay attention to the scale of the mammals because some catalogs sell a plastic dog that is larger than a horse in the same set.

- **Imitation animal fur fabric.** Fur fabric can be used for pretending. Placing large pieces of fur fabric with just a piece of elastic to connect the edges are all children need to become dogs, cats, or other mammals during play.

Extras If You Have More Funds

- **Animal mounts.** It is possible to purchase real animal mounts or replicas and provide an opportunity for children to get a good look at mammals they might otherwise not be able to study closely. However, some educators and families are less comfortable with stuffed, dead animals than others.

- **Real or imitation animal fur.** Fur can be used in displays. Children get the sense of what the animals feel like, not just look like.

- **Plastic scat replicas and track and scat cards.** These are available through Acorn Naturalists. They are plastic replicas of the scat (poop) and foot- or hoofprints of different animals. These can be especially handy on walks to identify what type of mammals have been present.

"PLEASE, PLEASE, PLEASE, I WANT A PET!"

Dear Families,

Adding a pet to your family can be a wonderful experience for your children. They will love something that needs them rather than being the only "cared for" member of the family. They will learn responsibility if they are included in care. They learn to appreciate the natural world in a very personal way. They also may get the opportunity to learn hard lessons about the life cycle before experiencing the death of a human family member.

What kind of pet should you adopt? Many families think of dogs when they think of pets, but a dog can require a major change to your daily family life. Most preschoolers are not ready for the responsibility of a dog. We recommend that you "think outside the crate" and start small.

- **A snail, an insect, or a worm.** They don't live very long, and your children will have the chance to start learning about pet responsibility.

- **A hermit crab.** This can be a wonderful first pet. A small hermit crab will have a small claw, and it won't hurt if it clamps onto a finger.

- **Fish.** Start with fish that require less work than fancy tropical fish. A goldfish, guppy, or betta can be a good "starter" fish.

- **Reptiles.** Lizards and turtles can make fascinating pets. Just make sure to get accurate information about how to control the temperature in the habitat, proper feeding, and safety precautions depending on the age of children in your household. Reptiles, especially snakes and turtles, require a long-term time commitment over the course of their lifespans, which can be fifty years or more for some species of turtles and often twenty years or more for many popular lizards, snakes, and turtles.

- **Small mammals.** Rats are a surprisingly good choice. They are very social and easy to care for. Guinea pigs don't tend to live as long (about three years) but are easy to handle. Hamsters and gerbils are popular, but they are more likely to bite and often are nocturnal, which makes them less engaging for children. Rabbits can make lovely pets if you are committed to their care. Rabbits get nervous in loud situations, so it is important when constructing their habitat to have a space for them to feel secure.

Involve your children in the lives of your pets. Pets can easily become "part of the furniture" or a resented demand. Make a habit of spending time with your pets every day.

- **Take them out of their habitat.** Find safe ways for the pet to leave the terrarium or cage to be handled, to crawl around, or to use a maze. Doing so will keep your children interested in and learning about your pet.

- **Take turns with pet care.** Feeding, cleaning, brushing, and so on are tasks that all family members can share in. These tasks help children learn about nature. Involve your children in research about new foods; take them to the pet store to get supplies, and so on.

- **Take your pet for a walk.** Special leashes are made for rabbits, and even some cats like to go for walks.

- **Avoid modeling negative feelings about the pet.** Yes, pets make messes, require care when you are busy, and can bite. Modeling patience and understanding will help your children develop these skills not just with animals but also with life.

CHAPTER 13

BENEATH THE SURFACE

Diving into Aquatic Life

Life beneath the surface in many areas is more diverse than the land above, but it is often difficult for children to explore underwater. Offering experiences in your program for children to investigate dragonfly larvae that live completely underwater until they are ready to fly, turtle hatchlings making their way in the world alone, or the migration of whale families near the beach can be an amazing experience for young children and for all of us.

WHAT PRESCHOOLERS ARE READY TO UNDERSTAND

- **Animals have adapted to live underwater but human beings can't.** Many animals that live underwater have adaptations that allow them to stay underwater for long periods of time, but some also visit the surface to breathe. This is a fascinating concept for young children.

- **Many different types of animals can live underwater.** A large variety of bugs, mammals, reptiles, amphibians, and even some birds can be found eating and playing beneath the surface.

- **Some animals can only live in the ocean and some can live in rivers or lakes.** Depending on where you are exploring with young children, you may be able to investigate the differences between animals that live in oceans and ones that live in lakes and rivers. Children who have traveled to other regions may also be able to share some of the knowledge they have gained about who lives where in our world.

What Is Too Abstract for Preschoolers to Understand

- **The names of different body parts.** This rote type of learning will not help children gain knowledge and understanding about aquatic animals.

- **The mechanics of how fish swim or how they breathe through their gills.** This can be hard for adults to understand as well and can be explored with older children when they are interested.

TOPICS FOR DIFFERENT ECOSYSTEMS

In the coastal areas, learning about aquatic animals is a part of daily life for many families in your community. Offering opportunities for children to continue their explorations in the classroom can extend the learning and offer chances to build a strong connection between home and school.

In areas with wetlands, streams, and lakes, children may or may not interact with these areas on a regular basis, but they may drive near them often. In Minneapolis children may pass over the Mississippi River several times a day; however, because it is a powerful body of water, many don't visit it often.

In the deserts, prairies, and cities, finding aquatic animals for children to study can be difficult. However, many places like dentist offices, pet stores, zoos, or aquariums can offer spaces where children can explore these animals. If you are unable to travel to other spaces, you can always introduce an aquarium into your classroom.

From Sheila: The Lab School hallway was a little plain, so the staff decided an aquarium would be a nice addition. I volunteered to take this on with a small group of children. After asking the teachers about which class might be best to work with, it was clear that there would be children throughout the school interested in participating. I planned to have small groups explore where a fish tank might go, how big should it be, what should live there, and so on. Each day different children were involved. We began by drawing a full-size aquarium on a large piece of butcher paper and the children drew plants, fish, and other special aquarium items. We then took two field trips with different small groups on the city bus to visit the local pet store. We asked an employee about building a fish tank and he told us the most important thing to remember is that some fish get along with other fish and some don't, so we started exploring compatibility charts, sizes of fish, and of course all the colors of fish the children wanted represented. The children were very interested in all the aquarium decor. We voted on items that would most fit in our school, and a sunken pirate ship won.

We did online research to find the right size aquarium and aquarium tank stand for the hallway. We ordered the tank and stand and when the items arrived, the children and families helped assemble the stand and prepare the aquarium. Every child in the school had the opportunity to add water, rocks, and plants. We took one more trip on the bus to the pet store with our buckets in hand, and many onlookers enjoyed seeing a group of preschoolers on the city bus with buckets that contained bags of colorful fish. The children continue to enjoy the aquarium each day, and it has eased transitions. It has also given children who needed a little extra time and attention an opportunity to feed the fish or just watch them swimming. Children help clean the sides and add more water when needed.

DIPPING YOUR TOE IN

- **Take advantage of teachable moments.** Stop to notice a bubble trail when you are walking by a still body of water. Avoid "cute" comments like "You can hear the ocean in the seashell," and instead take time to investigate the shell.

- **Read stories with bodies of water as a theme.** Examples of water-themed stories are located in appendix 2.

WADING IN

- **Make displays of seashells.** You can pair them with reference books that contain photos of seashells. This gives children an opportunity to compare, sort, and learn about the classification of species as well as learn important exercise observation skills.

- **Make math games with aquatic themes.** Sorting types of seashells or sizes of river rocks, or making lotto games with fish are all relatively easy activities to set up. They can provide opportunities for children to gain experience with basic math concepts like measurement, sorting, classification, and patterns.

DIVING IN

- **Learn about a body of water near your program.** You can offer a complex study of rivers, ponds, creeks, lakes, or oceans. Children can return to the same place at a nearby creek or pond over time to journal, take samples of water, or enjoy observations and discussions about the environment. Studies around larger bodies of water can involve photos, journals, and gathering samples of water to take back to the classroom to look at through microscopes and observe any creatures found in the samples. A great microscope for children to use is the Zoomy by Learning Resources. It connects directly to a computer for an onscreen view of small organisms or details of other objects.

- **Build an aquarium that reflects the local life in your area.** Create an aquarium installation in your program and find local species that children and families can observe, care for, and learn about at school.

INCLUSION OF ALL CHILDREN

When children have limited mobility or difficulty hearing, being near water can be a challenge. Having enough adults to supervise the play is important, while also giving all children opportunities to handle the aquatic life in similar ways. If you have children who are too impulsive to be near the water even with close supervision, you can collect water in buckets and set up a sample tub back at the classroom or in your water table.

CULTURAL CONSIDERATIONS

Beliefs about fish are important to know as you consider implementing studies on aquatic life. Families who are vegetarians will not want their children to eat fish or to be involved with activities that will result in the death of a fish. If all your families eat fish and it is an important part of their culture, having fish for a snack can be a meaningful activity. A related issue is whether to offer children the opportunity to try the Japanese art form of fish printing. This activity allows children to see subtle differences in the shape of fish and texture of fish scales, but it is done with dead fish, which can be considered wasteful as the fish is no longer edible. In desert areas, especially cities experiencing droughts, there may be restrictions on water usage. It is important to be thoughtful about families' abilities to access fresh water and understand that accessing water may be difficult.

HEALTH AND SAFETY ISSUES

When exploring aquatic animals, children are usually very excited to touch and feel them. Of course, some aquatic animals like fish or many aquatic insects aren't ones that we generally touch. If your program is located in a coastal area, you may have more opportunity for touching sea cucumbers, sea stars (starfish), and other marine life. Considering ways to keep both the animals and children safe is important. Venturing into the water just a little further for that cool shell can be tempting, so be sure children have plenty of supervision and appropriate protection.

From Sheila: For some reason, we had a small group of children who always wanted to feed our classroom fish a little bit of their play dough. It could have been that the colors of the fish food were often the same colors of the play dough, or that it can be made into tiny little pieces just like the flakes of food for our pets. This led to a high salt content in the water and was not healthy for the fish. We added a clip to the lid to prevent children from dropping bits of play dough and any other toys into the tank and continued to have them involved in feeding the fish. Using an item like a one-quarter teaspoon measuring spoon can be more effective than a pinch (which can vary widely) and will discourage overfeeding, which leads to dirtier fish tanks that need more frequent cleaning and health problems in your fish community.

RESOURCES

Author Favorites

- Julie's favorite: *Over in the Ocean: In a Coral Reef* by Marianne Berkes. 2004. Nevada City, CA: Dawn Publications. This book is another version of the folk song "Over in the Meadow," with sea creatures replacing the animals in the original.

It includes a variety of types of aquatic life and, because it is sung, is easy for children to become engaged with and remember.

- Sheila's favorite: *Dolphin's First Day: The Story of a Bottlenose Dolphin* by Kathleen Weidner Zoehfeld. Smithsonian Oceanic Collection. 1994. Norwalk, CT: Soundprints. This beautifully illustrated book explores the life of a dolphin calf.

Songs and Chants

- "Slippery Fish" by Charlotte Diamond
- "All Around Maui Blues" by Wayne Watkins
- "If I Was a Dolphin" by Wayne Watkins
- "Three Little Fishies," a traditional song

Materials to Support Learning about Aquatic Life

Free and Collectible Materials

- **Buckets and scoops.** You can include them on a list of things you want from families. Check buckets often for leaks and cracks and be sure they are not large enough to present a drowning hazard. Even if you do not have toddlers in your program, families may bring younger siblings to your center, and because toddlers have a higher center of gravity, they can drown if they fall into even a small amount of water in a container.

- **Large clear plastic jars and containers.** For exploring pond or ocean water samples, plastic jars are safer than glass. Look for large plastic containers used to sell snacks at big-box stores.

- **Mesh bags for collecting shells and rocks.** Save bags from onions, nuts, and tomatoes. This is another thing to add to your "wish list" from families.

Best Materials to Purchase If You Have Limited Funds

- **Aquatic life replicas.** Find plastic replicas of different sizes to use in sensory play, pretend play, and the block area. These can be purchased from early childhood and nature catalogs. Try to find replicas that are as realistic as possible rather than smiling octopuses or bright pink dolphins.

Extras If You Have More Funds

- **Fish mounts.** Real fish mounts or replicas can be purchased from stores like Acorn Naturalists.

- **Fish skeletons.** Select fish from your region. You can ask others in your community for donations of fish skeletons or purchase them online.

COASTAL LIVING

Dear Families,

Living near or visiting the ocean, a lake, river, pond, or stream can be quite an adventure and an amazing learning experience. Large bodies of water can produce an unparalleled sense of calm and wonder. There are, of course, safety concerns with young children around water. Because children don't know the properties of water, such as the strength of a current or how to measure depth, they are not prepared to keep themselves safe.

When we investigate bodies of water with your children, we often go in small groups so children can be easily monitored. We encourage children to lie on their bellies on the dock to discourage leaning over too far and falling in, plus they get a very close look. When exploring areas like streams or shallow bays, a teacher investigates in the same area and wades in with children when appropriate to accurately assess any dangers. When investigating areas like tide pools, children are encouraged to examine closely, and a teacher can facilitate any interactions with wildlife that may occur. Tide pools can be wondrous because they can vary in a small area and change throughout the day.

When exploring at home, bringing the right tools is important. A small bucket with an old spoon, a net, and a magnifying glass are all you need for hours of adventure. Also, be sure to bring sun protection and water for hydration. This will help prevent children from trying to drink the water they are playing in at the moment.

CHAPTER 14

WHERE DO YOU LIVE?

Habitats in Nature

All living creatures must call something home—either a shelter they have built, borrowed, or stolen. Habitats make a nice topic for young children's nature studies because they are easy for children to relate to. Children are also able to construct habitats for animals indoors and outdoors.

WHAT PRESCHOOLERS ARE READY TO UNDERSTAND

- **Habitats are specific to the creatures using them and to the ecosystem.** For instance, not all birds build nests in trees.

- **Animals use many strategies for their habitats.** You will discover everything from animals building their own homes to using ones naturally found in nature, to stealing homes from other animals.

- **We can learn about creatures based on their habitats.** Can they fly? Do they have sharp teeth to cut items to use? How can they use their bodies to move materials from one location to another? Do they need a habitat that protects them from predators or the elements?

WHAT IS TOO ABSTRACT FOR PRESCHOOLERS TO UNDERSTAND

- **The complexities and definitions of an ecosystem or a biome.** Learning about your home area and the concept of habitats is enough.

- **How climate change will alter habitats.** This is a scary idea for young children who have little power to make a difference right now. The skills and knowledge they gain during their early years will help them understand these complex issues. However, children should feel empowered to make a difference in their homes and community by turning off lights, recycling, composting, and other small changes that make a big impact.

TOPICS FOR DIFFERENT ECOSYSTEMS

Migration. Some types of migration are more relevant to some ecosystems than others. For instance, Maui has a lot of humpback whales that migrate to our waters from winter to spring. Do birds go south in the winter in your environment?

What nests are made from and where birds place them. This can be especially interesting in the desert where birds use cacti and the ground for their nests. Does the habitat need to protect from cold or hot weather? Children playing outside can relate to this and may ask the question about where the animals are when it is hot or cold. What kind of predators does the habitat need to withstand? For some animals, it is easy to see their predators, such as when a bird is digging for a worm or a cat is chasing a mouse. However, for many animals, humans are their greatest predator, and that can be too difficult for a young child to understand.

Is camouflage a part of the habitat? Children tend to become very interested in camouflage, and venturing out to see how animals in your region survive with this technique can be wonderful.

Stories from the Field

At the University of Chicago Lab Schools, in the heart of the city, children and nature can teach us. In the fall, several birds had crashed into the windows of our first-floor classroom. I had a good birder friend who lived nearby, and we walked over in a small group to ask for his help. We brought in one of the birds that had died for identification, and we wanted ideas to keep other birds from hitting the windows. My friend showed the children how to wrap their hands gently around a bird to keep it warm, safe, and calm in hopes it would recover. He explained why the birds were hitting the windows (migration routes, glass reflection, angle of sun, etc.). We came back with much to report and discuss.

Some children wanted to leave the windows open. "No," said another, "that would interrupt group time if birds were coming in and out." "Let's build nests for them so they will still like to be around us," said one child. "Yes, and put eggs in them so they will want to have babies," said another. So we gathered a collection of bird nests to see how they were built. We started with small plastic fruit baskets and wove through grass and small twigs, string, and hair/fur from family pets—anything we found in a bird's nest. We discovered the difficult task involved, even with ten fingers to do the work. After consulting reference book examples, the children created eggs out of clay, and fired and painted them. Some children wanted to write notes to the birds to ensure that they felt welcome and to warn them about the windows. More discussion followed—can birds read our language? Does anyone know bird language? It was decided that mother birds teach their children to read, just like humans, and we would write notes. We laminated the notes, attached them, and suction-cupped a nest to each window. We eliminated the problem of crashing birds, though that goal became just one of many. —**Sarah Sivright,** MEd, director, All Seasons Preschool, Inver Grove Heights, Minnesota

• • •

"Tail or no tail?" asks teacher Les. "Tail!" exclaims four-year-old Charlie, rushing a tiny tadpole to a bucket of pond water. Only two miles west of downtown Minneapolis, this pond is teeming with life. Frogs and toads are found in all stages, invertebrates swim about, and small snails gather on rocks and logs. Duckweed coats everything. Eighteen preschoolers participating in the Minneapolis Nature Preschool's debut summer camp work diligently to collect life from the pond. Containers are scattered along the shoreline, offering habitats of leaves, grass, or water. Children work in small groups to help each other sort their discoveries according to habitat. Others hold hands, anchored to a tree to reach as far off shore as possible without filling their boots with pond water. Older children help the youngest participants gingerly coax tiny toads out of nets and into dry land containers. No fences contain the group; instead, they remain focused by enthusiasm alone. It looks as though these children have been working alongside each other for an entire school year. In reality, they met only two hours earlier. The children come from different educational, language, and economic backgrounds. I watch, amazed by the community forming so quickly among this group. Four children squat by Charlie, celebrating her successful catch of a froglet. Never in fifteen years of my work with high school–aged youth have I seen friendships form so effortlessly. It is beautiful. I reflect on my favorite childhood memories of catching amphibians and am filled with gratitude. In our complex world, I am thankful to see children can still be filled with joy by simply catching a toad. —**Alyson Quinn,** board chair, Minneapolis Nature Preschool, Minneapolis, Minnesota

DIPPING YOUR TOE IN

- **Take advantage of teachable moments.** Take note of animal habitats in storybooks. Talk to children about where their pets sleep and play at their house.

- **Take time to follow slow-moving animals around their habitats.** Where does the trail of ants go? Where did the bird go?

- **Utilize technology.** Watch a bear or eagle cam online to observe the creature in its home.

WADING IN

- **Design activities to help children understand habitats.** For example, leaving brightly colored yarn near the bird feeder will make it easier for children to notice if the yarn appears in a nest.

- **Create simple habitats for creatures to visit the classroom for short periods of time.** For example, a butterfly habitat for caterpillars that you find or purchase, or a pond in a jar (see the activity on page 178).

DIVING IN

- **Create complex habitats for creatures.** You will find some ideas for creating habitats indoors and outdoors in appendix 1. Complex habitats like those for long-term pets indoors or wildlife outdoors will be more challenging to create but will also offer deeper experiences to observe and support animals in your environment.

- **Explore ways to make the space around your program a friendlier habitat for animals in your region.** For example, add bird feeders or birdhouses, or leave small piles of sticks for birds or squirrels to gather resources.

INCLUSION OF ALL CHILDREN

When learning about habitats, exploring your own classroom can be a great place to start the discussion. In a classroom at the Lab School, there was a freestanding door in a teacher's classroom that led to the dramatic play kitchen. Children would often knock to enter and treat it like their home. A few years ago, a child entered the program who was taller than the door. The children realized this, and the classroom formed a small group to measure and build a new door to their dramatic play area. This exploration about the needs of all in the play space can help children look deeper into habitat needs. When exploring habitats, be sure that all children can navigate the terrain. Generally, going out the day before an exploration can let you know if you need a wagon, carrier, or other assistance.

CULTURAL CONSIDERATIONS

The variety of homes that animals inhabit can mirror the differences in the homes of humans. Remembering that not all children have access to a stable home structure, while others may have access to multiple homes of varying sizes, is important. If you have children or families in your program who are experiencing homelessness, or are highly mobile and move often, discussing habitats and homes can be valuable as well as challenging. Instead of asking families to send in pictures of their homes, be more inclusive by instead saying, "Tell us about your favorite place to read a book," or "Describe your habitat—you can draw or send in a photo as well."

RESOURCES

Author Favorites

- **Julie's favorite:** *Home for a Bunny* by Margaret Wise Brown. 1956. New York: Golden Press. Another oldie but goodie. This beautifully illustrated book tells the story of a rabbit trying to find a habitat. While there is some anthropomorphizing (the animals talk), it provides realistic information about where animals live and why.

- **Sheila's favorite:** *The Salamander Room* by Anne Mazer. 1994. New York: Dragonfly Books. This book explores the very idea of habitat and why everything we need to be healthy and safe is a part of our habitat. It also emphasizes proper consideration for preparing habitats for the care of animals.

Resource Books for Adults

- *Animal Architects: Amazing Animals Who Build Their Homes* by Julio Antonio Blasco and Daniel Nassar. 2015. London: Laurence King Publishing. This book can be read with children or used as a resource for planning experiences around animals' habitats.

- *The Curious Nature Guide: Explore the Natural Wonders All Around You* by Clare Walker Leslie. 2015. North Adams, MA: Storey Publishing. This book made for adults beautifully illustrates many simple ways to enjoy nature.

Songs and Chants

- "Little White Duck" by Bernard Zaritsky and Walt Barrows

- "Safe at Home" by Banana Slug String Band

- "Going on a Bear Hunt," traditional chant

Materials to Support Learning about Habitats

Free and Collectible Materials

- **Abandoned birds' nests.** Find nests and place them in clear plastic containers to protect the nests and protect children from possible parasites.

- **Small logs.** These can be placed in an aquarium and can be an important part of a habitat for a variety of bugs and animals.

- **Handmade birdhouses.** These can be made by using wood glue and leftover pieces of wood from a construction project.

Best Materials to Purchase If You Have Limited Funds

- **Birdhouse kits.** Kits can vary in price and size. Consider the birds native to your area and what types of houses they need.

- **Bat houses.** In many areas, bats are an important part of the overall ecosystem and can help reduce the numbers of mosquitoes.

- **Butterfly or ladybug houses and a pollinator garden.** These habitats will allow pollinators to eat and sleep near your school.

Extras If You Have More Funds

- **Outdoor enclosed habitats.** These habitats could include a fenced area for a rabbit or turtle or any classroom pet.

- **Plant a tree.** The larger tree you can afford, the more animals will be provided for in this habitat.

HOMES AND HABITATS

Dear Families,

Studying habitats as a family can be a wonderful experience. Comparing the homes that we make as humans to those that animals make, both in complexity and beauty, can illuminate the work of animals throughout the world. When we explore the work it takes to build a home—how birds carefully construct nests with their beaks, how ants create different sleeping and eating spaces in intricate tunnels, how desert tortoises spend so much time creating the perfect underground burrows, and how bees create hives as a community—we can grow greater appreciation for the lives of other species and help build an ethic of care for animals.

Be aware of safety concerns when studying animal habitats. First, never enter an animal's cave, den, or nest, and be sure to keep children back a safe distance. If there are young inside, the animals can be very protective. If you find a nest in your yard, try to be sensitive and protect it until the young are old enough to leave the nest. Occasionally rabbits may burrow in a small hole in a yard or birds may build a nest on your home. Although this can be an inconvenience for mowing your lawn or entering your home, the time that those animals have young in the nest goes by quickly and your child will have an opportunity to see the babies grow and develop.

CHAPTER 15

STRENGTHENING THE BONDS

Getting Families in Nature

One of the best ways we can help children connect with nature is through helping their families connect with nature. Children will be in our programs for only a short time, but if we have impacted their families' connection to nature, it will last. We can support families' connection to the natural world in several ways.

Help families understand how nature is good for both children and adults in their family. Family newsletters about the benefits of nature will help them understand why it matters. Other ways to share information about nature include these:

- **Offering information about what nature activities happen at school in multiple ways.** You can post photos on the school's Facebook page, documentation boards, and schoolbooks.

- **Creating ways for family members to learn about nature through school programs.** Having guest speakers or book clubs gives parents opportunities both to learn about nature topics and to connect with other families in your program.

- **Inviting family members to take part in school field trips and nature experiences.** This will give you the opportunity to model nature education and provide you with more adults to help!

Helping parents and other adult family members cope with fears about the natural world. One of the most common reasons for a lack of connection with the natural world is fear. By helping families cope with fears about nature, you will lessen the transference of these fears to the children and make it more likely that families will spend time in nature.

- **Providing realistic information about nature and safety.** Information is powerful. If you share honest information about dangers as well as what is safe, fearful parents will be more apt to trust you.

- **Making suggestions for similar experiences if family members are too fearful to take part in what is first offered.** Are hikes in the mountains too scary? Offer ideas for hiking trails in flatter areas. Is tent camping too scary? Maybe finding a cabin rental is a better alternative.

Helping families find ways to make nature a part of their daily lives. Some families value nature and are not fearful but just can't figure out how to fit it into their busy lives.

- Sharing information about nature-based community events
- Providing maps with walking trails near school and near families' homes
- Creating a family garden at school
- Creating a lending library of nature-based books
- Sharing information about memberships to zoos, nature centers, aquariums, and the like
- Planning family-school events that engage folks with nature.

TOPICS FOR DIFFERENT ECOSYSTEMS

Plan for or share information about nature activities families can take part in. Being informed of events for each season of the year can help families think of getting out into nature in different ways. Provide a clothing exchange so families can pass on weather gear to each other. Families are not as likely to tell you that they don't go hiking because they don't have appropriate footwear as they are to stop and try on some things on their way in and out of school.

- **School hikes for different times of year.** These might help some families who are less likely to hike develop confidence in nature.
- **Holiday-related events, such as trips to a pumpkin patch or Christmas tree cutting.** These can become school and family traditions.
- **Family fishing trips to local parks or other water sources.** Catch and release becomes a good way to enjoy nature without having to clean and eat fish.
- **Color tours for regions with trees that change color.** Walks around your community to observe the change in seasons firsthand can be a great way to help children notice small changes in their environment. This ritual can become another tradition, and over time children and families can connect with trees and the natural world.
- **Snowshoe making.** Kits can be purchased, and when parents get together to make snowshoes, the social atmosphere can be like a quilting circle.
- **Biking days.** Even a short day where your parking lot is blocked off to car traffic can be an exciting opportunity to get outdoors with your families.
- **Farmers market field trip.** Trips to collect seasonal fruits and vegetables at a local indoor or outdoor market can get families in the habit of eating more fruits and vegetables.

- **Tour of local parks with a person from the neighborhood or a local historic society.** You can find these opportunities around your community by contacting your local library or historical society. Often these organizations have a strong knowledge of the community and can help deepen your knowledge of different cultural and historical perspectives.

- **Snow tubing.** If you live in a snowy climate, this is a way of enjoying the outdoors in the winter that doesn't require the skill of skiing or skating.

- **Desert safety classes at a nature center or desert botanical garden.** By learning what is safe in the desert, families are more likely to take advantage of the outdoors.

- **Family cleanups of a local outdoor space.** This is a wonderful way to involve families in both nature and community participation.

From Julie: When I worked at University of Hawaiʻi at Mānoa Children's Center, I told the teachers in the class for four-year-olds about the family camping trips we used to take in Minnesota. They decided to give it a try and reserved a large camping area at the beach. Most families came—some eagerly, some with trepidation. The trip was magical! Families who had never been without internet access found themselves unplugged and engaged with their children more than ever before. Children went to their friends' tents without having to be walked there or ask for permission. We built a giant bonfire around which the children sang for their families and the adults spontaneously told the children a story round-robin style. After dark the teachers took the children down to the shore to look for crabs. In the morning, several families decided they weren't ready for the trip to end and stayed longer.

Stories from the Field

My son Nathan's first camping experience outside of the backyard was the school camping trip! It was a great way to experience such an adventure alongside familiar teachers and friends from school. We had fun picking out the perfect spot for our tent, putting the poles together and setting it up, joining friends for a picnic dinner, singing campfire songs, and reading bedtime stories in our tent with a flashlight. Our evening was complete with weather-related adventures, and our tent got soaked, but we had a great time and even took a hike the next morning to the river. It made us want to return year after year for the annual tradition. Our family has really enjoyed getting to know other school families better, and it has been great for the children to interact with each other's families. The campground is big enough for adventure but small enough to run into familiar faces along the paths everywhere. My boys are already asking when we will be going on the next school camping trip! —Parent perspective: story from Claire Sanga, preschool parent, Minneapolis, Minnesota

DIPPING YOUR TOE IN

- **Take walks around your community with the families.** Short walking field trips to explore the space around your program will help children and families notice the nearby nature that they have access to each day.

- **Host nature events at your school.** Invite a naturalist from a nature center or parks and recreation board to visit your program, and invite the families.

- **Encourage families to attend events that highlight time outdoors.** If the Banff Centre Mountain Film and Book Festival or another outdoor festival is playing in your area, you can set up a group event to attend as a school. There may also be other nature-based learning events in your area. Check your local REI calendar or websites like www.naturalstart.org.

WADING IN

- **Host a nature-focused event with a community service aspect.** After exploring the community, we often find that our natural spaces need care and attention. Earth Day can be a great time to do a playground or community cleanup by picking up trash, composting leaves, and building composts or garden beds.

- **Celebrate International Mud Day.** This celebration of the joys of mud that is held annually on June 29 can be a great way to get families engaged in nature. Seeing adults enjoying a mudslide as much as the young children can be a lot of fun. This also tends to be an attractive event for siblings of any age.

DIVING IN

- **Lead a family camping trip.** Finding a good youth campground in your area can be a great way to introduce families to camping. These sites are often made for children to be able to explore and have resources that make first-time camping for young families an easier transition, like indoor bathrooms or wagons for carting gear.

- **Host a family nature club.** Your program can help provide support for interested parents to organize a family hiking club. Resources are available at www.childrenandnature.org and www.hikeitbaby.com.

- **Organize a family education night focused on adventuring with children: backpacking, international camping, and the like.** The magic of these moments is the time together, so choose a presenter who will make adventuring accessible for your families.

INCLUSION OF ALL CHILDREN

When family members have disabilities, constructing inclusive events is important. For example, if you have a family with vision limitations, a hike along a trail or familiar pathway will be more successful than going off trail. The best way to find what your families would want or need in these situations is to have a conversation about your goal for the event and solicit ideas from the families.

CULTURAL CONSIDERATIONS

Many cities are focused on improving their natural areas, and more natural areas are becoming accessible for families in their communities. There are also movements within transit systems to provide more transportation options to area parks and natural spaces. For example, the Sierra Club in Minnesota started a campaign called Transit to Green Space to highlight the many green spaces around the Twin Cities that are accessible by light rail, commuter rail, bus, walking, or biking. More information on that program can be found at www.sierraclub.org/minnesota/transit-green-space.

When nature learning becomes controversial: what to do when families' beliefs or values conflict with your plans.

Sometimes discussions come up in a nature-related area that turns out to be controversial with one or more families. Prepare yourself for these possibilities to avoid potential conflicts.

- **Be proactive.** Are there positions that are central to the values of the program that families should know about before enrolling their children? If so, make sure to mention them in promotional materials. You can learn about families' beliefs and values during intake either through a questionnaire or interview. When families share information on an intake form or through your conferences, be sure to talk with your team and others in your program. In programs with emergent curriculum, it is essential that all the staff that may interact with that child or family know their concerns.

- **Use language that is respectful of differing opinions.** Let families know that you will try to support their values without compromising your own. Examples of respectful language include, "Some people think . . ." and "Some families. . . ."

- **Avoid the temptation to indoctrinate.** It can be hard to stay quiet when adults' actions can have a negative impact on their children or society (such as not vaccinating their children) or on the environment (such as refusing to recycle). You are less likely to change people's minds through arguing or lecturing than through quiet example and providing resources or information when requested. Providing reasons for the school's policies and practices that are based on science can be done in a matter-of-fact manner that is less likely to make people defensive. For example, you can provide reasons for using nondisposable tableware with information about landfills or cost savings for the program in either purchasing or disposal fees. You can describe your program's use of integrated pest management and share the research and resources you use to construct your policies. You can explain why children who are not immunized will be excluded from school during an outbreak of disease rather than just quoting health department requirements.

- **Let families know when there has been a debate on a related topic between children.** Sharing points of view in a positive manner helps families understand the benefits of such discussions in developing children's cognitive skills as well as subtly sharing a position with the families. Even when we do our best to reflect the values of our families, there will be times during our programs where we need to let a family know that a difficult conversation occurred or their child has been exploring some big topic like life and death, mating, or gender roles.

Some of These Beliefs/Values Include:

- Climate Change

  From Sheila: While climate change is too abstract a topic to plan activities around for preschoolers, discussions are likely to come up. "If it is winter, why is there no snow?" asked a young child this year. In Minnesota you can generally count on snow to fall November through March. Sometimes the earlier snow doesn't stick and there isn't any depth of snow until January. The winter of 2017 was typical in that manner. However, when there was no snow in January and February, the children started to question if it was spring. I wanted to say no, it's just an unseasonably warm day or week or month. But the truth is, when you have seen crocuses budding in January or hostas sprouting in February and that has occurred more than once, you start to see a pattern. And that is exactly what scientists are finding. There is a pattern, and our climate is changing. This will affect different parts of the country in a variety of different ways. It could be more severe storms, more dry days, or more wet days, but either way we will have to be open to saying, "Maybe it *is* spring," which is what I told a preschooler in February 2017. I continued with, "Usually spring comes later, but it does look like spring, doesn't it? You are noticing the signs of spring, like the warmer days, the plants sprouting, and trees budding."

- Hunting

  From Julie: We found two common populations attracted to our nature center preschool: hunters and vegetarians. Both groups tend to consider themselves committed to the environment. We were careful to support both lifestyles without judgment. Children do not choose their family's belief system, but by providing a venue for children to hear alternative beliefs, they will be better prepared for developing their own values when they become adults.

- **Eating animals.** Children are likely to reflect their family's beliefs about the health and/or morality of eating animals. You may hear strong feelings as children notice what other children are eating if they bring their lunches to school, or conversations may come up around Thanksgiving.

- **Pesticides.** Some families feel very strongly about any exposure to pesticides. If your program uses pesticides, keep families informed about what was used and when so they can choose whether to keep their children home during this period.

- **GMOs.** Many parts of the country are having contentious debates about the safety of genetically modified organisms (GMOs). Keep families informed about food provided in your program.

- **The age of the earth.** This most typically comes up when examining fossils. Children may tell you that dinosaurs and people were on the earth together. You may have families who for religious reasons would like you not to encourage discussions about dinosaurs or other prehistoric life. You can say, "Many scientists say . . ." if the topic comes up.

- **Evolution.** This is another area in which you might not be prepared for a debate. For religious reasons, families may want you to refrain from talking about how evolution occurs. In the early childhood setting, this is not a difficult task since the concept can be a difficult one to grasp because it occurs over such a long period of time.

- **Sex.** Exposure to living creatures invites questions about reproduction. If your families have diverse beliefs about how these questions are answered, you can refer children to their families for explanations.

- **Death.** Religious beliefs impact how families want questions answered regarding death.

From Julie: In my preschool in Tucson we had the parents of three children die within the same year. One family was Latter-day Saints, one Christian Scientists, one Jewish. We discussed the family beliefs with the remaining parent and used the same language when talking to the child.

GUIDANCE ISSUES

Be proactive regarding guidance when families are with you on school outings. Let adults know about behavior expectations and consequences before problems arise. Most parents will respond to your direction if you are sure to be nonjudgmental. Word rules in terms of what works best at school, not what should be expected of children of this age. You will have families who are stricter and families who are more lenient than you. We recommend breaking children into small groups with specific adults in charge of each group. Giving a list to chaperones will help them stay focused. Be sure that children who often experience challenges during outings stick with a classroom teacher. All children should be supervised by school staff while on outings and parents can offer a helpful hand when exploring, however, be sure to take into consideration how much challenge each adult can handle. A parent who is a former teacher or has gone on lots of outings with you is more likely to handle challenges better than a novice parent. Let chaperones know they can ask for help. We also suggest that you ask chaperones to refrain from talking on their cell phones, taking photos, or chatting with other adults. These activities make it more difficult for the chaperone to be present. Parents bringing younger siblings on the outing can also be too challenging.

RESOURCES

Children's Books Better Suited for Families to Read

Some books are too long to keep children's interest in a large or even small group. Other books encourage children to ask questions that are best answered by families, with topics such as global warming or pollution. Here are some examples:

- *One Less Fish* by Kim Michelle Toft and Allan Sheather. 1997. Watertown, MA: Charlesbridge. This book shares the effect of people on fish. Because young children have less control than adults when it comes to making good choices for the environment, this book can be shared with families.

- *In the Tall, Tall Grass* by Denise Fleming. 1991. New York: Henry Holt. This beautifully illustrated book ends with a line about disappearing nature. Parents can read this story to their children and talk about what they are doing to protect the environment.

Author Favorites

- **Julie's favorite:** *Parent Engagement in Early Learning* by Julie Powers. 2016. St. Paul, MN: Redleaf Press. Yes, it is tacky to select a book I wrote, but I hope readers find helpful suggestions for working with families.

- **Sheila's favorite:** *Adventuring with Children: An Inspirational Guide to World Travel and the Outdoors* by Nan Jeffrey. Avalon House Travel Series. 1995. New York: Avalon House. When preparing to take children outdoors for extended excursions or travel abroad, this book has wonderful inspiration and great tips.

LESSON PLANS

WHERE DO CRITTERS GO WHEN IT RAINS?

Ecosystems: All • **Age group:** Two and up • **Group size:** Small group

Objectives

● Develop comfort outdoors in rain

● Learn about a variety of animals' adaptations for different weather

● Sharpen use of senses to learn about nature

Materials

☐ Appropriate rain gear

☐ Reference books about insects and other creatures for your ecosystem

☐ Cameras, tape recorders, or cell phones

Directions

1. Get rain gear ready for each child.

2. If possible, walk around outdoors first to look for signs of where animals might hide from the rain.

3. Read the story *Where Does the Butterfly Go When It Rains?* By May Garelick.

4. Gather the group of children. Ask children where you can look for critters.

5. Invite children to use the bathroom before putting on rain gear.

6. Help children get into their rain gear.

7. Walk in the rain, slowly. Even if you find no animals, you can still meet two of the objectives. Encourage use of senses through modeling listening, looking carefully, and smelling and tasting the rain. Look for animal tracks in the mud, windblown nests, or pieces of eggshells. If there is evidence of animals, take photos and/or record sounds.

8. Return to the classroom as children's interest begins to drift. Even if you only stay out for a couple of minutes, children have had an experience in nature!

Related Standards

Next Generation Science Standards (NGSS)

● K-ESS2-1. Use and share observations of local weather conditions to describe patterns over time.

● K-ESS3-2. Ask questions to obtain information about the purpose of weather forecasting to prepare for, and respond to, severe weather.

● K-LS1-1. Use observations to describe patterns of what plants and animals (including humans) need to survive.

Modifications: Children with mobility difficulties might need strollers or wagons. Visually impaired children can succeed in a small group to find critters. You may need to help the child feel the area.

Including Families: Place a documentation panel near the sign-in area and encourage children to share it with their families. Create a book about the walk, and allow children to take turns taking the book home overnight to share with family members. Email video and audio recordings to families.

RAIN-FAT CACTUS

Ecosystems: Desert • **Age group:** Three and up • **Group size:** Small group

Objectives

- Awareness of the effect of rain on plants in the desert
- Appreciation of cacti
- Better understanding of how cacti survive during long dry spells
- Experience with estimation

Materials

- ☐ Sidewalk chalk
- ☐ Photo of cactus you will use
- ☐ Thick ball of string
- ☐ Tape measure
- ☐ Display space in classroom

Directions

This activity has two parts—one before rainy season and one afterward.

- Familiarize children with the cacti near the program by taking several walks and discussing characteristics of the cactus.
- Find a cactus that children can safely approach—saguaros work well.
- Clear the area of fallen cactus thorns.
- Take photos of the cactus.
- Read books about cacti, such as *Cactus Hotel* by Brenda Z. Guiberson, *Cactus Café* by Kathleen Weidner Zoehfeld, or *Desert Giant: The World of the Saguaro Cactus* by Barbara Bash (see appendix 2).
- Familiarize children with measurement through activities using various types of tape measures.

Part 1 - During the Dry Season

1. Ask children how big they think the cactus is around. Invite them to draw a circle on the ground using sidewalk chalk of their estimated width.
2. Walk to the cactus. Wrap the string around the cactus and cut a piece that wraps around once.
3. Return to chalk drawings. Use the string along the border of each drawing to test the estimates.
4. Post the photo of the cactus with the length of string where children and families can see it.

Part 2 - After the Rainy Season

1. Refer children to the photos and string. Ask if they think the cactus has changed size.
2. Return to the cactus with the original string and a ball to remeasure.
3. If the cactus is now thicker, cut a new piece of string that reflects this change.
4. Take a new photo of the cactus.
5. Return to the posted photo of the cactus and have a conversation about what might have caused the change.
6. Write children's ideas on a poster to post near the two photos of the cactus and the strings.

Related Standards

Head Start Early Learning Outcomes Framework

Scientific Skills and Methods: The skills to observe and collect information and to use it to ask questions, predict, explain, and draw conclusions.

- Uses senses and tools, including technology, to gather information, investigate materials, and observe processes and relationships.

- Observes and discusses common properties, differences, and comparisons among objects.
- Participates in simple investigations to form hypotheses, gather observations, draw conclusions, and form generalizations.
- Collects, describes, and records information through discussions, drawings, maps, and charts.
- Describes and discusses predictions, explanations, and generalizations based on past experience.

Conceptual Knowledge of the Natural and Physical World: The acquisition of concepts and facts related to the natural and physical world and the understanding of naturally occurring relationships.

- Observes, describes, and discusses living things and natural processes.
- Observes, describes, and discusses properties of materials and transformation of substances.

Modifications: Children with visual impairments can take part by feeling the length of the string before and after rain.

WHAT WILL HAPPEN TO IT IN THE WATER?

Ecosystems: All · **Age group:** Two and up · **Group size:** Small or large group

Objectives

- Sharpen observation skills
- Experience cause and effect
- Experience firsthand the power of water
- Experience scientific method

Materials

☐ A water table or clear tubs on tables low enough for children to look down into

☐ Writing pad and waterproof markers for writing predictions

☐ A source of water to allow you to change the water when it gets cloudy

☐ Items to use in the water table, such as marbles, golf balls, Nerf balls, plastic Easter eggs, water-soluble and insoluble packing peanuts, seashells, wood, rocks, and pumice

Directions

1. Set up the items on a tray or baskets near the water table.

2. Fill the table or tubs with enough water for items to be completely submerged.

3. Invite a small group of children to take part in the activity. Tell them that it is a water experiment.

4. Have them wash their hands (this helps minimize the spread of disease, which happens easily when children splash water into their faces).

5. Ask children to select an item. Ask them to make a prediction about what will happen to the item when placed in the water. Write their predictions on the paper.

6. As children experiment, ask open-ended and probing questions to help children focus on what is happening to items.

7. When children are ready to try a new item, ask them first if their prediction was correct, reading it back to them. Ask the other children in the group if they agree. Encourage debate by asking, "How can you tell?" If they give you the wrong answer, still write it down.

8. Invite children to select another item until they lose interest in the activity.

Related Standards

NAEYC Accreditation

- 2.G.02 P-K Children are provided varied opportunities and materials to learn key content and principles of science, such as structure and property of matter (e.g., characteristics that include concepts such as hard and soft, floating and sinking) and behavior of materials (e.g., transformation of liquids and solids by dissolving or melting).

- 2.G.03 P-K Children are provided varied opportunities and materials that encourage them to use the five senses to observe, explore, and experiment with scientific phenomena.

- 2.G.04 P-K Children are provided varied opportunities to use simple tools to observe objects and scientific phenomena.

- 2.G.06 P-K Children are provided varied opportunities and materials that encourage them to think, question, and reason about observed and inferred phenomena.

- 2.G.07 P-K Children are provided varied opportunities and materials that encourage them to discuss scientific concepts in everyday conversation. Scientific concepts include things such as life cycles of organisms; structure and property of matter (hard, soft; floating/not floating; transformation of liquids and solids); speed; weather, seasons, time; light and shadow.
- 2.G.08 P-K Children are provided varied opportunities and materials that help them learn and use scientific terminology and vocabulary associated with the content areas.

Modifications: For two-year-olds or children with developmental delays, ensure that items are not too small to present a choking hazard. You can also limit the number of choices.

Including Families

- Post children's predictions and results where parents will see them.
- Invite parents to send items from home for future experiments.

PAINTING WITH MUD

Ecosystems: All • **Age group:** Two and up • **Group size:** Small group

Objectives

● Notice changes to soil in the different states of dry and wet

● Experience the texture of different types of mud (from clay, sand, etc.)

● Self-expression using natural materials

Materials

If Offered Outdoors:

☐ Sturdy containers for children to gather soil, such as buckets or pots and pans

☐ Trowels, spoons, shovels, or other tools for scooping soil

☐ Rolls of paper, such as butcher paper, or large sheets of paper

☐ Sticks long enough for children to reach paper while standing

☐ Source of water

If Offered Indoors:

☐ Sturdy containers for children to use to gather soil or containers filled with a variety of soil if children are unable to gather it from outdoors

☐ Sticks of a variety of widths, lengths, thicknesses, and shapes

☐ Containers of water

☐ Spoons to mix water and soil

☐ Sheets of paper

Directions

Begin by reading a story about mud, such as *Muddypaws* by Moira Butterfield or *Mud! Mud! Mud!* by Leonore Klein (see appendix 2).

If Offered Outdoors:

1. Find areas outdoors ahead of time that have a variety of types of soil that the children can access. Look for sandy areas, soft soil around trees, mulch from gardens, sticky claylike soil, etc.

2. Prepare containers so each has a tool for scooping soil, one for each child who will take part in the activity.

3. Find a flat, hard surface for children to use for the activity, such as a sidewalk.

4. Place containers of water near area to be used, and have towels ready.

5. Gather a small group of interested children to collect soil. Ask them where they can find different kinds of dirt.

6. Take children outdoors; give each child a container and scooping tool. Allow them to find soil. If children need to leave the fenced area to gather soil, an adult must accompany them.

7. Have children bring containers to work area and invite them to add water to soil to make mud.

8. Allow children to select a stick. Invite them to use the stick as a "paintbrush" to paint with mud.

9. Place finished painting out to dry.

If Offered Indoors:

1. Find areas outdoors ahead of time that have a variety of types of soil the children can access if you plan to allow children to collect soil. Look for sandy areas, soft soil around trees, and mulch from gardens, sticky claylike soil, etc.

2. Set up a table with pieces of paper, water to add to the soil, and space for the containers.

3. If children will be able to gather their own soil:

    a. Gather a small group of interested children to gather soil. Ask them where they can find different kinds of dirt.

    b. Take children outdoors; give each child a container and scooping tool. Allow them to find soil.

    c. If children need to leave the fenced area to gather soil, an adult must accompany them.

    d. Have children bring containers indoors to tables, and invite them to add water to soil to make mud.

If children are unable to collect soil themselves:

    a. Invite children to the table.

    b. Allow them to examine the different types of soil, and invite them to talk about where the soil came from.

4. Once at the table, invite them to add water to soil to make mud.

5. Allow children to select a stick. Invite them to use the stick as a "paintbrush" to paint with mud.

6. Place finished paintings away to dry.

Related Standards

NAEYC Accreditation

- 2.G.02 P-K Children are provided varied opportunities and materials to learn key content and principles of science, such as the difference between living and nonliving things (e.g., plants versus rocks); life cycles of various organisms (e.g., plants, butterflies, humans); earth and sky (e.g., seasons; weather; geologic features; light and shadow; and sun, moon, and stars); structure and property of matter (e.g., characteristics that include concepts such as hard and soft, floating and sinking); and behavior of materials (e.g., transformation of liquids and solids by dissolving or melting).

- 2.G.03 P-K Children are provided varied opportunities and materials that encourage them to use the five senses to observe, explore, and experiment with scientific phenomena.

- 2.G.06 P-K Children are provided varied opportunities and materials that encourage them to think, question, and reason about observed and inferred phenomena.

- 2.G.07 P-K Children are provided varied opportunities and materials that encourage them to discuss scientific concepts in everyday conversation. Scientific concepts include things such as life cycles of organisms; structure and property of matter (hard, soft; floating/not floating; transformation of liquids and solids); speed; weather, seasons, time; light and shadow.

- 5.A.06 I-T-P-K Children of all ages have daily opportunities for outdoor play (when weather, air quality, and environmental safety conditions do not pose a health risk).

Modifications: Children with mobility limitations will need support. A child who uses a walker can take part in this activity both indoors and outdoors as long as the mud and other materials are close enough for children to access.

Including Families

- If parents are available, invite them to take part in the activity. With more adults, you can gather soil with smaller groups of children and venture farther from the play yard.

- Use school-made books or documentation panels to share the experience with parents visually.

WHERE IS THE SEED?

Ecosystems: All • **Age group:** Two and up • **Group size:** Small or large group

Objectives

- Developing understanding of seeds
- Sharpening observation skills
- Refining fine-motor coordination
- Developing more understanding of the growth cycle of plants
- Provide children opportunities to explore fruits that are commonly eaten in their homes and communities

Materials

- ☐ Safe knives such as "pumpkin carvers"
- ☐ Cutting boards
- ☐ A variety of fruits such as berries, avocados, apples, citrus, cherries, or plums
- ☐ Towels for children to wipe their hands on (to help them resist putting their fingers in their mouths and contaminating the fruit)
- ☐ A camera for documentation

Directions

1. Read *Seeds* by Melanie Mitchell (see appendix 2) for younger children or *A Fruit Is a Suitcase for Seeds* by Jean Richards (see appendix 2) for older children.

2. Create a safe place for children to work. A table set up near a sink will make it easiest for children to wash hands often and keep fruit free of germs.

3. Have a separate cutting board for each child taking part in the activity.

4. Set a variety of fruit out for children to choose between.

5. Invite a small group of children to take part in the activity.

6. Have children wash their hands well using running water and soap. A nailbrush is helpful in removing germs, and children enjoy the novelty of using one. Resist rushing children to hurry when washing hands.

7. Have each child select a piece of fruit. Ask the child where the seeds are. Encourage them to cut out the seeds.

8. Save the seeds and fruit in separate bowls.

9. Take photographs to document the experience.

Related Standards

NAEYC Accreditation

- 2.A.04 I-T-P-K The curriculum can be implemented in a manner that reflects responsiveness to a family's home values, beliefs, experiences, and language.

- 2.G.02 P-K Children are provided varied opportunities and materials to learn key content and principles of science, such as the difference between living and nonliving things (e.g., plants versus rocks); life cycles of various organisms (e.g., plants, butterflies, humans); earth and sky (e.g., seasons; weather; geologic features; light and shadow; and sun, moon, and stars); structure and property of matter (e.g., characteristics that include concepts such as hard and soft, floating and sinking); and the behavior of materials (e.g., transformation of liquids and solids by dissolving or melting).

- 2.G.03 P-K Children are provided varied opportunities and materials that encourage them to use the five senses to observe, explore, and experiment with scientific phenomena.

- 2.G.04 P-K Children are provided varied opportunities to use simple tools to observe objects and scientific phenomena. Simple tools include materials such as bug boxes, binoculars, magnifying glasses, gears, levers, and can be many other tools as well.

- 2.G.05 P-K Children are provided varied opportunities and materials to collect data and to represent and document their findings (e.g., through drawing or graphing). The process of data collection and documentation is inherently scientific; the subject matter of what is collected and documented does not have to refer to science topics such as biology or physics.

- 2.G.06 P-K Children are provided varied opportunities and materials that encourage them to think, question, and reason about observed and inferred phenomena.

- 2.G.07 P-K Children are provided varied opportunities and materials that encourage them to discuss scientific concepts in everyday conversation. Scientific concepts include things such as life cycles of organisms; structure and property of matter (hard, soft; floating/not floating; transformation of liquids and solids); speed; weather, seasons, time; light and shadow.

- 2.G.08 P-K Children are provided varied opportunities and materials that help them learn and use scientific terminology and vocabulary associated with the content areas.

- 2.K.02 T-P-K Children are provided varied opportunities and materials to help them learn about nutrition, including identifying sources of food and recognizing, preparing, eating, and valuing healthy foods.

Modifications: Children with fine-motor challenges will need cutting implements that they can control.

Including Families

- Create a book or post the photos of the experience on your website.

- Invite parents to send seeds from cucumbers, melons, etc.

SEED SOCKS

Ecosystems: All · **Age group:** Three and up · **Group size:** Small or large group

Objectives

- Make connection between seeds and plants
- Develop understanding of how plants spread
- Enjoy an outdoor activity

Materials

☐ Oversized socks

☐ Sandwich bags

Directions

1. Read books about seeds and plants, such as *A Fruit Is a Suitcase for Seeds* by Jean Richards or *From Seed to Plant* by Gail Gibbons (see appendix 2).

2. Find an area within walking distance with seeds on the ground.

3. Gather a group of children who would like to take part in the activity. Tell them that you are going to gather seeds, just not with your hands.

4. Have children pull socks onto the outside of their shoes.

5. Walk with children in an area that has seeds that have dropped from plants. Stop from time to time so children can see if they have seeds stuck to their socks.

6. Return to school. Offer each child a plastic bag for their socks. Add a small amount of water to the bags and tape them to a window that gets sun.

7. Watch the bags in the days and weeks to come, looking for signs of germination.

Related Standards

Head Start Early Learning Outcomes Framework

Conceptual Knowledge of the Natural and Physical World: The acquisition of concepts and facts related to the natural and physical world and the understanding of naturally-occurring relationships.

- Observes, describes, and discusses living things and natural processes.
- Observes, describes, and discusses properties of materials and transformation of substances.

Modifications: If you have nonambulatory children, socks can be attached to the wheels of a wheelchair.

Including Families

- Invite parents to donate old socks to be a part of the experience.
- Share the experiences through documentation panels or books.

COLOR WALK

Ecosystems: All • **Age group:** Three and up • **Group size:** Small or large group

Objectives

- Enjoying the beauty of nature through focused attention to color

- Understanding changes of specific plants depending on the season

- Developing mathematical concepts through identifying and matching gradations and hues in color

Materials

- ☐ A wide variety of colors of crayons (Have duplicates of crayons that are likely to match plants, including a wide range of greens, browns, yellows, and colors for flowers you may encounter.)

- ☐ Scissors to take plant cuttings

- ☐ Paper and tape

Directions

1. Read a story about the type of plants you will be visiting. Some examples include *Cactus Café* by Kathleen Weidner Zoehfeld, *My Hawaiin Farm* by Pearl Maxner, *Evergreens are Green* by Susan Canizares, and *Planting a Rainbow* by Lois Ehlert (see appendix 2). Talk to children about the colors of plants in the stories.

2. Gather a small group of children who are interested in a color walk. Ask them to make predictions about what colors they will see. Invite them to select one crayon to take on the walk to match to a plant. Don't discourage children from selecting crayons that are less likely to match a plant.

3. Walk with children. Carry a basket of scissors and extra crayons.

4. Encourage children to find a part of a plant that matches their crayon. If they can, take a cutting of the leaf, stick, petal, etc. If children are unable to find a match for their color, invite them to select a different crayon from the basket.

5. Return to the classroom and invite children to tape their plant part onto paper and to use the crayon to color a section near the plant part. If a child discovers the match isn't as good as he or she hoped, invite them to use other crayons until the best match is found.

6. Display the product from the color walk.

Related Standards

NAEYC Accreditation

- 2.G.02 P-K Children are provided varied opportunities and materials to learn key content and principles of science, such as the difference between living and nonliving things (e.g., plants versus rocks); life cycles of various organisms (e.g., plants, butterflies, humans); earth and sky (e.g., seasons; weather; geologic features; light and shadow; and sun, moon, and stars); structure and property of matter (e.g., characteristics that include concepts such as hard and soft, floating and sinking); and the behavior of materials (e.g., transformation of liquids and solids by dissolving or melting).

- 2.G.03 P-K Children are provided varied opportunities and materials that encourage them to use the five senses to observe, explore, and experiment with scientific phenomena.

● 2.G.04 P-K Children are provided varied opportunities to use simple tools to observe objects and scientific phenomena. Simple tools include materials such as bug boxes, binoculars, magnifying glasses, gears, levers, and can be many other tools as well.

● 2.G.05 P-K Children are provided varied opportunities and materials to collect data and to represent and document their findings (e.g., through drawing or graphing). The process of data collection and documentation is inherently scientific; the subject matter of what is collected and documented does not have to refer to science topics such as biology or physics.

● 5.A.06 I-T-P-K Children of all ages have daily opportunities for outdoor play (when weather, air quality, and environmental safety conditions do not pose a health risk).

Modifications: Children with fine-motor limitations will need large, sturdy crayons.

Including Families: Share the activity with families and invite them to take home crayons so they can duplicate the experience with plants at home.

MAKING BUTTER

Ecosystems: All · **Age group:** Three and up · **Group size:** Small or large group

Objectives

- Understand a simple connection between dairy products
- Experience a transformation from liquid to solid
- Build fine-motor coordination and motor planning
- Enjoying the taste of fresh butter and buttermilk

Materials

- ☐ A container of heavy cream (About a pint is a good amount for a class of 18 to have a taste or spread onto crackers.)
- ☐ A clear plastic container such as a clean mayonnaise jar
- ☐ Popsicle sticks to use for tasting the cream and later the butter
- ☐ Small cups to taste the buttermilk when done
- ☐ Container for butter
- ☐ Small pitcher for buttermilk

Directions

1. Read a story about dairy cows, such as *The Milk Makers* by Gail Gibbons (see appendix 2).
2. Show children the carton of cream. Ask what might be inside.
3. Slowly pour the cream into the plastic jar so that children notice how thick it is.
4. Allow children to taste the cream by dipping a popsicle stick into the jar.
5. Screw the top on the jar, ensuring that it is tight.
6. Ask children to make predictions about what will happen to the cream if they shake the jar.

7. Pass the jar from child to child, allowing each to shake the jar. You may want to sing a farm-related song as children are taking turns to make it easier to wait. It will take about 10 minutes to change from whipping cream to solid butter and liquid buttermilk.
8. The jar will change from a clouded appearance to clear as the butter separates from the buttermilk.
9. Once the butter is a semisolid mass, carefully open the jar and pass it around for each child to view.
10. Pour the buttermilk into a pitcher. Use a spoon to move the butter into a container.
11. Invite children to have a taste of the buttermilk and the butter.

Related Standards

NAEYC Accreditation

- 2.G.02 P-K Children are provided varied opportunities and materials to learn key content and principles of science, such as the difference between living and nonliving things (e.g., plants versus rocks); life cycles of various organisms (e.g., plants, butterflies, humans); earth and sky (e.g., seasons; weather; geologic features; light and shadow; and sun, moon, and stars); structure and property of matter (e.g., characteristics that include concepts such as hard and soft, floating and sinking); and the behavior of materials (e.g., transformation of liquids and solids by dissolving or melting).
- 2.G.03 P-K Children are provided varied opportunities and materials that encourage them to use the five senses to observe, explore, and experiment with scientific phenomena.

- 2.G.06 P-K Children are provided varied opportunities and materials that encourage them to think, question, and reason about observed and inferred phenomena.

- 2.G.07 P-K Children are provided varied opportunities and materials that encourage them to discuss scientific concepts in everyday conversation. Scientific concepts include things such as life cycles of organisms; structure and property of matter (hard, soft; floating/not floating; transformation of liquids and solids); speed; weather, seasons, time; light and shadow.

- 2.G.08 P-K Children are provided varied opportunities and materials that help them learn and use scientific terminology and vocabulary associated with the content areas.

- 2.K.02 T-P-K Children are provided varied opportunities and materials to help them learn about nutrition, including identifying sources of food and recognizing, preparing, eating, and valuing healthy foods.

Modifications: Accommodations may be needed for children with fine-motor limitations, such as using a larger container to shake or one with a handle.

Including Families: Make directions and photos of the activity available by printing or sending electronically.

COMBING WOOL

Ecosystems: All • **Age group:** Three and up • **Group size:** Small or large group

Objectives

- Understand the relationship between sheep and wool
- Enjoy a natural sensory experience
- Sustain interest in an individual activity

Materials

- ☐ A few pounds of raw wool
- ☐ Wool combs or brushes

Directions

In preparation for this activity, set up a table where children can sit and comb wool. Children will benefit from displays of photos of sheep, sheepskin, and wool yarn. While firsthand experience with sheep is the best pre-activity, reading a storybook about sheep shearing can also help to provide context (see appendix 2).

1. Pass around the bag of sheep's wool. Encourage conversation about what is in the bag, what it feels like, how it smells, etc. Encourage children to try carrying it around the room to feel how heavy it is.

2. Sing "Baa, Baa, Black Sheep." This experience will bring new meaning to the song.

3. Pass around wool combs. Invite children to handle them and notice the wool that is caught between the teeth. Let children know that they will be able to comb the wool as an activity.

4. Assist children in pulling off sections of wool and using combs to clean and soften the wool with a back-and-forth motion with a comb in each hand.

Related Standards

Head Start Early Learning Outcomes Framework

Social Studies Knowledge and Skills: The understanding of the relationship between people and the environment in which they live.

- Recognizes that people share the environment with other people, animals, and plants.

Scientific Skills and Methods: The skills to observe and collect information and to use it to ask questions, predict, explain, and draw conclusions.

- Uses senses and tools, including technology, to gather information, investigate materials, and observe processes and relationships.
- Observes and discusses common properties, differences, and comparisons among objects.
- Describes and discusses predictions, explanations, and generalizations based on past experience.

Conceptual Knowledge of the Natural and Physical World: The acquisition of concepts and facts related to the natural and physical world and the understanding of naturally occurring relationships.

- Observes, describes, and discusses living things and natural processes.
- Observes, describes, and discusses properties of materials and transformation of substances.

Modifications: Children with vision impairment can benefit from this highly tactile experience.

Including Families

- Take photos of children combing wool with explanations.
- Invite a family member who knits to demonstrate for the class.

SILKWORMS

Ecosystems: All • **Age group:** Three and up • **Group size:** Large group

Objectives

- Better understanding of the life cycle of moths
- Experience caring for a classroom pet
- Develop some understanding of the interconnection between plants and insects

Materials

- ☐ Silkworm eggs
- ☐ Mulberry leaves or silkworm food
- ☐ Habitat
- ☐ Reference books about silkworms
- ☐ Silkworm life cycle poster
- ☐ *Silkworms* by Sylvia A. Johnson (see appendix 2)

Directions

1. Order silkworm eggs from a catalog.
2. Wait until mulberry leaves appear on trees before defrosting eggs.
3. Create a habitat for the worms.
4. Show children the eggs. Brainstorm what might hatch from the eggs. Make a list of predictions.
5. Place eggs on mulberry leaves in a habitat that will limit the worms' movement and protect the silkworms from the children when needed, such as a plastic shoebox. Include sticks and twigs for the worms to use to attach their chrysalises.
6. Encourage the children to check on the eggs daily to watch for hatching. Tiny threadlike worms will emerge.
7. Replace mulberry leaves daily. As the worms grow, they will eat the leaves quickly.
8. As the worms grow, allow children to handle them gently. Make sure children wash their hands before and after handling worms.

9. Watch for the worms to begin to make chrysalises. They may be yellow or white or both. When all the worms are encased in a chrysalis, you will no longer need to feed them.
10. Watch for the moths to emerge from the chrysalises. You can remove a chrysalis to be closely examined by the children, but handle it by lifting the stick or twig rather than touching the chrysalis.
11. You don't need to feed the moths. They will die after laying eggs. You don't need to worry about them flying away as they do not fly.
12. Carefully save the eggs and freeze for next year.

Related Standards

Head Start Early Learning Outcomes Framework

Scientific Skills and Methods: The skills to observe and collect information and to use it to ask questions, predict, explain, and draw conclusions.

- Uses senses and tools, including technology, to gather information, investigate materials, and observe processes and relationships.
- Observes and discusses common properties, differences, and comparisons among objects.
- Participates in simple investigations to form hypotheses, gather observations, draw conclusions, and form generalizations.
- Collects, describes, and records information through discussions, drawings, maps, and charts.
- Describes and discusses predictions, explanations, and generalizations based on past experience.

Conceptual Knowledge of the Natural and Physical World: The acquisition of concepts and facts related to the natural and physical world and the understanding of naturally occurring relationships.

- Observes, describes, and discusses living things and natural processes.
- Observes, describes, and discusses properties of materials and transformation of substances.

Modifications: Children with visual impairments will benefit from high-powered magnifying glasses. Children who tend to be impulsive will need to be supervised closely to ensure that they do not injure the eggs, silkworms, chrysalises, or moths.

Including Families

- Ask families who have mulberry trees to bring in leaves.
- Invite families to send in items made from silk to display.

WORM BEDS

Ecosystems: All • Age group: Three and up • Group size: Small or large group

Objectives

- Opportunities to see a natural process that worms provide in our ecosystem
- Learning about waste and waste reduction
- Helping children develop comfort and confidence handling worms
- Developing fine-motor coordination

Materials

- ☐ Two plastic totes of similar size, one with holes drilled in the bottom, and one with a lid with holes drilled in it for ventilation
- ☐ Newspaper or dried leaves
- ☐ 40–50 earthworms or red wigglers (can be dug up in your soil or purchased at a bait store)

Directions

1. Read books about composting, such as *The Little Composter* by Jan Gerardi and/or *Compost Stew* by Mary McKenna Siddals (see appendix 2).
2. Invite children and/or families to assist in providing the newspaper, dried leaves, and garden clippings.
3. Drill six holes in the bottom of one of the plastic bins (children can help do this with a hand drill if you draw dots in the places you would like the holes drilled and supervise the drilling).
4. Place the bin with holes inside of the other bin.
5. Layer the bottom of the bin about halfway up with dried leaves or newspaper. Place about ¼ of the bin with green material like food scraps or garden clippings. Stir it in slightly.

6. Add the worms and place the lid on top.
7. Add food scraps when they are available, such as:
   - leftover vegetable peels from preparing snack
   - leftover fruits or vegetables
   - bread crusts or ends
   - apple cores

Related Standards

Next Generation Science Standards

- K-LS1-1. Use observations to describe patterns of what plants and animals (including humans) need to survive.
- K-ESS2-2. Construct an argument supported by evidence for how plants and animals (including humans) can change the environment to meet their needs.
- K-ESS3-1. Use a model to represent the relationship between the needs of different plants or animals (including humans) and the places they live.
- K-ESS3-3. Communicate solutions that will reduce the impact of humans on the land, water, air, and/or other living things in the local environment.

Including Families

- Ask any families that compost at home to help construct your worm bin or outdoor compost.
- Have a family "build night" and help other families create their own worm bins or composts.

RAISING TADPOLES

Ecosystems: Freshwater • **Age group:** Three and up • **Group size:** Small or large group

Objectives

- Opportunity to observe the metamorphosis of an animal and learn about growth
- Learn responsible animal care through returning to habitat or caring for new pet

Materials

- ☐ A tank with a lid
- ☐ Freshwater from the same area that the tadpoles were caught (if you need to supplement with tap water or add it to keep the level up, be sure to use a dechlorinator)
- ☐ Magnifying lenses for children's observations
- ☐ Nets
- ☐ A bucket to carry the tadpoles back to the classroom

Directions

If you are in an area with wetlands or freshwater, you can often catch tadpoles along the edges of water and near the grasses. One of the benefits of catching the tadpoles in your local area is that you can release those frogs in the same place. Make sure that the tadpoles you catch are nontoxic. Use a field guide or the internet to learn more about the species in your area. Any purchased tadpoles, frogs, or other animals cannot be released into the environment, because introducing invasive species can lead to devastating consequences for ecosystems. Some migratory insects like butterflies can be exceptions to this rule, but always be sure to know what is native to your area to ensure your classroom experience will not adversely affect the environment around you.

1. Read about tadpoles and frogs (see appendix 2).

2. Prepare journals for children to document changes they see in the tadpoles.

3. Set up a tank with a lid in the classroom.

4. Gather freshwater from the same area that the tadpoles will be caught or supplement with tap water treated with a dechlorinator.

5. Catch or purchase tadpoles for the aquarium. Be sure to also gather some plants and bugs native to the water area.

6. Provide opportunities for children to regularly feed the tadpoles or frogs.

7. If you choose to purchase tadpoles, those frogs must be kept as pets through their lifetime by having them as classroom pets, offering them to families in your program, or asking a local school or nature center if they would like to provide a home for the frogs.

Related Standards

Head Start Early Learning Outcomes Framework

Social Studies Knowledge and Skills: The understanding of the relationship between people and the environment in which they live.

- Recognizes aspects of the environment, such as roads, buildings, trees, gardens, bodies of water, or land formations.
- Recognizes that people share the environment with other people, animals, and plants.

Scientific Skills and Methods: The skills to observe and collect information and to use it to ask questions, predict, explain, and draw conclusions.

- Uses senses and tools, including technology, to gather information, investigate materials, and observe processes and relationships.
- Observes and discusses common properties, differences, and comparisons among objects.

- Participates in simple investigations to form hypotheses, gather observations, draw conclusions, and form generalizations.

- Collects, describes, and records information through discussions, drawings, maps, and charts.

- Describes and discusses predictions, explanations, and generalizations based on past experience.

Conceptual Knowledge of the Natural and Physical World: The acquisition of concepts and facts related to the natural and physical world and the understanding of naturally occurring relationships.

- Observes, describes, and discusses living things and natural processes.

- Observes, describes, and discusses properties of materials and transformation of substances.

Modifications: Always be sure to have a lid on top of the tank with a screen to keep young children's hands out and to prevent children from dropping things into the tank. If you are using a glass tank, be sure to have it secured on a table where it cannot be pulled over by children.

Including Families: If you purchased frogs and they need care over school breaks, a frog can be a great pet to travel to and from homes in a lightweight tank.

BUILDING HABITATS FOR REPTILES

Ecosystems: All • **Age group:** Three and up • **Group size:** Small group

Objectives

- Opportunity to examine habitats and recreate them based on what children have observed and learned about the needs and preferences of the animal
- Teaching children responsible care for animals includes appropriate habitats

Materials

Depending on the animal you are creating a habitat for, you will need a variety of different materials. Here are a few examples:

Salamander

- Substrate: Coconut fiber bedding, topsoil, or forest floor soil mixes from a pet store are good natural substrate choices
- Thermometer (keep temperature around 70 degrees)
- Spray bottle with filtered water for keeping the salamander and substrate moist
- Pieces of rock or small logs
- Container for water (a small plant pot saucer works well)

Box Turtle

- A large plastic tote with a lid (can be deep or shallow, at least 10 gallons, but the bigger the better)
- Substrate: Coconut fiber bedding, topsoil, or forest floor soil mixes from a pet store are good natural substrate choices
- Pieces of flat rock or small half logs

- Container for water (a small plant pot saucer works well)
- Heat lamp to keep the temperature above 70 degrees
- Space for food (a flat rock will work well)

Directions

1. Read books about the pets you are interested in adding to the classroom (see appendix 2).
2. Research the food, temperature, and specific needs for the pet you would like to create a habitat for in your classroom.
3. Place the substrate in the tub and place the logs, water dish, and rocks around the tank.
4. The substrate should be at least four inches deep and changed out every month or two.
5. Fill the water dish with filtered water and replace each day.
6. Provide opportunities for children to feed the pets.

Related Standards

Head Start Early Learning Outcomes Framework

Social Studies Knowledge and Skills: The understanding of the relationship between people and the environment in which they live.

- Recognizes aspects of the environment, such as roads, buildings, trees, gardens, bodies of water, or land formations.
- Recognizes that people share the environment with other people, animals, and plants.

- Understands that people can take care of the environment through activities, such as recycling.

Modifications: If you have children who have trouble controlling their impulses, be sure to use acrylic aquariums or glass aquariums on the ground so there will be no danger of them getting pushed or pulled onto a child.

Including Families

- Ask families for donations such as aquariums, lamps, flagstone, or rocks for the habitat.

- Invite families to join you on walks around the neighborhood or a visit to the pet store.

BIRD WATCHING WALK

Ecosystems: All · **Age group:** Three and up · **Group size:** Small group

Objectives

- Become engaged in nature through supported discovery
- Learn about local birds and their habitats
- Improve observation skills

Materials

- ☐ Field guides or photos of local birds, their nests, and information about where they nest
- ☐ Binoculars if the children are old enough to successfully use them
- ☐ Apps of birdcalls
- ☐ Camera

Directions

1. Prepare a group of children for a bird watch. Ask questions to help children think about and discuss what behaviors are likely to make it easier to spot birds (walking quietly, watching carefully) and less likely (running toward birds, shouting, looking at the ground instead of in trees, telephone poles, and sky).

2. Walk with children, stopping to listen and look for birds.

3. Take photos of birds if possible.

Related Standards

NAEYC Accreditation

- 2.G.02 P-K Children are provided varied opportunities and materials to learn key content and principles of science, such as the difference between living and nonliving things (e.g., plants versus rocks); life cycles of various organisms (e.g., plants, butterflies, humans); earth and sky (e.g., seasons; weather; geologic features; light and shadow; and sun, moon, and stars); structure and property of matter (e.g., characteristics that include concepts such as hard and soft, floating and sinking); and the behavior of materials (e.g., transformation of liquids and solids by dissolving or melting).

- 2.G.03 P-K Children are provided varied opportunities and materials that encourage them to use the five senses to observe, explore, and experiment with scientific phenomena.

- 2.G.04 P-K Children are provided varied opportunities to use simple tools to observe objects and scientific phenomena. Simple tools include materials such as bug boxes, binoculars, magnifying glasses, gears, levers, and can be many other tools as well.

- 2.G.07 P-K Children are provided varied opportunities and materials that encourage them to discuss scientific concepts in everyday conversation. Scientific concepts include things such as life cycles of organisms; structure and property of matter (hard, soft; floating/not floating; transformation of liquids and solids); speed; weather, seasons, time; light and shadow.

- 2.G.08 P-K Children are provided varied opportunities and materials that help them learn and use scientific terminology and vocabulary associated with the content areas.

- 5.A.06 I-T-P-K Children of all ages have daily opportunities for outdoor play (when weather, air quality, and environmental safety conditions do not pose a health risk).

Modifications: Children with motor impairments can take part in a walk using a wagon or sled, depending on the time of the year. Children with visual limitations will benefit from binoculars. Children with limited hearing can benefit from personal sound amplifiers.

Including Families

- Write a newsletter about the experience on the walk.
- Invite family members to join you on the walk.

INCUBATING CHICKS

Ecosystems: All • **Age group:** Three and up • **Group size:** Small or large group

Objectives

- Gain experience with the life cycle of birds
- Gain experience learning to care for an animal

Materials

☐ Incubator

☐ Thermometer

☐ Hygrometer (measures humidity)

☐ At least six fertilized chicken eggs (you can get them from a local farm if you can gather your own eggs, or purchase)

☐ 10–20 gallon aquarium

☐ Heat lamp

Directions

When considering whether to hatch chicks, it is important to find a home for your chicks to go to at the end of the classroom experience. Ask families ahead of time if they have a backyard chicken coop or have a relationship with a farm that might want more chickens.

Choose a primary teacher to oversee turning the eggs and adding water to the incubator.

1. Have books and posters or signs available that show what is happening inside the egg (see appendix 2).

2. Setting up the incubator:

   a. Follow the incubator instructions on heating and adjustment.

   b. Set the incubator up several days in advance so children can get used to the incubator and start to read books about chicks and their growth inside the egg.

3. Incubator maintenance:

   a. To properly incubate eggs, open the incubator only to turn the eggs and add water, or purchase an automatic turner. An automatic turner makes it more likely that more chicks will successfully hatch, but it can rob children of a hands-on experience. A combination of using the automatic turner and having children take a turn rotating eggs may work as well.

   b. The fewer times you open the incubator, the better success you will enjoy with the eggs.

   c. The chicks will take 21 days to hatch.

   d. Turn the chicks at least three times per day.

   e. Maintain the humidity at 40–50 percent during the first 18 days.

   f. After day 18, raise the humidity to 70 percent and stop turning the eggs.

4. Preparing for chicks:

   a. Don't help any chicks out of their eggs, and be sure to keep the humidity up so they don't dry out. They can take several hours to hatch. You may find it hard to resist helping when you see a chick exhausted from trying to hatch, but it will not survive if you "help" it.

   b. Set up an aquarium with a lid and a heat lamp to be ready when the chicks arrive.

   c. Purchase chick food online, at a pet store, or at a local farm supply store, and have a water source with plenty of available water but not deep enough that a chick could drown.

Related Standards

Head Start Early Learning Outcomes Framework

Conceptual Knowledge of the Natural and Physical World: The acquisition of concepts and facts related to the natural and physical world and the understanding of naturally occurring relationships.

- Observes, describes, and discusses living things and natural processes.

Modifications: Securely tape a baby food jar over the temperature control once it has become stable at 100 degrees. This will keep children from altering the sensitive temperature to the incubator (remember that glass is unsafe for children to handle).

If you have children with true egg allergies (not egg sensitivity), you may want to skip this activity to keep them safe.

Including Families: If you have families that are considering backyard chickens, they may be willing to provide the eggs and take the chicks when they are ready for a home.

POND IN A JAR

Ecosystems: Wetlands • **Age group:** Three and up • **Group size:** Large group

Objectives

- Observe and study small aquatic life in the classroom
- Opportunity to observe changes in small plants and animals
- Opportunity to observe and study unique movement of small aquatic life
- Opportunity for children to learn about collecting data by documenting their findings through photographs or drawings of the pond in a jar

Materials

- ☐ One-gallon glass jar (such as one for pickles) with a few holes cut in the lid
- ☐ Nets and empty plastic containers with lids (such as 32 oz. yogurt containers) for catching aquatic life and gathering water
- ☐ Magnifying lenses
- ☐ Nature journals
- ☐ Colored pencils
- ☐ Field guides featuring aquatic life native to your area
- ☐ Wagon for carrying water (optional)

Directions

1. Clean the glass jar with a vinegar and water solution (1 cup white vinegar and fill remainder of the jar with water) and let it set for at least an hour.
2. Recruit volunteers to help supervise children while collecting samples.
3. Find a window with some sun throughout the day, but not full sun.
4. Collect water and carry it back to school.
5. Try to collect a variety of pond aquatic life, including insects and plants.
6. Place the water and pond life in the jar in your classroom.
7. Securely attach the lid.
8. As needed, fill with water from the pond to keep it full.

Related Standards

NAEYC Accreditation

- 2.G.04 P-K Children are provided varied opportunities to use simple tools to observe objects and scientific phenomena. Simple tools include materials such as bug boxes, binoculars, magnifying glasses, gears, levers, and can be many other tools as well.
- 2.G.05 P-K Children are provided varied opportunities and materials to collect data and to represent and document their findings (e.g., through drawing or graphing). The process of data collection and documentation is inherently scientific; the subject matter of what is collected and documented does not have to refer to science topics such as biology or physics.
- 2.G.06 P-K Children are provided varied opportunities and materials that encourage them to think, question, and reason about observed and inferred phenomena.
- 2.G.07 P-K Children are provided varied opportunities and materials that encourage them to discuss scientific concepts in everyday conversation. Scientific concepts include things such as life cycles of organisms; structure and property of matter (hard, soft; floating/not floating; transformation of liquids and solids); speed; weather, seasons, time; light and shadow.

- 2.G.08 P-K Children are provided varied opportunities and materials that help them learn and use scientific terminology and vocabulary associated with the content areas.
- 5.A.06 I-T-P-K Children of all ages have daily opportunities for outdoor play (when weather, air quality, and environmental safety conditions do not pose a health risk).

Modifications: Be sure to have the jar out of the reach of children when not supervised.

Including Families: Invite families to help with supervision near the water while collecting and returning the water.

PRETEND CENTER: THE BEACH

Ecosystems: All • **Age group:** Two and up • **Group size:** Small or large group

Objectives

- Increase understanding of coastal areas through pretend play
- Understand beach safety through pretending to follow safety rules
- Develop literacy skills through use of beach signs

Materials

- ☐ Beach equipment, including towels, beach chairs, umbrellas, coolers, pretend beach food, empty sunscreen bottles, cameras, and radios
- ☐ Textured, tan ground cover (a canvas drop cloth from a hardware store or an indoor/outdoor jute rug will work well)
- ☐ Blue tarp to simulate water
- ☐ Watercraft that will fit in your space—in a large space, you can place a kayak, paddleboard, or canoe; in smaller spaces you can place pool noodles, skim, surf, or body boards
- ☐ Life vests
- ☐ Beach signs with symbols, including danger signs for sharks, riptides, or high surf; signs for trash; etc.
- ☐ Dress up clothing, including swimming suits that are large enough to fit over children's clothing, beach cover-ups, fins, goggles, and beach sandals (called "slippers" in Hawaii)
- ☐ Fishing equipment, including fishing poles, tackle box, pretend fish, buckets, fishing vests and hats, rubber boots, and waders (optional)

Directions

Find an area large enough for big-body pretend play, including pretending to swim and surf. If you have an area outdoors for this center, you can just spread sand on a tarp and place the blue "water" tarp at the edge. If indoors, use a textured ground cover in place of the real sand. Arrange beach chairs and umbrella in sand areas and watercraft in the "water."

1. Read a story about the ocean, such as *Wave* by Suzy Lee or *Going to the Tide Pools in Hawaii Nei* by Joy S. Au (see appendix 2).

2. Start with limited equipment for the center to avoid overwhelming the children. You can add more later.

3. Draw children's attention to the pretend center. You may need to add a sign-up for children waiting for turns if your space is limited.

4. Take your cues from each group of children regarding how much you should be involved. Children who quickly engage in appropriate play may not need anything from you. If a group of children seems less competent at the pretend play activity, you can join the play and model pretending.

5. Add complexity to the play by adding a new pretend role (such as inviting one of the children to be the "surfing teacher"), adding a new activity (such as fishing), or adding a dramatic element (placing the "Danger! Sharks Sighted!" sign).

6. Add safety suggestions in the context of pretend play, such as putting on sunscreen and drinking water.

Related Standards

Head Start Early Learning Outcomes Framework

Initiative and Curiosity: An interest in varied topics and activities, desire to learn, creativeness, and independence in learning.

- Demonstrates flexibility, imagination, and inventiveness in approaching tasks and activities.
- Demonstrates eagerness to learn about and discuss a range of topics, ideas, and tasks.
- Asks questions and seeks new information.

Modifications: Children with mobility issues may need assistance getting onto a beach chair or lying down on a towel. Provide pretend watercraft with appropriate support.

Including Families: Ask families to share photos from their trips to the beach.

ROCK HUNT

Ecosystems: All • **Age group:** Three and up • **Group size:** Small or large group

Objectives

- Develop appreciation for rocks and minerals
- Notice differences between rocks
- Make connections between books and personal experience

Materials

☐ *Everybody Needs a Rock* by Byrd Baylor (see appendix 2)

☐ Chart paper

☐ Markers

Directions

1. Read the story *Everybody Needs a Rock* by Byrd Baylor.

2. Ask children what rules they think are important for finding your own rock. Write their ideas on chart paper. You can suggest some of the rules from the story and see if the children agree.

3. Ask children to find the pocket they will use for the rock they choose. This will help them remember to select one rock.

4. Take the children to find a rock. If children pick up more than one, ask them which one they will keep. Ask open-ended and probing questions about the rocks they see, rocks they like, and why.

5. Ensure that each child has a rock before the children return to school or that the child is sure that he or she doesn't want one.

6. Regather the group to share their rocks and invite children to say what they like about their rocks.

Related Standards

NAEYC Accreditation

- 2.G.02 P-K Children are provided varied opportunities and materials to learn key content and principles of science, such as the difference between living and nonliving things (e.g., plants versus rocks); life cycles of various organisms (e.g., plants, butterflies, humans); earth and sky (e.g., seasons; weather; geologic features; light and shadow; and sun, moon, and stars); structure and property of matter (e.g., characteristics that include concepts such as hard and soft, floating and sinking); and the behavior of materials (e.g., transformation of liquids and solids by dissolving or melting).

- 2.G.04 P-K Children are provided varied opportunities to use simple tools to observe objects and scientific phenomena. Simple tools include materials such as bug boxes, binoculars, magnifying glasses, gears, levers, and can be many other tools as well.

- 2.G.06 P-K Children are provided varied opportunities and materials that encourage them to think, question, and reason about observed and inferred phenomena.

- 2.G.07 P-K Children are provided varied opportunities and materials that encourage them to discuss scientific concepts in everyday conversation. Scientific concepts include things such as life cycles of organisms; structure and property of matter (hard, soft; floating/not floating; transformation of liquids and solids); speed; weather, seasons, time; light and shadow.

- 2.G.08 P-K Children are provided varied opportunities and materials that help them learn and use scientific terminology and vocabulary associated with the content areas.

- 5.A.06 I-T-P-K Children of all ages have daily opportunities for outdoor play (when weather, air quality, and environmental safety conditions do not pose a health risk).

Modifications: Children with gross-motor disabilities may need an adaptation to move safely on rocky terrain. Also, be sensitive to cultural issues regarding rocks—for example, taking a rock and moving it to another place can be culturally insensitive in Hawaii.

Including Families: Share the plan with families beforehand. If families do not understand the activity, they may expect their child to throw the rock away.

INVESTIGATING ROCKS

Ecosystems: All • **Age group:** Two and up • **Group size:** Small group

Objectives

- Increase interest in minerals through noticing differences
- Develop skills in using scientific tools
- Developing sensory awareness

Materials

- ☐ A variety of rocks of different sizes, colors, textures, weights, and composition. Pumice stones, rocks with mica embedded, gravel, slate, and pyrite are all good types to include.
- ☐ Balance scale
- ☐ Small food scale
- ☐ Paint cups with water and small brushes
- ☐ Magnifying glasses
- ☐ Small makeup brushes
- ☐ Reference books on rocks, gems, and minerals
- ☐ Journals and markers for children to log their discoveries

Directions

1. Alert children to the rock investigation center. Allow them to work for as long as they are interested.

2. If equipment is new for some children, provide individual explanations and instructions as needed rather than boring children with an explanation at group time.

3. Provide scaffolding for children based on their interest. Ask open-ended questions, such as "What did you notice about that rock?" Invite children to make predictions, such as "Which one do you think is heavier?" as well as to evaluate their results. For children who are interested in drawing and writing, invite them to document their discoveries.

Related Standards

NAEYC Accreditation

- 2.G.02 P-K Children are provided varied opportunities and materials to learn key content and principles of science, such as the difference between living and nonliving things (e.g., plants versus rocks); life cycles of various organisms (e.g., plants, butterflies, humans); earth and sky (e.g., seasons; weather; geologic features; light and shadow; and sun, moon, and stars); structure and property of matter (e.g., characteristics that include concepts such as hard and soft, floating and sinking); and the behavior of materials (e.g., transformation of liquids and solids by dissolving or melting).

- 2.G.04 P-K Children are provided varied opportunities to use simple tools to observe objects and scientific phenomena. Simple tools include materials such as bug boxes, binoculars, magnifying glasses, gears, levers, and can be many other tools as well.

- 2.G.06 P-K Children are provided varied opportunities and materials that encourage them to think, question, and reason about observed and inferred phenomena.

- 2.G.07 P-K Children are provided varied opportunities and materials that encourage them to discuss scientific concepts in everyday conversation. Scientific concepts include things such as life cycles of organisms; structure and property of matter (hard, soft; floating/not floating; transformation of liquids and solids); speed; weather, seasons, time; light and shadow.

- 2.G.08 P-K Children are provided varied opportunities and materials that help them learn and use scientific terminology and vocabulary associated with the content areas.

Modifications

- Children with visual disabilities will benefit from a large lighted magnifying glass, the type used by crafters.
- Children who struggle with impulsivity would need an adult close enough to stop a rock from being thrown.

- Provide close supervision when using rocks that are small enough to be choking hazards.

Including Families: Create a class book or documentation panel for children to share with their families.

GROUPING ROCKS

Ecosystems: All · **Age group:** Three and up · **Group size:** Small group

Objectives

- Increase appreciation for rocks through noticing similarities
- Develop understanding that the same mineral can look different depending on its state (raw, polished, cut, used in jewelry, etc.)
- Develop discrimination skills through sorting and classifying

Materials

- ☐ A variety of minerals such as quartz, pyrite, mica, or agate
- ☐ Minerals in different states, including rough rocks, polished rocks, cut rocks, and gems in jewelry
- ☐ Photos of each type of mineral in a variety of states

Directions

To set up the center, prepare a table with baskets or other containers for each type of mineral with the photo displayed near the container. Place a variety of minerals in a larger basket. Provide enough magnifying glasses for the number of children who will take part in the activity at one time.

1. During group time, read a story about rocks, gems, and minerals, such as *Rocks* by Robin Nelson (see appendix 2).

2. Alert children to the activity choice of rock classification.

3. Ask probing questions to help children focus on similarities between rocks and between individual rocks and photos. You can also guide children through making observations, such as "Look, when I hold this one up to the light, it sparkles. Are there any others that do that?"

4. Focus on the investigation process rather than correct classification.

Related Standards

Head Start Early Learning Outcomes Framework

Social Studies Knowledge and Skills: The understanding of the relationship between people and the environment in which they live.

- Recognizes aspects of the environment, such as roads, buildings, trees, gardens, bodies of water, or land formations.

Scientific Skills and Methods: The skills to observe and collect information and to use it to ask questions, predict, explain, and draw conclusions.

- Uses senses and tools, including technology, to gather information, investigate materials, and observe processes and relationships.
- Observes and discusses common properties, differences, and comparisons among objects.
- Participates in simple investigations to form hypotheses, gather observations, draw conclusions, and form generalizations.
- Describes and discusses predictions, explanations, and generalizations based on past experience.

Conceptual Knowledge of the Natural and Physical World: The acquisition of concepts and facts related to the natural and physical world and the understanding of naturally occurring relationships.

- Observes, describes, and discusses living things and natural processes.
- Observes, describes, and discusses properties of materials and transformation of substances.

Modifications: Children with visual impairments will need large pictures and/or the activity could be modified as a purely tactile activity with grouping based on touch.

Including Families

- Make a documentation panel of children's discoveries.
- Invite parents to send in minerals for children to examine at school.

BUILDING A SNOW FORT

Ecosystems: Snowy environments • **Age group:** Three and up • **Group size:** Small or large group

Objectives

- Deeper understanding of snow, including how it compacts, how it responds to water, and how it provides insulation from the cold
- Focused play and attention over several hours
- Deeper understanding of sequence

Materials

☐ Snow shovels

☐ Three to four 2-foot-long thin sticks or wooden dowels

Directions

Make several piles of snow on the playground and put cones around one of them to help children get used to not climbing on the one that will be used for a snow fort. This will also give teachers an opportunity to see the interest in snow piles, who may need closer support to not step on the protected one, and how many piles may need to be created. It will take a while to dig out the structure so it is large enough for children and possibly adults to play inside. Be sure it will stay near or below freezing for several days to make it worth the work.

1. Pile snow at least as tall as the children. Any snow can be used for this, but heavy wet snow can take longer to pile because of its weight. Make sure the pile is about twice as wide as it is tall.

2. Allow snow to set for 24 hours. This allows the water molecules to solidify a little bit and will make a much stronger structure.

3. Place a thin, long stick or wooden dowel (at least 2 feet) into the top of the structure about 8–12 inches. If you have a few, that is even better, and you can also do one on each side of the structure. This will allow you to let children do most of the digging out of the hole without them going

through the walls or the sides since they will be able to see when they are getting close.

4. If you have a lot of snow, building more than one fort is best, and you can make a few that are tunnels instead of forts. This can be a good introduction to the structures for children or teachers who may be uncomfortable going into a snow-built structure for the first time.

Related Standards

Head Start Early Learning Outcomes Framework

Social Studies Knowledge and Skills: The understanding of the relationship between people and the environment in which they live.

- Recognizes aspects of the environment, such as roads, buildings, trees, gardens, bodies of water, or land formations.
- Recognizes that people share the environment with other people, animals, and plants.
- Understands that people can take care of the environment through activities, such as recycling.

Scientific Skills and Methods: The skills to observe and collect information and to use it to ask questions, predict, explain, and draw conclusions.

- Uses senses and tools, including technology, to gather information, investigate materials, and observe processes and relationships.
- Observes and discusses common properties, differences, and comparisons among objects.
- Participates in simple investigations to form hypotheses, gather observations, draw conclusions, and form generalizations.
- Describes and discusses predictions, explanations, and generalizations based on past experience.

Conceptual Knowledge of the Natural and Physical World: The acquisition of concepts and facts related to the natural and physical world and the understanding of naturally occurring relationships.

- Observes, describes, and discusses living things and natural processes.
- Observes, describes, and discusses properties of materials and transformation of substances.

Modifications: Build a snow slide or tunnel for those children uncomfortable with small enclosed spaces.

Including Families: Ask families to help with stacking snow, especially if they have a snowblower, which can help you get a head start and possibly build a small snow village with several snow forts. This can be done after school or on weekends, which may allow families who normally can't volunteer to help at school.

DEEP-FRIED DANDELIONS

Ecosystems: All • **Age group:** Three and up • **Group size:** Small group

Objectives

- Give children an opportunity to learn about wild edibles
- Give children an opportunity to cook.

Materials

- ☐ Dandelions in bloom
- ☐ Colander
- ☐ Electric frying pan or stove top with a quart-sized pan or pot
- ☐ Vegetable oil
- ☐ Batter (can be pancake or tempura) that meets the allergy needs of the group (A recipe for an easy batter can be found in appendix 6.)
- ☐ Cinnamon and sugar mixture for coating (optional)
- ☐ Two bowls (one for batter and one for cinnamon and sugar mixture)
- ☐ Two cookie sheets (one for uncooked flowers and one for cooked flowers lined with paper towels)

Directions

1. Collect dandelion flowers.
2. Wash the flowers and let them dry in a colander or dry them with a paper towel.
3. Have the children mix the batter.
4. When the dandelions are dry, have the children dip the dandelions and set them on a cookie sheet.
5. In a frying pan (electric or on the stove top) heat ½ inch of vegetable oil (once the oil begins heating, children will not be allowed near the frying pan).
6. When the children have dipped several flowers, place 3–4 in the vegetable oil and fry until golden brown on both sides.
7. When they are golden brown on both sides, remove them from the pan and dip them in the cinnamon and sugar mixture.
8. Allow to cool on a cookie sheet with paper towels.
9. Serve when completely cool.

Related Standards

NAEYC Accreditation

- 2.G.03 P-K Children are provided varied opportunities and materials that encourage them to use the five senses to observe, explore, and experiment with scientific phenomena.
- 2.K.02 T-P-K Children are provided varied opportunities and materials to help them learn about nutrition, including identifying sources of food and recognizing, preparing, eating, and valuing healthy foods.
- 5.A.06 I-T-P-K Children of all ages have daily opportunities for outdoor play (when weather, air quality, and environmental safety conditions do not pose a health risk).

Modifications: Have support nearby to help children with special needs collect dandelions and dip them in batter.

Including Families: Using family volunteers with this activity helps with supervision and gives a novel experience to families.

APPENDIX 2

CHILDREN'S BOOKS

Book Title	INTRODUCTION	INDIVIDUALIZATION	INDOORS	OUTDOORS	WEATHER	WATER	ROCKS, SAND, & SOIL	PLANTS	BUGS	BIRDS	REPTILES & AMPHIBIANS	MAMMALS	AQUATIC LIFE	HABITATS	FAMILIES
About Birds: A Guide for Children by Cathryn Sill. 1997. Atlanta: Peachtree Publishers.				●						●					
Among the Flowers by David M. Schwartz. 1997. Cypress, CA: Creative Teaching Press.				●				●							
Angus and the Ducks by Marjorie Flack. 1930. New York: Doubleday.				●						●		●			
Animal Babies in Ponds and Rivers by Jennifer Schofield. 2004. London: Kingfisher.				●									●		
Animal Homes: Pop-Up Book by Jeffrey Terreson. 1989. Washington, DC: National Geographic Society.				●										●	
Animals Born Alive and Well by Ruth Heller. 1989. New York: Scholastic.												●			●
Animals Should Definitely Not Wear Clothing by Judi Barrett. 1970. New York: Atheneum Books for Young Readers.	●														●
Apple Farmer Annie by Monica Wellington. 2001. New York: Dutton.								●							
Apple Tree by Barrie Watts. 1987. Englewood Cliffs, NJ: Silver Burdett Press.				●				●							
Are You a Butterfly? by Judy Allen. 2000. London: Kingfisher.				●					●						
Awesome Amphibians by Jeff Bauer. 2009. New York: Scholastic.				●							●				
Be Good to Eddie Lee by Virginia Fleming. 1993. New York: Philomel Books.		●													
Be Nice to Spiders by Margaret Bloy Graham. 1967. New York: HarperCollins.			●	●					●						
Beaks! by Sneed B. Collard III. 2002. Watertown, MA: Charlesbridge.				●						●					
Beans to Chocolate by Inez Snyder. 2003. New York: Children's Press.								●							
Before After by Matthias Arégui and Anne-Margot Ramstein. 2014. Somerville, MA: Candlewick Press.								●	●	●	●	●	●		
Better Move On, Frog! by Ron Maris. 1982. Livermore, CA: Discovery Toys.				●							●				
The Bird Alphabet Book by Jerry Pallotta. 1986. Watertown, MA: Charlesbridge.				●						●					
Birds, Nests and Eggs by Mel Boring. 1996. Minocqua, WI: NorthWord Press.				●						●					
Blueberries for Sal by Robert McCloskey. 1948. New York: Viking.				●				●							
Bluestem Horizon: A Story of a Tallgrass Prairie by Evelyn Lee. 1998. Norwalk, CT: Soundprints.				●				●				●		●	

Book Title	INTRODUCTION	INDIVIDUALIZATION	INDOORS	OUTDOORS	WEATHER	WATER	ROCKS, SAND, & SOIL	PLANTS	BUGS	BIRDS	REPTILES & AMPHIBIANS	MAMMALS	AQUATIC LIFE	HABITATS	FAMILIES
Box Turtle at Long Pond by William T. George. 1989. New York: Greenwillow Books.				●							●				
The Bug Book by Kathy Kranking. 1998. New York: Golden Books.				●					●						
Bugs, Bugs, Bugs! by Mary Reid and Betsey Chessen. 1998. New York: Scholastic.				●					●						
Bumblebee, Bumblebee, Do You Know Me?: A Garden Guessing Game by Anne Rockwell. 1999. New York: HarperCollins.				●					●						
Busy Chickens by John Schindel. 2009. New York: Tricycle Press.				●						●					
Butterfly by Susan Canizares. 1998. New York: Scholastic.				●					●						
Butterfly and Moth by Paul Whalley. 1988. New York: Knopf.				●					●						
Cactus Café by Kathleen Weidner Zoehfeld. 1997. Norwalk, CT: Soundprint.				●	●			●						●	
Cactus Hotel by Brenda Z. Guiberson. 1991. New York: Henry Holt.				●	●			●							
The Carrot Seed by Ruth Krauss. 1945. New York: HarperCollins.				●				●							●
Chameleon! by Joy Cowley. 2005. New York: Scholastic.									●						
The Chick and the Duckling by Mirra Ginsburg. 1988. New York: Aladdin Paperbacks.				●		●				●					
Chickens Aren't the Only Ones by Ruth Heller. 1981. New York: Grosset & Dunlap.									●	●	●		●		
Clouds by Anne Rockwell. 2008. New York: HarperCollins.				●	●										
Come On, Rain! by Karen Hesse. 1999. New York: Scholastic.				●	●										
Compost Stew by Mary McKenna Siddals. 2010. Berkley, CA: Tricycle Press.			●	●				●							
A Cool Drink of Water by Barbara Kerley. 2002. Washington, DC: National Geographic Society.				●		●									
Coral Reef by Susan Canizares and Mary Reid. 1998. New York: Scholastic.				●									●	●	
Curious about Fossils by Kate Waters. 2016. New York: Grosset & Dunlap.							●								
A Day at the Pumpkin Patch by Megan Faulkner and Adam Krawesky. 2006. New York: Scholastic.				●				●				●	●		
The Dead Bird by Margaret Wise Brown. 1938. New York: William Morrow & Co.				●						●					

Book Title	INTRODUCTION	INDIVIDUALIZATION	INDOORS	OUTDOORS	WEATHER	WATER	ROCKS, SAND, & SOIL	PLANTS	BUGS	BIRDS	REPTILES & AMPHIBIANS	MAMMALS	AQUATIC LIFE	HABITATS	FAMILIES
Desert Giant: The World of the Saguaro by Barbara Bash. 2010. San Francisco: Sierra Club Books for Children.								●							
A Dolphin Is Not a Fish by Betsey Chessen and Pamela Chanko. 1998. New York: Scholastic.				●								●	●		
A Drop of Water by Gordon Morrison. 2006. New York: Houghton Mifflin.				●	●	●									
Earthquakes by Deborah Heiligman. 2002. New York: Scholastic.				●			●								
Eating the Alphabet by Lois Ehlert. 1996. New York: HMH Books for Young Readers.								●							
The Eensy-Weensy Spider by Mary Ann Hoberman. 2000. Boston: Little, Brown.				●					●						
An Egg Is Quiet by Dianna Hutts Aston. 2006. San Francisco: Chronicle Books.				●					●	●	●				
Emergency! by Gail Gibbons. 1995. New York: Holiday House.					●										
Evergreens Are Green by Susan Canizares. 1998. New York: Scholastic.								●							
Everybody Needs a Rock by Byrd Baylor. 1985. New York: Aladdin Paperbacks.				●			●								
The Fascinating World of Bats by Maria Angels Julivert. 1994. New York: Barron's.				●								●			
The Fascinating World of Beetles by Maria Angels Julivert. 1995. New York: Barron's.				●					●						
Feathers: Not Just for Flying by Melissa Stewart. 2014. Watertown, MA: Charlesbridge.										●					
A First Look at Nature Book: The Frog by Angela Sheehan. 1976. New York: Warwick Press.				●							●				
Fish by Gallimard Jeunesse. First Discovery Book series. 1998. New York: Scholastic.				●		●							●	●	
Fish Is Fish by Leo Lionni. 2015. New York: Random House.				●		●							●		
Flashlight by Lizi Boyd. 2014. San Francisco: Chronicle Books.			●	●	●										
Flies Are Fascinating! by Valerie Wilkinson. 1994. Chicago: Children's Press.									●						
Flowers by Melanie Mitchell. 2004. Minneapolis: Lerner Publishing.				●				●							
The Fossil Girl: Mary Anning's Dinosaur Discovery by Catherine Brighton. 1999. London: Frances Lincoln.				●			●								
Frogs by Gail Gibbons. 1993. New York: Holiday House.				●							●				

Book Title	INTRODUCTION	INDIVIDUALIZATION	INDOORS	OUTDOORS	WEATHER	WATER	ROCKS, SAND, & SOIL	PLANTS	BUGS	BIRDS	REPTILES & AMPHIBIANS	MAMMALS	AQUATIC LIFE	HABITATS	FAMILIES
Frogs, Toads, and Turtles by Diane Burns. 1997. Minocqua, WI: NorthWord Press.				●							●				
From Seed to Plant by Gail Gibbons. 1991. New York: Holiday House.								●							
From Tadpole to Frog by Kathleen Weidner Zoehfeld. 2001. New York: Scholastic.											●				
A Fruit Is a Suitcase for Seeds by Jean Richards. 2002. Minneapolis: Millbrook Press.								●							
Gilberto and the Wind by Marie Hall Ets. 1978. New York: Puffin.				●	●										
Going Home: The Mystery of Animal Migration by Marianne Berkes. 2010. Nevada City, CA: Dawn Publications.										●		●	●	●	
Going to the Tide Pools in Hawaii Nei by Joy S. Au. 1995. Honolulu: Mutual Publishing.				●		●							●	●	
The Goodnight Gecko by Gill McBarnet. 1991. Pu'unene, HI: Ruwanga Trading.				●							●				
The Growing-Up Tree by Vera Rosenberry. 2003. New York: Holiday House.				●				●							
Growing Vegetable Soup by Lois Ehlert. 1987. San Diego: Harcourt Books.								●							
A Gull's Story: A Tale of Learning about Life, the Shore, and the ABCs by Frank Finale. 2002. Bay Head, NJ: Jersey Shore Publishing.				●						●			●		
Hide and Seek Fog by Alvin Tresselt. 1965. New York: HarperCollins.				●	●										
Home by Carson Ellis. 2015. Somerville, MA: Candlewick Press.			●	●										●	
Honeybees by National Geographic Society. 1973. Washington, DC: National Geographic Society.				●					●						
The Honey Makers by Gail Gibbons. 1996. New York: Morrow Junior Books.				●					●						
Hop Frog by Rick Chrustowski. 2003. New York: Henry Holt.				●							●				
I Can Read about Earthquakes and Volcanoes by Deborah Merrians. 1996. New York: Troll Communications.				●			●								
I Love Guinea Pigs: Read and Wonder by Dick King-Smith. 2001. Somerville, MA: Candlewick Press.												●			
I Went Walking by Sue Williams. 1996. San Diego: Harcourt.				●								●			
I Wish I Had a Pet by Maggie Rudy. 2014. New York: Beach Lane Books.															●
If You Find a Rock by Peggy Christian. 2008. Orlando: Harcourt.							●								

Book Title	INTRODUCTION	INDIVIDUALIZATION	INDOORS	OUTDOORS	WEATHER	WATER	ROCKS, SAND, & SOIL	PLANTS	BUGS	BIRDS	REPTILES & AMPHIBIANS	MAMMALS	AQUATIC LIFE	HABITATS	FAMILIES
I'm a Pill Bug by Yukihisa Tokuda. 2006. La Jolla, CA: Kane/Miller Book Publishers.			●	●											
In My Family/En mi familia by Carmen Lomas Garza. 2000. San Francisco: Children's Press.															●
In November by Cynthia Rylant. 2009. New York: Harcourt.				●	●							●		●	●
Incredible Plants edited by Barbara Taylor. 1997. London: DK Publishing.			●	●				●							
An Instant Guide to Reptiles and Amphibians by Pamela Forey and Cecilia Fitzsimons. 1987. New York: Gramercy Books.				●							●				
It Looked Like Spilt Milk by Charles G. Shaw. 1947. New York: Harper & Row.				●	●										
Jake the Gardener: Guide Dog Digs Treasure by E. S. Aardvark. 2006. Fort Bragg, NC: Macaronic Press.								●							
Jennie's Hat by Ezra Jack Keats. 1966. New York: Harper & Row.				●	●										
Jump, Frog, Jump! by Robert Kalan. 1989. New York: Greenwillow Books.				●		●					●		●		
Jungle Jack Hanna's Pocketful of Bugs by Jack Hanna. 1996. New York: Scholastic.				●					●						
Just Me by Marie Hall Ets. 1965. New York: Viking Press.				●						●		●			
Know Your Fishes in Hawai'i: A Fun Fish Identification Book for Kids by Wilfred Toki. 2005. Ewa Beach, HI: BeachHouse Publishing.				●		●							●		
Ladybugs and Other Insects by Pascale de Bourgoing, Gallimard Jeunesse, and Sylvaine Perols. First Discovery Book series. 1991. New York: Cartwheel Books.				●					●						
Leaves by Melanie Mitchell. 2004. Minneapolis: Lerner Publications.				●				●							
Let's Get Turtles by Millicent E. Selsam. 1965. New York: Harper & Row.											●				
Let's Go Rock Collecting by Roma Gans. 1997. New York: HarperCollins.				●			●								
A Letter to Amy by Ezra Jack Keats. 1968. New York: Viking Press.				●	●										
The Life and Times of the Ant by Charles Micucci. 2003. Boston: Houghton Mifflin.				●					●						
Light (Science Emergent Readers) by Samantha Berger. 1998. New York: Scholastic.			●	●	●										
The Little Composter by Jan Gerardi. 2010. New York: Random House.				●					●						
The Little Lamb by Judy Dunn. 1977. New York: Random House.				●								●			

Book Title	INTRODUCTION	INDIVIDUALIZATION	INDOORS	OUTDOORS	WEATHER	WATER	ROCKS, SAND, & SOIL	PLANTS	BUGS	BIRDS	REPTILES & AMPHIBIANS	MAMMALS	AQUATIC LIFE	HABITATS	FAMILIES
Looking for a Moose by Phyllis Root. 2006. Somerville, MA: Candlewick Press.				●								●		●	
Make Way for Ducklings by Robert McCloskey. 1941. New York: Viking Press.				●						●				●	
Mama Built a Little Nest by Jennifer Ward. 2014. New York: Beach Lane Books.				●						●					
Max and the Tag-Along Moon by Floyd Cooper. 2013. New York: Philomel Books.				●											
McDuff Moves In by Rosemary Wells. 1997. New York: Hyperion Books.			●									●		●	●
Meeting Trees by Scott Russell Sanders. 1997. Washington, DC: National Geographic Society.				●				●							
Miss Rumphius by Barbara Cooney. 1982. New York: Viking.	●	●		●				●							
Mister Seahorse by Eric Carle. 2004. London: Puffin Books.													●		●
The Mitten by Jan Brett. 1989. New York: G.P. Putnam's Sons.				●	●							●		●	●
Momo's Kitten by Mitsu and Tarō Yashima. 1961. New York: Viking Press.												●		●	●
Moonbear's Shadow by Frank Asch. 2000. New York: Aladdin Paperbacks.				●											
Moon Dance by Christian Riese Lassen. 2005. Carlsbad, CA: Penton Overseas.				●											
Muddypaws by Moira Butterfield. 2008. New York: Parragon.					●							●		●	
My Hawaiin Farm by Pearl Maxner. 2005. Waipahu, HI: Island Heritage Publishing.								●						●	
My Night Forest by Roy Owen. 1994. New York: Four Winds Press.								●						●	
Natural Objects by Mir Tamim Ansary. 1997. Crystal Lake, IL: Rigby Interactive Library.							●	●	●					●	
A Nest Is Noisy by Dianna Hutts Aston. 2015. San Francisco: Chronicle Books.				●						●				●	
Next Time You See a Seashell by Emily Morgan. 2012. Arlington: NSTA Kids Press.				●									●		
Next Time You See a Sunset by Emily Morgan. 2012. Arlington, VA: NSTA Kids Press.				●										●	
Night Creatures by Gallimard Jeunesse and Sylvaine Peyrols. First Discovery Series. 1998. New York: Scholastic.				●					●	●		●			
Not a Stick by Antoinette Portis. 2006. New York: HarperCollins.								●							

Book Title	INTRODUCTION	INDIVIDUALIZATION	INDOORS	OUTDOORS	WEATHER	WATER	ROCKS, SAND, & SOIL	PLANTS	BUGS	BIRDS	REPTILES & AMPHIBIANS	MAMMALS	AQUATIC LIFE	HABITATS	FAMILIES
Ocean: A Photicular Book by Dan Kainen and Carol Kaufmann. 2014. New York: Workman.				●		●							●	●	
The Ocean Alphabet Board Book by Jerry Pallotta. 2003. Watertown, MA: Charlesbridge.				●		●							●		
One-Dog Canoe by Mary Casanova. 1999. DK Publishing.				●	●										
An Orange in January by Dianna Hutts Aston. 2007. New York: Penguin.					●			●						●	
Over in the Ocean: In a Coral Reef by Marianne Berkes. 2004. Nevada City: Dawn Publications.				●		●							●		
Owl Moon by Jane Yolen. 1987. New York: Philomel Books.			●							●					
Pet Show! by Ezra Jack Keats. 1972. London: Hamish Hamilton.			●						●	●		●			
Planting a Rainbow by Lois Ehlert. 1998. New York: Harcourt.				●											
Play with Me by Marie Hall Ets. 1955. New York: Viking.	●	●		●										●	
Pond Life by George K. Reid. Golden Guides from St. Martin's Press. 2001. New York: St. Martin's Press.				●		●							●	●	
Pop-Up Tadpole to Frog by Elizabeth Rodger. 1996. New York: Scholastic.				●							●				
Questions and Answers about Bees by Betty Polisar Reigot. 1983. New York: Scholastic.				●					●						
Rain by Robert Kalan. 1978. New York: Greenwillow Books.				●	●	●									
Rain Feet by Angela Johnson. 1994. New York: Orchard Books.				●	●	●								●	
The Reason for a Flower: A Book about Flowers, Pollen, and Seeds by Ruth Heller. 1983. New York: Puffin Books.				●				●	●						
Riley's Pockets by Nicole Winter Tietel. 2015. Edina, MN: Beaver's Pond Press.				●											●
River of Life by Debbie S. Miller. 2000. New York: Clarion Books.				●		●									
A Rock Can Be . . . by Laura Purdie Salas. 2015. Minneapolis: Millbrook Press.				●			●								
A Rock Is Lively by Dianna Hutts Aston. 2012. San Francisco: Chronicle Books.				●			●								
Rocks by Robin Nelson. 2005. Minneapolis: Lerner.				●			●								
Rocks: Hard, Soft, Smooth, and Rough by Natalie M. Rosinsky. Amazing Science Books. 2003. Mankato, MN: Picture Window Books.				●			●								

Book Title	INTRODUCTION	INDIVIDUALIZATION	INDOORS	OUTDOORS	WEATHER	WATER	ROCKS, SAND, & SOIL	PLANTS	BUGS	BIRDS	REPTILES & AMPHIBIANS	MAMMALS	AQUATIC LIFE	HABITATS	FAMILIES
Rocks, Rocks, Big and Small by Joanne Barkan. 1990. Englewood Cliffs, NJ: Silver Burdett Press.				●			●								
Roots by Melanie Mitchell. 2004. Minneapolis: Lerner.				●				●							
Round Trip by Ann Jonas. 1990. San Diego: Harcourt School Publishers.				●											
Roxaboxen by Alice McLerran. 1991. New York: HarperCollins.				●			●								
The Salamander Room by Anne Mazer. 1994. New York: Dragonfly Books.			●	●					●	●	●			●	●
Sally Goes to the Vet by Stephen Huneck. 2004. New York: Harry N. Abrams Books.			●									●			
Sand to Sea: Marine Life of Hawaii by Stephanie Feeney and Anne Fielding. 1989. Honolulu: University of Hawai'i Press.				●	●	●	●						●	●	
Sea Creatures by Pamela Chanko. 1998. New York: Scholastic.				●		●							●	●	
Seashells, Crabs and Sea Stars: Take-Along Guide by Christiane Kump Tibbitts. 1999. Minocqua, WI: NorthWord Press.				●		●							●	●	
See-Through Reptiles by Steve Parker. 2004. Philadelphia: Running Press.				●							●				
Seeds by Melanie Mitchell. 2004. Minneapolis: Lerner.				●				●							
Shadows and Reflections by Tana Hoban. 1990. New York: Greenwillow Books.				●	●										
Silkworms by Sylvia A. Johnson. 1982. Minneapolis: Lerner.				●					●					●	
The Skeleton Book: An Inside Look at Animals by Madeleine Livaudais and Robert Dunne. 1972. New York: Scholastic.										●	●	●	●		
The Skull Alphabet Book by Jerry Pallotta. 2002. Watertown, MA: Charlesbridge.										●		●			
Snails by Jens Olesen. 1985. Englewood Cliffs, NJ: Silver Burdett Press.				●					●						
Snakes and Lizards by Daniel Moreton and Pamela Chanko. 1998. New York: Scholastic.				●							●			●	
Snakes, Salamanders, and Lizards by Diane Burns. 1995. Minocqua, WI: NorthWord Press.											●				
The Snowy Day by Ezra Jack Keats. 1996. New York: Viking.	●			●	●									●	
Southwest Desert Wildlife. 1988. Mesa, AZ: Smith-Southwestern.				●				●	●	●	●	●		●	
Squeek Goes Adventuring by Olga Wierbicki. 2016. St. Louis, MO: McDonald & Associates Publishing.	●													●	●

Book Title	INTRODUCTION	INDIVIDUALIZATION	INDOORS	OUTDOORS	WEATHER	WATER	ROCKS, SAND, & SOIL	PLANTS	BUGS	BIRDS	REPTILES & AMPHIBIANS	MAMMALS	AQUATIC LIFE	HABITATS	FAMILIES
Starfish by Edith Thacher Hurd. 2000. New York: HarperCollins.				●		●							●		
Stems by Melanie Mitchell. 2004. Minneapolis: Lerner.				●				●							
The Stick Book: Loads of Things You Can Make or Do with a Stick by Fiona Danks and Jo Schofield. 2012. London: Frances Lincoln Children's Books.				●				●							
The Story of Hina by Patrick Ching. 1998. Waipahu, HI: Island Heritage Publishing.				●								●	●	●	
The Stray Dog by Marc Simont. 2001. New York: HarperCollins.			●	●								●		●	●
Sun by Daniel Moreton and Susan Canizares. 1998. New York: Scholastic.				●	●										
Sun and Rain: Exploring Seasons in Hawaii by Stephanie Feeney. 2008. Honolulu: University of Hawai'i Press.				●	●	●	●	●							
Sunflower House by Eve Bunting. 1997. New York: Scholastic.				●				●							
Super Spiders by Jason Blake. 2006. New York: Scholastic.				●					●						
A Swim through the Sea by Kristin Joy Pratt-Serafini. 1994. Nevada City, CA: Dawn Publications.				●		●							●		
Thunder Cake by Patricia Polacco. 1997. New York: Puffin Books.			●	●	●										●
The Tiny Seed by Eric Carle. 1991. New York: Simon & Schuster Books for Young Readers.				●	●			●							
To Be a Bee by Ellsworth Rosen. 1969. Boston: Houghton Mifflin.				●					●						
Tomatoes to Ketchup by Inez Snyder. 2003. New York: Children's Press.								●							
Tough Boris by Mem Fox. 1998. New York: HMH Books for Young Readers.		●													
Trash! by Charlotte Wilcox. 1988. Minneapolis: Carolrhoda Books.	●		●	●											
The Tree Farmer by Chuck Leavell and Nicholas Cravotta. 2005. Lorton, VA: VSP Books.				●				●							
A Tree Is Growing by Arthur Dorros. 1997. New York: Scholastic.				●				●							
Trees to Paper by Inez Snyder. 2003. New York: Children's Press.								●							
Twilight Comes Twice by Ralph Fletcher. 1997. New York: Clarion Books.				●											
Ultimate Explorer Field Guide: Rocks and Minerals by Nancy Honovich. 2016. Washington, DC: National Geographic Kids.				●			●								

Book Title	INTRODUCTION	INDIVIDUALIZATION	INDOORS	OUTDOORS	WEATHER	WATER	ROCKS, SAND, & SOIL	PLANTS	BUGS	BIRDS	REPTILES & AMPHIBIANS	MAMMALS	AQUATIC LIFE	HABITATS	FAMILIES
The Umbrella by Jan Brett. 2004. New York: G.P. Putnam's Sons Books for Young Readers.				●	●	●						●			
Umbrella by Tarō Yashima. 1958. New York: Viking.				●	●	●									●
Volcanoes by Lily Wood. 2000. New York: Scholastic.				●			●								
Wait! Wait! by Hatsue Nakawaki. 2013. New York: Enchanted Lion.				●		●			●	●	●	●	●		
Water by Susan Canizares and Pamela Chanko. 1998. New York: Scholastic.				●		●									
The Water Princess by Susan Verde. 2016. New York: G.P. Putnam's Sons Books for Young Readers.				●		●								●	●
Wave by Suzy Lee. 2008. San Francisco: Chronicle Books.				●	●	●							●		
What Do Insects Do? by Susan Canizares and Pamela Chanko. 1998. New York: Scholastic.				●					●						
What is the Difference between a Frog and a Toad? by Mary Firestone. 2009. Mankato, MN: Picture Window Books.				●							●				
What Lives in a Shell? by Kathleen Weidner Zoehfeld. 1994. New York: HarperCollins.				●					●				●	●	
What Pete Ate from A–Z by Maira Kalman. 2003. New York: Puffin Books.												●			
When I Go Camping with Grandma by Marion Dane Bauer and Allen Garns. 1995. Mahwah, NJ: BridgeWater Books.				●											●
Where Does the Butterfly Go When It Rains? by May Garelick. 1961. New York: Scholastic.				●	●	●			●	●	●	●	●	●	
Where the Wild Things Are by Maurice Sendak. 1963. New York: Harper & Row.			●	●											●
Who Has This Tail? by Laura Hulbert. 2012. New York: Henry Holt.										●	●	●			
Whose Egg? by Lynette Evans. 2013. San Rafael, CA: Insight Kids.									●	●	●				
Whose Nest? by Victoria Cochrane. 2013. San Rafael, CA: Insight Kids.									●	●	●	●			
Why Does Lightning Strike?: Questions Children Ask about the Weather by Terry Martin. 1996. New York: DK Publishing.				●	●										
Wild Weather: Hurricanes! by Lorraine Jean Hopping. 1995. New York: Cartwheel Books.				●	●										
The Wind Blew by Pat Hutchins. 1974. New York: Scholastic.				●	●										
A Windy Day by Gilda Berger and Melvin Berger. 2003. New York: Scholastic.				●	●										

Book Title	INTRODUCTION	INDIVIDUALIZATION	INDOORS	OUTDOORS	WEATHER	WATER	ROCKS, SAND, & SOIL	PLANTS	BUGS	BIRDS	REPTILES & AMPHIBIANS	MAMMALS	AQUATIC LIFE	HABITATS	FAMILIES
A Windy Day by Robin Nelson. 2001. Minneapolis: Lerner.				●	●										
The Wonderful Journey by Gill McBarnet. 1986. Pu'unene, HI: Ruwanga Trading.				●		●						●	●		
Wonders of the Pond by Francine Sabin. 1982. Mahwah, NJ: Troll Communications.				●		●							●		
World's Weirdest Reptiles by M. L. Roberts. 1994. Mahwah, NJ: Watermill Press.				●							●				
You Belong Here by M. H. Clark. 2016. Seattle, WA: Compendium.														●	●
Yucky Worms by Vivian French. 2010. Somerville, MA: Candlewick Press.				●					●						

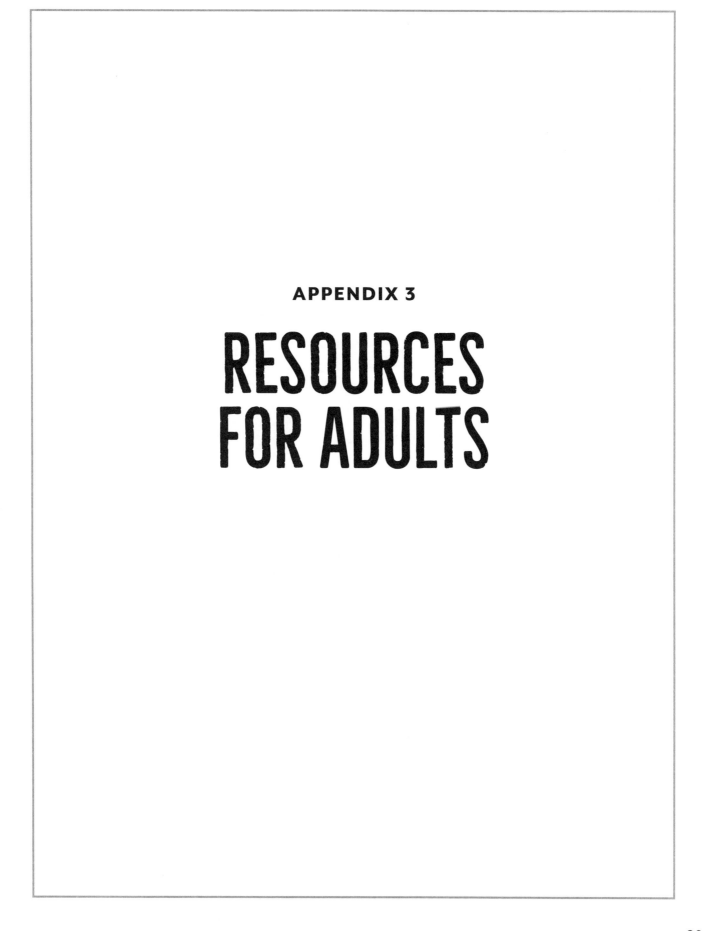

APPENDIX 3

RESOURCES FOR ADULTS

Book Title	INTRODUCTION	INDIVIDUALIZATION	INDOORS	OUTDOORS	WEATHER	WATER	ROCKS, SAND, & SOIL	PLANTS	BUGS	BIRDS	REPTILES & AMPHIBIANS	MAMMALS	AQUATIC LIFE	HABITATS	FAMILIES
Access Anything: I Can Do That! Adventuring with Disabilities by Andrea and Craig Kennedy. 2007. Parker, CO: Outskirts Press.	●	●													
Adventuring with Children: An Inspirational Guide to World Travel and the Outdoors by Nan Jeffrey. 1995. New York: Avalon House.	●	●		●											●
Babies in the Rain: Promoting Play, Exploration, and Discovery with Infants and Toddlers by Jeff A. Johnson. 2009. St. Paul, MN: Redleaf Press.				●	●	●								●	●
Babies Outdoors by Jan White and Glynn Galley. 2010. Siren Films.				●	●									●	●
Balanced and Barefoot: How Unrestricted Outdoor Play Makes for Strong, Confident, and Capable Children by Angela Hanscom. 2016. Old Saybrook, CT: Tantor Media.	●	●		●											●
Bird field guides: Check your local library or *Acorn Naturalists*.										●					
The Bird Watching Answer Book: Everything You Need to Know to Enjoy Birds in Your Backyard and Beyond by Laura Erickson. 2009. North Adams, MA: Storey Publishing.				●						●					
Black and Brown Faces in America's Wild Places: African Americans Making Nature and the Environment a Part of Their Everyday Lives by Dudley Edmonson. 2006. Cambridge, MN: Adventure Publications.	●	●		●											●
Black Faces, White Spaces: Reimagining the Relationship of African Americans to the Great Outdoors by Carolyn Finney. 2014. Chapel Hill: University of North Carolina Press.	●	●		●											
Care guides for specific animals: Check your local library or *Acorn Naturalists*.			●						●	●	●	●	●	●	
Celebrate Nature!: Activities for Every Season by Angela Schmidt Fishbaugh. 2011. St. Paul, MN: Redleaf Press.			●	●	●		●	●							
Colors of Nature: Culture, Identity, and the Natural World by Alison Hawthorne Deming and Lauret E. Savoy. 2002. Minneapolis, MN: Milkweed Editions.	●	●													●
Connecting Animals and Children in Early Childhood by Patty Born Selly. 2014. St. Paul, MN: Redleaf Press.	●	●	●	●					●	●	●	●		●	
Cultivating Outdoor Classrooms: Designing and Implementing Child-Centered Learning Environments by Eric Nelson. 2012. St. Paul, MN: Redleaf Press.				●											
Designs for Living and Learning: Transforming Early Childhood Environments by Margie Carter and Deb Curtis. 2003. St. Paul, MN: Redleaf Press.			●												

Book Title	INTRODUCTION	INDIVIDUALIZATION	INDOORS	OUTDOORS	WEATHER	WATER	ROCKS, SAND, & SOIL	PLANTS	BUGS	BIRDS	REPTILES & AMPHIBIANS	MAMMALS	AQUATIC LIFE	HABITATS	FAMILIES
Disaster Planning and Preparedness in Early Childhood and School-Age Care Settings by Charlotte M. Hendricks and Michele B. Pettibone. 2015. St. Paul, MN: Redleaf Press.	●		●	●											
Discovering Nature with Young Children Teacher's Guide by Ingrid Chalufour, Karen Worth, and Education Development Center, Inc. 2003. St. Paul. MN: Redleaf Press.	●	●													
The Early Sprouts Cookbook by Karrie Kalich, Lynn Arnold, Carole Russell. 2011. St. Paul, MN: Redleaf Press.	●														
Embracing Rough-and-Tumble Play Family Companion by Mike Huber. 2016. St. Paul, MN: Redleaf Press.	●	●	●	●											●
Establishing a Nature-Based Preschool by Rachel A. Larimore. 2011. Fort Collins, CO: InterpPress Books.	●														
Exploring Water with Young Children Teacher's Guide by Ingrid Chalufour, Karen Worth, and Education Development Center, Inc. 2005. St. Paul, MN: Redleaf Press.						●									
Field guide specific to your region: Check your local library or catalogs such as *Acorn Naturalists*.	●						●	●	●	●	●	●	●		
Field guide for reptiles and amphibians: Check your local library.											●				
Gardening with Young Children (Hollyhocks and Honeybees) by Sara Starbuck, Marla Olthof, and Karen Midden. 2nd edition. 2014. St. Paul, MN: Redleaf Press.				●				●							
The Great Outdoors: Restoring Children's Right to Play Outside by Mary S. Rivkin. 1995. Washington, DC: NAEYC.	●	●		●											
Green Thumbs: A Kid's Activity Guide to Indoor and Outdoor Gardening by Laurie M. Carlson. 1995. Chicago: Chicago Review Press.	●		●	●											
How to Raise a Wild Child: The Art and Science of Falling in Love with Nature by Scott Sampson. 2016. New York: Mariner Books.	●														●
I Love Dirt!: 52 Activities to Help You and Your Kids Discover the Wonders of Nature by Jennifer Ward. 2008. Boston: Trumpeter Books.							●								
I'm OK! Building Resistance through Physical Play by Jarrod Green. 2016. St. Paul, MN: Redleaf Press.	●	●													
Insect Adventures by J. Henri Fabre and Louise Seymore Hasbrouck. 2014. CreateSpace Independent Publishing.									●						

Book Title	INTRODUCTION	INDIVIDUALIZATION	INDOORS	OUTDOORS	WEATHER	WATER	ROCKS, SAND, & SOIL	PLANTS	BUGS	BIRDS	REPTILES & AMPHIBIANS	MAMMALS	AQUATIC LIFE	HABITATS	FAMILIES
Last Child in the Woods: Saving Our Children from Nature-Deficit Disorder by Richard Louv. 2005. Chapel Hill, NC: Algonquin Books.	●														●
Learning Gardens and Sustainability Education: Bringing Life to Schools and Schools to Life by Dilafruz Williams and Jonathan Brown. 2011. New York: Routledge.	●	●		●				●						●	
Learning in Bloom: Cultivating Outdoor Explorations by Ruth Wilson. 2016. Lewisville, NC: Gryphon House.	●	●	●	●											●
Leave No Child Inside: A Study of ECE Outdoor Program Environments by Ronda Rae. 2008. LinkedIn SlideShare. https://www.slideshare.net/RondaRae /leave-no-child-inside.	●	●		●											●
Lens on Outdoor Learning by Wendy Banning and Ginny Sullivan. 2010. St. Paul, MN: Redleaf Press.	●	●		●											
A Little Bit of Dirt: 55+ Science and Art Activities to Reconnect Children with Nature by Asia Citro. 2016. Seattle: Innovation Press.	●	●		●	●	●	●							●	●
Loose Parts: Inspiring Play in Young Children and *Loose Parts 2: Inspiring Play with Infants and Toddlers* by Lisa Daly and Miriam Beloglovsky. 2014; 2016. St. Paul, MN: Redleaf Press.			●	●											
Medical Emergencies in Early Childhood and School-Age Settings, Revised Edition by Charlotte Hendricks, PhD. 2016. St. Paul, MN: Redleaf Press.				●	●										
Moving and Learning with Your Child by Rae Pica. 2015. St. Paul, MN: Redleaf Press.	●	●													●
Mud Kitchen in a Day: How to Quickly Get Your Kids Outside, Playing in the Dirt, and Enjoying Creative Play by Jason Runkel Sperling. 2016. CreateSpace Independent Publishing.				●		●									
National Audubon Guide to Seashore Creatures: North America by Norman Meinkoth. 1981. New York: Knopf; Chanticleer Press.						●							●		
Nature for the Very Young: A Handbook of Indoor and Outdoor Activities by Marcia Bowden. 1989. Hoboken, NJ: John Wiley and Sons.	●		●	●											
Nature Preschools and Forest Kindergartens: The Handbook for Outdoor Learning by David Sobel. 2016. St. Paul, MN: Redleaf Press.	●														
Nature Ranger (Nature Activities) by Richard Walker. 2010. London: DK Publishing.				●											
The Outside Play and Learning Book: Activities for Young Children by Karen Miller. 1989. Lewisville, NC: Gryphon House.	●			●											

Book Title	INTRODUCTION	INDIVIDUALIZATION	INDOORS	OUTDOORS	WEATHER	WATER	ROCKS, SAND, & SOIL	PLANTS	BUGS	BIRDS	REPTILES & AMPHIBIANS	MAMMALS	AQUATIC LIFE	HABITATS	FAMILIES
Parent Engagement in Early Learning: Strategies for Working with Families by Julie Powers. 2nd edition. 2016. St. Paul, MN: Redleaf Press.	●														●
Pedagogy and Space: Design Inspirations for Early Childhood Classrooms by Linda M. Zane, EdD. 2015. St. Paul, MN: Redleaf Press.			●	●										●	
Pet Bugs: A Kids Guide to Catching and Keeping Touchable Insects by Sally Kneidel. 1994. New York: John Wiley and Sons.									●					●	
Pets in a Jar : Collecting and Caring for Small Wild Animals by Seymour Simon. 1975. New York: Viking Press.									●					●	
Plants (Wildlife Watchers) by Terry Jennings. 2009. Irvine, CA: QEB Publishing.								●							
Pond Life: An Introduction to Familiar Plants and Animals Living In or Near Ponds, Lakes, and Wetlands by James Kavanagh. 2003. Tampa, FL: Waterford Press.						●			●	●	●	●	●		
The Power of Physical Play by Siren Films and David Whitebread. 2015. St. Paul, MN: Redleaf Press. 2 DVDs, 114 min.	●	●	●	●											
Risk, Challenge and Adventure in the Early Years: A Practical Guide to Exploring and Extending Learning Outdoors by Kathryn Susan Solly. 2014. Abingdon, UK: Taylor and Francis.	●	●													
The Rock Factory: The Story About the Rock Cycle by Jacqui Bailey. 2006. Mankato, MN: Picture Window Books.							●								
Rooted in the Earth: Reclaiming the African American Environmental Heritage by Dianne D. Glave. 2010. Chicago: Lawrence Hill Books.	●			●											●
SAFE and Fun Playgrounds: A Handbook by Heather M. Olsen, Susan D. Hudson, and Donna Thompson. 2015. St. Paul, MN: Redleaf Press.	●			●											
Science Experiences for the Early Childhood Years: An Integrated Affective Approach by Jean D. Harlan and Mary S. Rivkin. 2012. Hoboken, NJ: Pearson.	●	●	●	●	●	●	●	●							
Snow Play: How to Make Forts and Slides and Winter Campfires by Birgitta Ralston. 2010. New York: Workman Publishing.	●	●		●	●										
Square Foot Gardening with Kids: Learn Together: Gardening Basics—Science and Math—Water Conservation—Self-Sufficiency—Healthy Eating by Mel Bartholomew. 2014. Nashville: Cool Springs Press.				●				●							

Book Title	INTRODUCTION	INDIVIDUALIZATION	INDOORS	OUTDOORS	WEATHER	WATER	ROCKS, SAND, & SOIL	PLANTS	BUGS	BIRDS	REPTILES & AMPHIBIANS	MAMMALS	AQUATIC LIFE	HABITATS	FAMILIES
Practical Solutions to Practically Every Problem: The Survival Guide for Early Childhood Professionals, 3rd Edition, by Steffen Saifer. 2017. St. Paul, MN: Redleaf Press.		●													
Toddlers Outdoors by Siren Films and Jan White. 2017. St. Paul, MN: Redleaf Press. DVD, 65 min.	●	●		●											
Two Year Olds Outdoors by Siren Films and Jan White. 2017. St. Paul, MN: Redleaf Press. DVD, 63 min.	●	●		●											
Vitamin N: The Essential Guide to a Nature-Rich Life by Richard Louv. 2016. Chapel Hill, NC: Algonquin Books.	●			●											●
Waterworks: Water Play Activities for Children Aged 1–6 by Jeanne C. James and Randy F. Granovetter. 1987. Lewisville, NC: Kaplan.						●									
The Wild Weather Book: Loads of Things to Do Outdoors in Rain, Wind and Snow by Fiona Danks and Jo Schofield. 2013. London: Frances Lincoln Publishers.				●	●										
Wildlife field guides: Check your local library or *Acorn Naturalists*.				●						●	●	●	●	●	
Worms, Shadows, and Whirlpools: Science in the Early Childhood Classroom by Karen Worth and Sharon Grollman. 2003. Portsmouth, NH: Heinemann.			●	●		●			●						
Your Brain on Nature: The Science of Nature's Influence on Your Health, Happiness, and Vitality by Eva M. Selhub, MD, and Alan C. Logan, ND. 2012. New York: John Wiley and Sons.	●	●													●

APPENDIX 4

WEBSITES AND APPS

Websites

All About Birds	www.allaboutbirds.org
The Old Farmer's Almanac	www.almanac.com/topics/birding-fishing/bird-sounds
Cornell Lab of Ornithology	www.birds.cornell.edu
Children and Nature Network	www.childrenandnature.org/initiatives/families
iNaturalist	www.inaturalist.org
HECHO	www.hechoonline.com
Latino Outdoors	http://latinooutdoors.org
NAEYC Guidelines on Time Outdoors	www.naeyc.org/
Green Hearts Institute for Nature in Childhood	www.greenheartsinc.org
NGSS Kindergarten Standards	www.nextgenscience.org
Outdoor Afro	www.outdoorafro.com
Nature Start Alliance	www.naturalstart.org

Apps

Animal Tracks	iTrack Wildlife
Bird Identification	EyeLoveBirds; Merlin Bird ID
Bird Songs and Calls	EyeLoveBirds
Bug Identification	Bug ID
Edible Plants	Edible and Poisonous Plants
Fish Identification	WhatFish
Fossil Identification	The Fossilator
Geocaching	Cachebot
Local Parks	Park Path
Moon Phases	The Moon
Plant Identification	Garden Answers; Plant ID
Planting and Gardening	Garden Time
Poisonous and Dangerous Plant Identification	Rash Plants
Reptile Identification	Regional Reptile
Rock Identification	Mineral Identifier
Weather	NOAA Weather Radar

MATERIALS, SUPPLIES, AND EQUIPMENT

Free and Collectible Materials

	INDIVIDUALIZATION	INDOORS	OUTDOORS	WEATHER	WATER	ROCKS, SAND, & SOIL	PLANTS	BUGS	BIRDS	REPTILES & AMPHIBIANS	MAMMALS	AQUATIC LIFE	HABITATS	FAMILIES
Clear plastic containers	●	●	●	●	●	●	●	●	●	●	●	●	●	●
Books from the public library	●	●	●	●	●	●	●	●	●	●	●	●	●	●
Standing tables, support chairs, and walkers	●													
Old beach or patio umbrellas			●	●										
Wood pallets			●											
Very large cardboard boxes			●										●	
Homemade rain gauges			●	●	●									
Real snow shovels			●	●	●									
Buckets, sand toys, Jell-O molds, and other items for playing in the snow			●	●										
Laminated black construction paper for looking closely at snowflakes			●	●	●									
Kite-making materials			●	●										
Natural materials like bamboo, leaves, driftwood, rocks, etc.			●			●							●	
Expired and used seed packets							●							
Gourds and other durable vegetables		●					●							
Materials for making gardens and terrariums		●	●				●			●			●	
Calendars with nature themes		●		●	●	●	●	●	●	●	●	●		
Leaves, stumps, sticks, bark, cones, and pods from trees in your ecosystem		●	●			●	●							
Variety of scoops, pots, and buckets for planting		●	●				●							
Discarded flowers from florist		●					●							
Abandoned birds' nests		●							●				●	
Handmade birdhouses			●						●				●	
Bug containers		●						●						
Butterfly houses		●						●					●	
Snakeskins		●								●				
Homemade temporary cages for collecting and observing animals or bugs		●	●					●		●			●	
Bird feathers		●							●					
Birdsong CD		●							●				●	

	INDIVIDUALIZATION	INDOORS	OUTDOORS	WEATHER	WATER	ROCKS, SAND, & SOIL	PLANTS	BUGS	BIRDS	REPTILES & AMPHIBIANS	MAMMALS	AQUATIC LIFE	HABITATS	FAMILIES
Free and Collectible Materials (*cont.*)														
Handmade bird feeders			●						●					
Buckets and scoops of many kinds to use in the water		●	●	●	●									
Large clear plastic jars for exploring pond or ocean water samples												●		
Jewelry made from different stones		●				●								
Logs and tree cookies—large and small for dramatic play		●	●				●							
Best Materials to Purchase If You Have More Funds														
Wagons with sides and room for 1–2 children to comfortably sit inside	●		●	●	●	●	●	●	●	●	●	●	●	●
Sleds if you live in a snowy area	●		●	●	●	●	●	●	●	●	●	●	●	●
Tubs, tables, or other systems that allow children easy access to water, sand, and other natural substances		●	●	●	●	●	●							
High-quality magnifying glasses, boxes, and loupes	●	●	●	●	●	●	●	●	●	●	●	●		
Flexible or fabric measuring tape for independent use		●	●			●	●							
High-quality journals with unlined pages for documentation by children	●	●	●	●	●	●	●	●	●	●	●	●	●	●
Gutters, plastic tubing, and other materials for moving water (These items are often on sale after the summer season at hardware stores.)			●	●	●		●					●		
Sandboxes that can be covered			●			●								
Real metal shovels			●		●	●	●						●	
Wheelbarrows (wooden or metal) that are functional and sturdy with big tires and a well-balanced wheel base			●		●	●	●							●
Nature posters	●	●	●	●	●	●	●	●	●	●	●	●		
Apps for recognizing birds, insect, and mammal sounds		●	●					●	●		●			
Keychain field guides			●			●	●	●	●	●	●	●		
Pocket guides														
Realistic and "to scale" plastic animal reproductions		●	●					●	●	●	●	●		
Rain gauges			●	●	●									
Gear for safe exploration outdoors			●	●										

Best Materials to Purchase
If You Have More Funds (cont.)

	INDIVIDUALIZATION	INDOORS	OUTDOORS	WEATHER	WATER	ROCKS, SAND, & SOIL	PLANTS	BUGS	BIRDS	REPTILES & AMPHIBIANS	MAMMALS	AQUATIC LIFE	HABITATS	FAMILIES
For rain—avoid using umbrellas, and instead invest in galoshes/boots/wellies, waterproof jackets with hoods, and waterproof pants.			●	●										
For snow—waterproof mittens, neck warmers or gaiters, snow pants, warm socks, and warm waterproof boots are essentials when exploring in below-freezing temperatures and snow.			●	●	●									
For sun—sunglasses to protect children's eyes			●	●										
Hats with chin straps			●	●										
Fresh seeds for plants that will grow successfully in your ecosystem	●		●				●							
Life cycle models (These are available in nature catalogs for life cycles of plants, flowers, insects, butterflies, etc.)	●						●	●				●		
Soil	●		●				●							
Good-quality observation containers	●		●					●		●		●		
Honeycomb and refined honey	●							●						
Good-quality bird feeders			●						●					
Birdseed specific to the birds in your area	●		●				●		●					
Clean gravel	●		●		●									
Field guides			●			●	●	●	●	●	●	●	●	●
Tools for exploration	●		●	●	●	●	●							
Tubes, gutters, droppers, turkey basters, funnels, etc.	●		●	●	●		●							
Items from hardware stores	●		●	●	●	●	●						●	
A variety of rocks, gems, and minerals	●		●			●								
Hay bales			●	●										
Thermos with enough capacity for servings for your class			●											

Extras If You Have More Funds

	INDIVIDUALIZATION	INDOORS	OUTDOORS	WEATHER	WATER	ROCKS, SAND, & SOIL	PLANTS	BUGS	BIRDS	REPTILES & AMPHIBIANS	MAMMALS	AQUATIC LIFE	HABITATS	FAMILIES
Shade screens			●	●	●		●							
Accessible water tables	●	●	●		●									
Accessible raised-bed gardens	●		●				●							
Strong magnifying glasses, lighted magnifiers, and binoculars	●	●	●	●		●	●	●	●	●	●	●	●	

Extras If You Have More Funds (*cont.*)

	INDIVIDUALIZATION	INDOORS	OUTDOORS	WEATHER	WATER	ROCKS, SAND, & SOIL	PLANTS	BUGS	BIRDS	REPTILES & AMPHIBIANS	MAMMALS	AQUATIC LIFE	HABITATS	FAMILIES
Personal sound amplifiers		●	●					●	●		●			
Specimens (Early childhood catalogs have specimens of insects, plant parts, etc., encased in clear plastic for purchase.)		●					●	●		●		●		
Replicas (Early childhood catalogs have specimens of animal scat, foot- and hoofprints, and bones for purchase.)		●	●					●	●	●	●		●	
Light tables		●												
Weather station			●	●										
Washer and dryer			●	●	●		●					●		●
Good outdoor storage			●	●	●	●	●		●	●	●	●	●	
Outlast Blocks by Community Playthings			●											
A variety of types of water and sensory tables	●	●	●		●	●	●					●		
High-quality, realistic creature puppets and stuffed animals		●						●	●	●	●	●		
Nature items to be used in pretend play	●	●	●		●	●	●					●	●	
Animal mounts		●							●	●	●	●		
Real or imitation animal fur		●									●			
Imitation animal fur fabric		●	●								●			
Puzzles, lotto games, seriation games of mammals, insects, plants, etc.	●	●				●	●	●	●	●	●	●	●	
Birdcalls			●						●					
Plastic scat replicas		●	●						●	●	●		●	
Track and scat cards		●	●						●	●	●		●	
Furniture and play equipment made with wood in its most visible forms		●					●							
Tree blocks		●					●							
Flower press			●				●	●					●	
Plants that attract butterflies			●					●						
Butterfly nets			●					●						
Bird egg replicas (You can purchase replica eggs that are specific to the birds in your environment—these are sturdier that real eggs.)		●							●					
Bird feathers		●							●					

Extras If You Have More Funds (cont.)

	INDIVIDUALIZATION	INDOORS	OUTDOORS	WEATHER	WATER	ROCKS, SAND, & SOIL	PLANTS	BUGS	BIRDS	REPTILES & AMPHIBIANS	MAMMALS	AQUATIC LIFE	HABITATS	FAMILIES
Binoculars		●	●	●	●		●	●	●	●	●	●	●	
Bird puppets and stuffed animals		●						●	●	●	●	●		
Large laminator for observing natural materials		●	●	●	●		●						●	●
Fish skeletons												●		
A variety of rocks, gems, and minerals		●				●								
Drills for rocks		●	●			●								
Variety of rocks in different states		●	●			●								
Rock tumbler		●			●									
Child-sized skis			●	●									●	
Child- and adult-sized snowshoes			●	●	●									●

APPENDIX 6

NATURE-BASED RECIPES

BUTTERMILK SCONES

Servings: 16

Ingredients

3 cups flour
⅓ cup sugar
1 teaspoon salt
2½ teaspoons baking powder
½ teaspoon baking soda
¾ cup cold cubed butter
1 cup buttermilk plus 1 tablespoon for brushing
    on tops

Directions

1. Preheat oven to 375° F.

2. Combine flour, sugar, salt, baking powder, and baking soda in a large bowl.

3. Cut in butter and mix with your fingertips to create a coarse meal.

4. Add buttermilk and mix just until combined.

5. Transfer dough to a floured board and divide into eight parts.

6. Roll each to one-inch thick rounds.

7. Cut each round in half and place slightly separated on a greased baking sheet.

8. Brush the tops with buttermilk, and bake 15 minutes or until light brown.

SUSHI RICE

Servings: 16

Ingredients

2 cups uncooked glutinous white rice
    (short grain or sushi rice)
3 cups water
½ cup rice vinegar
1 tablespoon vegetable oil
¼ cup white sugar
1 teaspoon salt

Directions

1. Rinse uncooked rice in a bowl, strainer, or colander until water runs clear.

2. Add rice and water in a medium saucepan.

3. Bring to a boil—then reduce heat to low, cover, and cook for 20 minutes or until water is absorbed.

4. Combine rice vinegar, oil, sugar, and salt, and cook over medium heat or in microwave until sugar and salt are dissolved.

5. Gently toss the mixture into the cooked rice.

6. Fan the rice and stir gently to cool.

ANY FRUIT POPSICLES

Servings: 12

4 cups any berries (fresh or frozen)
½ cup apple juice
4 tablespoons honey
1 lemon, juiced
1 pinch salt

Directions

1. Combine ingredients with a blender.

2. Pour the mixture into molds.

3. Freeze molds overnight.

SNOW CONES

Servings: 10

Ingredients

1 cup any flavor juice
2 tablespoons honey
Freshly fallen snow

Directions

1. In a small saucepan, boil any flavor juice and honey until thickened (about 10–15 minutes).

2. Let cool to room temperature (juice mixture can be made ahead of time).

3. Once completely cool, drizzle it over scoops of fresh snow.

MAPLE CANDY

Servings: 10

Ingredients

Maple syrup
Freshly fallen snow

Directions

1. During a snowfall, collect snow using a clean baking sheet. Pack down the snow and continue collecting snow. Repeat once more.

2. Heat 1 cup of real maple syrup in a small saucepan over medium heat until it reaches a boil or until candy thermometer reaches 245° F.

3. Before maple syrup cools, drizzle it over packed snow in long strips.

4. It will be ready to eat in about five seconds.

ICE CREAM MADE WITH FRESH SNOW

Servings: 8

Ingredients

8–10 cups of fresh snow
1 10-ounce can of sweetened condensed milk
1 teaspoon vanilla
Large metal bowl

Directions

1. Collect fresh snow in a large metal bowl.

2. Drizzle vanilla and sweetened condensed milk over fresh snow and mix until creamy.

SUMMER BERRY COBBLER

Servings: 8

Ingredients

Filling
6 cups fresh berries
½ cup sugar
2 tablespoons cornstarch
½ teaspoon salt
1 lemon, juiced

Topping
1½ cups flour
¼ cup plus 2 tablespoons sugar, divided
1 tablespoon baking powder
½ teaspoon salt
1 stick unsalted butter, cut in small pieces and chilled
¾ cup half-and-half

Directions

1. Preheat oven to 375° F.

2. In a large bowl, toss together filling ingredients.

3. Pile mixture into a 9-inch round baking dish or deep pie plate.

4. In another bowl, combine flour, ¼ cup sugar, baking powder, and salt.

5. Cut in the butter until mixture resembles coarse meal.

6. Lightly toss with half-and-half until it forms a soft dough.

7. Drop the dough in tablespoon-size pieces on top of the berries until the surface is almost covered.

8. Lightly pat the dough down to evenly distribute the dough, but leave spaces for berries to show through.

9. Sprinkle 2 tablespoons sugar on top.

10. Place baking dish on a cookie sheet and bake 40–45 minutes until top is golden and berries are bubbling.

11. Serve with ice cream or whipped cream.

THUNDER CAKE

by Patricia Polacco

Servings: 10

Ingredients

1 cup shortening

1¾ cups sugar

1 teaspoon vanilla

3 eggs, separated

1 cup cold water

⅓ cup puréed tomatoes

2½ cups cake flour

½ cup cocoa powder

1½ teaspoon baking soda

1 teaspoon salt

Directions

1. Preheat oven to 350° F.

2. Grease and flour two 8½-inch cake pans.

3. Cream together shortening and sugar.

4. Beat in vanilla and egg yolks.

5. Mix in cold water and puréed tomatoes.

6. Beat egg whites until they are stiff, and fold into egg and tomato mixture.

7. Sift cake flour, cocoa, baking soda, and salt.

8. Mix dry mixture into wet mixture.

9. Pour batter evenly into cake pans.

10. Bake 35–40 minutes.

11. Let cakes cool on wire racks before frosting with chocolate buttercream icing.

12. Top with fresh strawberries (optional).

EASY BATTER

(Can be used for dandelions, onions, or any other veggies you'd like to fry.)

Ingredients

1 cup flour

1 tablespoon sugar (optional to add a little sweetness)

1 teaspoon salt

1 cup sparkling water (plain, lemon, or lime)

Directions

1. Mix flour, sugar, and salt together.

2. Pour in sparkling water until mixed.

REFERENCES

American Academy of Child and Adolescent Psychiatry. 2015. "Screen Time and Children." www.aacap.org/aacap/families_and_youth/facts _for_families/FFF-Guide/Children-And-Watching -TV-054.aspx.

American Academy of Pediatrics Council on Communications and Media. 2013. "Children, Adolescents, and the Media." *Pediatrics* 132, no. 5 (November). https://doi.org:10.1542/peds.2013-2656.

Americans with Disabilities Act of 1990, PL 101-336, Title III, Sections 301and 302 [2] [A] [i]. www .congress.gov/bill/101stcongress/senate-bill/933.

Ball, D. J. 2002. "Playgrounds—Risks, benefits and choices" (Vol. 426/2002). London: Health and Safety Executive (HSE) contract research report, Middlesex University.

Bienefeld, M., Pickett, W., and Carr, P. A. 1996. "A descriptive study of childhood injuries in Kingston, Ontario, using data from a computerized injury surveillance system." Health Canada—Chronic Diseases in Canada, 17, 21–27.

Bowler, Diana, Lisette M. Buyung-Ali, Teri M. Knight, and Andrew Pullin. 2010. "A Systemic Review of Evidence for the Added Benefits to Health of Exposure to Natural Environments." *BMC Public Health* 10, no. 456 (August): 1–10. 10https://doi.org/10.1186/1471-2458-10-456.

Bryce, Emma. 2014. "Should We Eat Bugs?" TED video, 4:51. https://ed.ted.com/lessons/should-we -eat-bugs-emma-bryce.

Burdette, Hillary L., and Robert C. Whitaker. 2005. "Resurrecting Free Play in Young Children: Looking Beyond Fitness and Fatness to Attention, Affilia-tion, and Affect." *Archives of Pediatrics and Adolescent Medicine* 159 (1): 46–50. https://doi.org/10.1001 /archpedi.159.1.46.

Carson, Rachel. 1965. *The Sense of Wonder*. New York: Harper & Row.

Centers for Disease Control. 2017. "Healthy Pets, Healthy People." www.cdc.gov/healthypets/index .html.

Consumer Reports. 2018. "How Safe Is Deet?" www.consumerreports.org/insectrepellent/how -safe-is-deet-insect-repellent-safety.

Curiosity.com. 2016. "To Avoid Collision, Birds Always Veer Right." Staff blog article posted October 13, 2016. https://curiosity.com/topics/to -avoid-collision-birds-always-veer-right-curiosity.

Faber Taylor, Andrea, and Frances E. (Ming) Kuo. 2011. "Could Exposure to Everyday Green Spaces Help Treat ADHD? Evidence from Children's Play Settings." *Applied Psychology: Health and Well-Being* 3, no. 3 (August): 281–303. https://doi.org /10.1111/j.1758-0854.2011.01052.x.

Greenleaf, Arie T., Rhonda M. Bryant, and Joanna B. Pollock. 2014. "Nature-Based Counseling: Integrating the Healing Benefits of Nature into Practice." *International Journal for the Advancement of Counseling* 36, no. 2 (June): 162–74. https://doi.org/10.1007/s10447-013-9198-4.

Guinier, Lani, and Gerald Torres. 2002. *Enlisting Race, Resisting Power, Transforming Democracy.* Cambridge, MA: Harvard University.

Louv, Richard. 2005. *Last Child in the Woods: Saving Our Children from Nature-Deficit Disorder.* Chapel Hill, NC: Algonquin Books.

Mack, M. G., Hudson, S., and Thompson, D. 1997. "A descriptive analysis of children's playground injuries in the United States 1990–4." *Injury Prevention*, 3, 100–03.

Matsuoka, Rodney H. 2010. "Student Performance and High School Landscapes: Examining the Links." *Landscape and Urban Planning* 97, no. 4 (September): 273–82. https://doi.org/10.1016/j.landurbplan.2010.06.011.

Maybank, Aletha. 2013. "Yes Black People DO Get Sunburn." *Ebony*, May 2013.

National Association for the Education of Young Children (NAEYC). 2007. "The Value of School Recess and Outdoor Play." Education.com. Last modified July 26, 2017. www.education.com/reference/article/Ref_Value_School_Recess.

———. 2018. *NAEYC Early Learning Program Accreditation Standards and Assessment Items*. Washington, DC: NAEYC. www.naeyc.org/sites/default/files/globally-shared/downloads/PDFs/accreditation/early-learning/standards_and_assessment_web_0.pdf.

National Recreation and Park Association (NRPA). 2017. "Children in Nature: Improving Health by Reconnecting Youth with the Outdoors." Accessed July 2, 2018. www.nrpa.org/uploadedFiles/nrpa.org/Advocacy/Children-in-Nature.pdf

Noddings, Nel. 2003. *Happiness and Education*. New York: Cambridge University Press.

Phelan, K., Khoury, J., Kalkwarf, H., and Lamphear, B. 2001. "Trends and patterns of playground injuries in United States." *Ambulatory Pediatrics*, 1, 227–233.

Raanaas, Ruth Kjaersti, Grete Grindal Patil, and Terry Hartig. 2011. "Health Benefits of a View of Nature through the Window: A Quasi-Experimental Study of Patients in a Residential Rehabilitation Center." *Clinical Rehabilitation* 26, no.1 (August): 21–32. http://journals.sagepub.com/doi/abs/10.1177/0269215511412800?journalCode=cea.

Sawyers, J. K. 1994. "The preschool playground: Developing skills through outdoor play." *Journal of Physical Education, Recreation and Dance*, 65, 31–33.

Selly, Patty Born. 2014. *Connecting Animals and Children in Early Childhood*. St. Paul, MN: Redleaf Press.

Smithsonian Museum of Natural History, Oceans Exhibit, 2018.

Sobel, David. 2005. *Place-Based Education: Connecting Classrooms & Communities*. Great Barrington, MA: The Orion Society.

Swartz, M. K. 1992. "Playground safety." *Journal of Pediatric Health Care*, 6, 161–62.

Townsend, Mardi, and Rona Weerasuriya. 2010. "Beyond Blue to Green: The Benefits of Contact with Nature for Mental Health and Well-Being." Melbourne, Australia: Beyond Blue Limited. www.hphpcentral.com/wp-content/uploads/2010/09/beyondbluetogreen.pdf.

Wellhousen, Karyn, and Ingrid Crowther. 2004. *Creating Effective Learning Environments*. New York: Delmar Learning.

Williams, Dilafruz R., and Jonathan D. Brown. 2012. *Learning Gardens and Sustainability Education: Bringing Life to Schools and Schools to Life*. New York: Routledge.

Wu, Chih-Da, Eileen McNeely, J. G. Cedeño-Laurent, Wen-Chi Pan, Gary Adamkiewicz, Francesca Dominici, Shih-Chun Candice Lung, Huey-Jen Su, and John D. Spengler. 2014. "Linking Student Performance in Massachusetts Elementary Schools with the 'Greenness' of School Surroundings Using Remote Sensing." *PLOS ONE* 9, no. 10. http://dx.doi.org/10.1371/journal.pone.0108548.

INDEX

happiness, providing opportunities to experience, 4–5
Happiness and Education (Noddings), 4
Harrington, Kit, 101–102
Hartig, Terry, 13
"Health Benefits of a View of Nature through the Window: a Quasi-experimental Study of Patients in a Residential Rehabilitation Center" (Raanaas, Patil, and Hartig), 13
health issues
    tips for facilitating inclusion of children with, 23, 49
    See also safety issues
hearing impaired, tips for inclusion of, 21, 76–77, 131
heat exhaustion and heatstroke, 53
Hendricks, Charlotte, 53
herptiles. *See* reptiles and amphibians
hunting, 148
hydration and weather, 51–52, 53
hypothermia, 52

ice, bringing indoors, 62
illness
    myths about, 43–44
    true causes of, 49
inclusion
    all children in family experiences in nature, 147
    autistic children, 18
    children who do not speak, 22
    children with allergies to insects, 94
    children with behavioral issues, 7, 20–21, 131
    children with limited mobility, 21
        near water, 67, 131
        raised-bed gardens and planters for, 85
        rocky places, 76, 138
        wagons or sleds for, 49
    deaf or hearing-impaired children, 21
        near water, 131
        rocky places, 76–77
    disadvantaged youth, 17–18
    dual-language learners, 17–18
    sound and/or movement sensitive children, 104
    vision-impaired children, 21, 113
Individuals with Disabilities Education Act (IDEA), 22
indoor nature-based experiences
    access to water, 30, 65, 66
    animals as classroom pets, 27–28, 30
    birds as pets, 100–101

bringing animals into classroom, 123
bringing outdoors in, 28–30
creating mud kitchen, 38
cultural issues to consider, 30
Dipping Your Toe In ideas, 28–29, 84
Diving In ideas, 30
furnishings and environment and, 29–30
growing plants, 14, 83
habitats, 138
hatching chicks, 105
insects as temporary pets, 94, 96
materials for, 31–32, 97
pond in a jar, 27
resources about, 31
safety issues, 30–31
sample invitation to families to see nature in classroom, 33
Wading In ideas, 29
inquiry, nature education supports, 3
insects, spiders, and worms
    avoiding bites, 52
    concepts preschoolers are ready to understand, 91
    concepts too abstract for preschoolers to understand, 92
    Dipping Your Toe In ideas, 94
    Diving In ideas, 94
    families
        attitudes of, toward, 95
        treatment of, 91
    lesson plans
        silkworms, 167–168
        worm beds, 169
    materials for, 97
    resources about, 96
    safety issues, 91, 94, 95
    sample letters to families
        about adopting, 127–128
        about learning through interactions with bugs, 98
    as temporary pets, 38, 94, 96
    topics for different ecosystems, 93
    Wading In ideas, 94
irrigation systems, understanding, 63

Janquart, Amanda, 28

Katz, Lillian, 83
kayaking, 63

Larimore, Rachel, 10–11
Lazaroff, Cheryl, 75
learning standards, 7–8
lesson plans
    animals in rain, 152
    aquatic life

the beach, 180–181
pond in jar, 178–179
raising tadpoles, 170–171
birds
    bird watching walk, 174–175
    incubating chicks, 176–177
cacti and rain, 153–154
color in nature, 162–163
geology
    grouping rocks, 186–187
    investigating rocks, 184–185
    rock hunt, 182–183
insects, spiders, and worms
    silkworms, 167–168
    worm beds, 169
mammals
    combing wool, 166
    making butter, 164–165
mud painting, 157–158
plants, deep-fried dandelions, 190
reptiles and amphibians
    habitats for reptiles, 172–173
    raising tadpoles, 170–171
seeds' connection to plants, 161
seeds' locations, 159–160
snow fort building, 188–189
water, 155–156
licensing limitations, 6
lightning, 53
limited mobility, children with. *See* mobility issues, inclusion of children with
Lister, Marie, 37–38
Lite-Brite, 31
Louv, Richard, 5
low vision, children with, tips for inclusion of, 21, 131

mammals
    concepts preschoolers are ready to understand, 119
    concepts too abstract for preschoolers to understand, 120
    Dipping Your Toe In ideas, 122
    Diving In ideas, 123
    families, ideas about specific, 123–124
    health and safety issues, 123, 124
    lesson plans
        combing wool, 166
        making butter, 164–165
    materials for, 125–126
    resources about, 124–125
    sample letter to families about adopting, 127–128
    topics for different ecosystems, 120–121
    Wading In ideas, 122–123